Please note the information contained within this document is for educational and entertainment purposes only. All effort has been executed to present accurate, up to date, reliable, complete information. No warranties of any kind are declared or implied. Readers acknowledge that the author is not engaged in the rendering of legal, financial, medical, or professional advice. The content within this book has been derived from various sources. Please consult a licensed professional before attempting any techniques outlined in this book. By reading this document, the reader agrees that under no circumstances is the author responsible for any losses, direct or indirect, that are incurred as a result of the use of the information contained within this document, including, but not limited to, errors, omissions, or inaccuracies.

CONTENTS

INTRODUCTION

As a teen, I never dreamed the food habits I was developing would come back to haunt me. Growing up in a small town of less than 2,000 people, our restaurant choices were limited. Eating out was a special occasion and something I looked forward to.

The fried foods I ate when we were out became some of my favorites, but it wasn't until years later I realized my eating habits were causing my weight to continue to creep up.

The struggle to maintain a healthier weight has been an issue for me for years. Balancing life as a busy working mother isn't always easy. One area that often fell through the cracks for me was cooking healthy, balanced meals. It seemed to take a lot of time, effort, and energy to meal plan and prepare healthy dinners every night.

I tried different deprivation-themed diets, but I always ended up back at square one. As a registered nurse, I knew that these fad diets weren't the answer and I needed to start more simply.

As I have gotten older my body has changed, and it has become even harder to lose weight and keep it off. I was diagnosed with an autoimmune disease and some of the medications can interfere with my weight-loss efforts. Instead of giving up, I started looking for alternatives that didn't involve completely cutting out certain food groups or food items from my life.

I realized that if I was going to see success, I needed to find ways to make foods I love healthier. The air fryer has been a game changer for me. I can make so many of my favorite recipes significantly healthier, and they taste as good and some are even better than before.

There is a whole new world of opportunities available when it comes to making delicious vegetables that I look forward to eating. Protein is no longer limited to a few boring basics. The air fryer delivers a crispy texture to many of my favorite foods, and there is no guilt involved because only an insignificant amount of olive oil is required.

I am a firm believer that baby steps can change the world. Limiting my fat intake and reducing the calories on many recipes can make a difference on the scale. It also makes a difference inside my body and for my overall health.

This cookbook shows everyday families how to make easy and classic recipes a little bit healthier using the air fryer. This cookbook has recipes for real people. The ingredients are common and can easily be found at any grocery store. I adapted recipes my family has been eating for years, and my family is even more excited to come to the table when they see I am cooking their favorite meals with the air fryer!

I am 100 percent sold on the benefits of air frying. As you begin to use your air fryer, I think you will quickly see how easy it is to adapt regular recipes into healthier versions by cooking them this way. This is an appliance for everyday life, and it deserves space on the counter in your kitchen.

Get ready to learn all about air frying and how it can change how you cook your meals. Keep reading to find recipes that are simple, use just a few ingredients, and don't require you spend the whole evening in the kitchen.

How the Air Fryer Can Help You Lose Weight

Losing weight ultimately comes down to calories. In this chapter, you'll learn how the air fryer is a powerful tool to help you work toward your weight loss goals. It cooks foods using less oil, meaning fewer calories, without sacrificing any of the satisfying flavor and texture you associate with fried foods. Making these kinds of small changes in your diet can have a long-term impact on your overall weight and health.

Although it may be tempting to jump right into this book's delicious air fryer recipes, it's important that you read the first two chapters. Getting to know the air fryer will help make the cooking experience all the more enjoyable.

Why Air Fry?

Weight loss is a personal journey for each person. My struggles to lose weight have helped me realize that wellness isn't only about a number on the scale. There has been a shift in my thinking that has allowed me to see the value of incorporating healthier habits overall into my life and the lives of my family.

Crash diets, on the other hand, don't work for me. Depriving myself of certain foods has never helped me maintain my weight loss goals. If I'm forbidden from eating a food I love for very long, I end up reverting to my old eating habits. A slow-and-steady approach works much better for me, and that means finding ways to cook my favorite foods in healthier ways.

Which leads me to the air fryer. It allows me to enjoy the soul-satisfying flavor and texture of fried foods, without all the calories of traditional frying. It cooks food by circulating hot air around the food very quickly. Typical air fryers have a removable basket that doesn't have to be submerged into hot oil to get foods crispy. Instead, there are holes that let the very hot air move around the food.

Traditionally fried foods are often extremely high in unhealthy fats and very high in calories. It is hard to lose weight if fried foods are on the menu often. But completely eliminating fried foods from our diet can lead us to feel deprived and throws us off our weight-loss goals. Fortunately, French fries do not have to be an off-limits treat if they are made using the air fryer. It is possible to make crunchy homemade fish sticks, chicken strips, and even snacks in the air fryer. The calorie savings will be big, because you'll need much less oil to make these foods in the air fryer.

But it's not just carb-heavy foods that benefit from air frying. One of my favorite things about the air fryer is that it has made vegetables exciting to me again. I have always been a picky eater, and in the past, I wasn't overly eager to try new vegetables. Brussels sprouts were never on my menu until I started cooking them in the air fryer. So, cooking vegetables in the air fryer has been a game changer for me. It is so easy to create delicious and flavorful side dishes using fresh or frozen veggies.

Air frying can be as easy or as complicated as you choose. Start off making simple recipes with common ingredients. Roasted vegetables and shrimp are great choices for beginners. For a simple dish that impresses, you can get the job done with three components: a vegetable, some seasonings, and a little bit of olive oil will give you a scrumptious result.

When you are more comfortable with the appliance try your hand at some more complex recipes. Learning to cook salmon and other seafood recipes will bring healthy proteins and low calories to your plate. Lean cuts of meat turn out moist and delicious in the air fryer.

The more you use the air fryer, the more you will come to value this appliance as a resource in your weight-loss and wellness journey.

Foods to Enjoy

For a well-balanced diet that can still work with your weight loss goals, you'll want to focus on eating high-quality carbohydrates (mostly vegetables), healthy fats, and lean proteins. Fortunately, the air fryer is a great tool for preparing many different foods that fall into these categories.

Veggies

Vegetables are a key component for pretty much any weight loss program. Vegetables are packed with fiber, water, and nutrients, and they tend to be lower in calories than other foods. They're also a good source of healthy carbohydrates (more on that shortly).

The problem is that when we are trying to eat only healthy foods, vegetable boredom can hit quickly. We get stuck in a rut eating the same few choice all the time. Suddenly we find ourselves snacking on a bag of chips instead of carrot sticks.

Finding delicious new ways to prepare vegetables is imperative for long term weight loss. Air-fried veggies can have a roasted taste with a slightly crispy texture. These results are achieved without a lot of unnecessary oil. I love the flexibility of being able to air fry fresh vegetables with no pre-cooking required. Spicy Sweet Potatoes and Simple Roasted Cauliflower are on our menu almost every week.

Healthy Fats

Fats in general have a bad reputation. It's true that we want to avoid consuming trans fats and saturated fats, especially when trying to lose weight. But there are also healthy fats, which are critical for us to produce energy, support cell growth, absorb certain nutrients, and produce certain hormones.

Monounsaturated and polyunsaturated fats are considered good fats. Some common foods that are high in good fats include avocados, nuts, seeds, and fish. There are also specific oils that are lower in saturated fat thus making them a better choice. The oils lowest in saturated fats are avocado, canola, corn, olive, grapeseed, safflower, peanut, sesame, soybean, and sunflower.

When I am preparing foods in the air fryer and oil is needed, I typically use an olive oil spray. Very little oil is required for air frying. Lightly spraying foods with a spritz of olive oil can add that crunchy texture we crave from fried foods, but without all the calories that traditional deep-frying would add.

Lean Proteins

Protein helps you feel full longer, and if you aren't hungry, you won't be tempted to snack or eat as much during your next meal. An additional benefit of protein is the help it gives your body in maintaining lean muscle mass.

However, not all protein is created equal. Some sources of protein like fatty cuts of meat, hot dogs, bacon, and other processed meats are very high in saturated fat. It's important to choose lean proteins if you are trying to lose weight. Opt for turkey, chicken, and lean cuts of beef and pork when planning your meals. Easy Turkey Tenderloin, Whole Roasted Chicken, and Lemon-Garlic Tilapia are just a few of the protein-packed recipes in this cookbook.

Protein is known to reduce the hunger hormone ghrelin and boost levels of the peptide YY, which makes you feel full.

High-Quality Carbohydrates

Potatoes and sweet potatoes seem to be controversial vegetables when it comes to weight loss. Both of these potatoes are highly nutritious. They are rich in fiber and vitamins B_6 and C. There is a difference of where these potatoes fall on the glycemic index. Sweet potatoes have a lower glycemic index than regular white potatoes. Potatoes have a lot to offer and can help you feel full faster. The key is to pair them with lean protein and avoid slathering them with butter or other high-fat condiments.

In addition to vegetables, other high-quality carbohydrates include foods like beans and other legumes, fruits, and whole grains. In addition to being packed with nutrients and minerals, they also help limit fluctuations in our insulin levels and regulate our blood sugar.

It is common to feel hungry and overeat after a blood-sugar spike. Low-quality carbohydrates such as processed foods, white bread, desserts, juices, and other sugary drinks can cause these spikes to occur. It is very difficult to lose weight eating a diet high in low-quality carbohydrates.

I have discovered delicious swaps for highly processed carbs, and I don't feel at all deprived. Swapping out spaghetti noodles for zucchini noodles or using riced cauliflower in place of white rice are two easy replacements. The air fryer is a tool I use to turn plain high-quality carbohydrates into tasty dishes my whole family loves. The best part is that I am cooking with whole foods packed with nutrients my body needs.

Keep reading to learn how combining air frying with simple spices from the pantry can turn high-quality carbs into flavorful, healthy side dishes and snacks.

Foods to Avoid

There are certain foods and ingredients that should be avoided when you're trying to lose weight. The recipes in the books don't include these ingredients, but you'll find the air fryer is particularly good at producing satisfying results without them.

As mentioned previously, trans fat does nothing to enhance your body or your health. It raises the bad cholesterol level (LDL) and lowers the good cholesterol level (HDL) in our body. Trans fats have been shown to increase our risk of heart disease, stroke, and even type 2 diabetes. Trans fats tend to be found in processed foods and will be listed on packages as "partially hydrogenated oils" in the ingredient list. Common processed foods that are high in trans fat include crackers, chips, cookies, cakes, fast food, and vegetable shortening. There can be some hidden sources of trans fat in items like coffee creamer and baked goods.

Though many of us have a sweet tooth, sugar definitely goes on the forbidden list. And it lurks in many processed foods like salad dressings, pasta sauces, bread, canned fruit, and even in foods labeled as diet foods. Sugar adds calories without filling us up and can even lead to food cravings. High-carb snacks are a common pitfall when dieting. Chips, crackers, granola bars, and other highly processed foods fall into this category. They contain "empty" calories with little-to-no nutritional value for our bodies.

While low-fat foods may sound like a good option, unless they are a naturally low-fat whole food, it's best to avoid these items. They may be lower in fat, but it's usually replaced by sugar. Additionally, these foods are generally not as flavorful, and people tend to overeat them.

Fruit juice is not a healthy option. It is high in calories, which aren't very filling or satisfying when consumed in liquid form. The fiber from the fruit, which helps you to feel full, has been stripped away. Eating whole fruit is a much better choice.

The Plate Approach to Weight Loss

You may feel a little overwhelmed by the dos and don'ts we just covered when it comes to making smart food choices for weight loss. But don't worry, there's one area in which we are going to make things simple: This cookbook is not going to take a calorie-counting approach to weight loss. Instead, I want to focus on a simpler way to think about mealtime: the plate approach.

The plate approach focuses our attention on what's in front of us at mealtime and divides it up into sections. Half of our plate should be filled with vegetables. The other half of the plate should be filled with healthy fats, lean proteins, and high-quality carbohydrates. What I love about the plate approach is that it doesn't require a membership, calorie-counting, or even food tracking. It's a way of eating that anyone can do, and you can start immediately.

Keep in mind portion control when you are filling your plate. Using a smaller plate will help you keep your portions in control and also tricks your brain into thinking your plate is fuller.

A sectioned portion-control plate makes a wonderful tool to help you get used to the plate approach. But you can you also use something as easy as your own two hands to provide an easy visual reminder about portion sizes. Women should eat a palm-sized piece of lean protein plus a fistful of veggies at each meal. Add 25 percent more of each of those if you're a man. As for the rest of your plate, no one should have more than a cupped handful of high-quality carbs or a thumb's worth of healthy fats per meal.

This cookbook will make it easy for you to use the recipes to fill your plate appropriately. You won't have to take the time to count calories or input ingredients into a food tracker with the simple plate approach to dieting. All you need to do is fill your plate with healthy portion sizes of vegetables and other high-quality carbs, lean proteins, and healthy fats.

IF YOU'RE COUNTING CALORIES

Each person must decide the best approach to weight loss for themselves. For some, that means counting calories.

There are about 3,500 calories in one pound of stored body fat. If you can subtract 3,500 calories from your intake through diet and/or exercise you will lose one pound of body weight.

Experts say that the average person requires about 2,000 calories a day to maintain their current weight. This number will vary based on your height, weight, age, gender, and your current level of physical activity.

An easy way to begin counting calories is to use a food tracking app or website. It will help you calculate your basal metabolic rate (BMR), which is the amount of energy (calories) your body needs while resting. Knowing your BMR will help you set a daily calorie goal.

This cookbook contains calories counts for every recipe. There are also occasional tips on how to make a recipe even lower in calories.

My 10 Tips for Success

Whether you're using the plate method or following a diet that requires more specific tracking, there are some universal best practices that will help make your weight-loss goals a reality. Here are 10 tips to follow if you want to see a positive change on the scale.

1.Don't drink your calories. Stick to drinking water as much as possible. If you prefer flavored drinks, try adding some fruit slices to your water. Tea is another good option if you don't load it with sugar.

2.Get enough sleep each night. More and more research shows how sleep deprivation can lead to weight gain. Quality sleep is vital to good health and helps give us the energy to stay active during the day.

3.Plan your meals out each week. Even if you're not counting calories, meal planning can help you avoid spur of the moment trips through the fast-food drive-through. Be sure to account for breakfast, lunch, dinner, and snacks.

4.Prep your food. You'll start your week off right by prepping all your snacks for the week. Portion out food into baggies and containers so you can grab it and go. For snacks, wash and cut up vegetables and fruits so they are ready to eat. Mornings are a breeze if your lunches are prepped and ready to go the night before.

5.Stock up on healthy foods. It's hard to make healthy choices if your home is full of processed and unhealthy foods. Clear your refrigerator and pantry of these culprits and stock up on healthier alternatives.

6.Keep moving. Staying active is an important part of any weight loss plan, so find ways to exercise that you enjoy. Try to change your exercise routine from time to time so your body doesn't hit a plateau. Fitness trackers are an easy way to spot check how much you're moving throughout the day.

7.Purchase a smaller plate. There are special divided plates that are designed for weight loss, or you can get a child's plate. Just remember to always fill the largest section with vegetables at each meal.

8.Variety makes a difference. Eating the same thing all the time gets boring fast. Keep your diet varied and try new recipes and new foods each week. I like to keep a binder in the kitchen that's packed with healthy recipes and weight loss tips.

9.Visual reminders are helpful. I have found it useful to keep a picture of myself at a healthy weight in the kitchen. I see this picture when I open the refrigerator, and it helps me keep my food choices in perspective with my goals. If you are working to lose weight before a big vacation or event, it may help to hang a picture of that location as a reminder.

10.Positive affirmations are extremely motivating. What we say to ourselves can have a huge impact on our ability to find success with weight loss. Speak kindly to yourself and remain positive. I like to hang positive messages on the refrigerator to remind myself that I am worth the effort!

Fire Up the Air Fryer

One of the best things about the air fryer is how simple it is to use. Getting to know your air fryer will give you the confidence to start cooking your favorite foods with less oil and fewer calories. This chapter provides tips, tools, and troubleshooting advice that will allow you to get healthy meals on the table right away. You'll also learn to set up your kitchen in a way that will make it easy to stick to your goals. Finally, this chapter provides a meal plan to make starting your weight-loss journey as easy as possible.

My Kitchen Secrets

There are certain foods and accessories that will allow you to take full advantage of what the air fryer has to offer. Follow these guidelines to get your kitchen and pantry prepped and ready to start making healthy meals.

Healthy Air Fryer Staples

You will see some ingredients used over and over throughout this cookbook's recipes. To set yourself up for success, stock your refrigerator and pantry with these heathy air-fryer staples.

Boneless, Skinless Chicken Breasts: This protein is versatile and can be used in many different recipes. You can make quick lunches and dinners with boneless, skinless chicken breasts, and you'll be surprised by how tasty chicken can be in the air fryer.

Chickpeas: A high-fiber, high-protein snack, chickpeas only take minutes to cook in the air fryer and can be seasoned lots of different ways.

Eggs: An easy-to-get, inexpensive source of protein, eggs are surprisingly delicious in the air fryer and can be used in a variety of dishes.

Extra-Virgin Olive Oil: Olive oil is a must-have for air frying. There's a myth that no oil is needed when using an air fryer. Using small amounts of extra-virgin olive oil or avocado oil will give you that fried taste without the calories that come from deep-fat frying. Extra-virgin olive oil and avocado oil are both healthy fats and play an important part of any healthy diet. When I call for "olive oil" in the recipes, I always mean "extra-virgin olive oil."

Fresh Vegetables: As previously mentioned, veggies rise to delicious new heights when air-fried. Keep vegetables like sweet potatoes, broccoli, and cauliflower on hand for simple and delicious side dishes or snacks.

Lean Ground Turkey: A tasty lower-fat alternative to ground beef, lean ground turkey is a versatile protein. It can easily be made into meatballs or burgers in the air fryer.

Shrimp: Extremely easy to cook in the air fryer, shrimp can be made with a variety of seasonings and sauces and the outcomc is always delicious. I like to keep bags of frozen shrimp in the freezer all the time for fast, simple meals.

Whole Grains: Keep whole grains like quinoa or brown rice in the pantry to round out your meal. Or use them as base to turn veggies and protein into a full meal in a bowl.

Whole-Wheat Panko Bread Crumbs: Use bread crumbs to transform everyday dishes into a crunchy, addictive experience. They can be seasoned a variety of ways to change the flavor of a dish.

Spice Up Your Life

Spices can brighten up the flavor of otherwise boring ingredients and can be mixed and matched to add variety to your dining routine. You'll be more satisfied with your meals and less inclined to overeat.

All-Purpose Seasoning Salt: I love the convenience of salt blends. The combination of salt and other spices tastes great on almost any protein or vegetable.

Black Pepper: This universal spice adds subtle heat to dishes and also offers digestive health benefits.

Cajun Seasoning: My personal favorite spice blend, this lively, brightly flavored combination of spices such as paprika, cayenne pepper, chili flakes, and more can bring a vibrant kick to any dish.

Cayenne Pepper: It only takes a tiny amount of cayenne to bring a delightful heat to a recipe. It has also been said to boost metabolism and curb hunger.

Cinnamon: One of the healthiest spices, cinnamon brings a depth of flavor to sweet and savory dishes. Two big benefits of cinnamon are the ability to help lower blood sugar levels and to reduce heart disease risk factors.

Cumin: With its aromatic, nutty flavor, cumin is a staple in many spice blends. It also helps aid digestion and is a source of iron.

Garlic Powder: Made from dehydrated, ground garlic cloves, garlic powder has anti-inflammatory qualities and adds a homey flavor to many recipes.

Onion Powder: Get the flavor of onion without the hassle of teary eyes. Onion powder is made of dehydrated, ground onions. It contains the helpful mineral magnesium which can aid in the production of energy.

Paprika: Use this spice to add a wonderful peppery, smoky flavor to foods. Since it's made from ground bell peppers, it's loaded with vitamins, minerals, and antioxidants.

Salt: A mainstay of pretty much every recipe, salt can help bring out new flavors in foods. The essential minerals of sodium and chloride in salt act as important electrolytes in the body. These minerals are essential for fluid balance, nerve transmission, and muscle function. There are several kinds of salt to keep on hand: table salt, kosher salt, and sea salt.

Seafood Seasoning: You can make an amazing air-fried seafood dish with basic seafood seasoning. This seasoning will save you time and add a lot of flavor to your fish. Seafood seasonings usually contain a mixture of allspice, celery seed, salt, mustard powder, pepper, paprika, and more.

MUST-HAVE TOOLS

While using the air fryer is as simple as can be, there are some helpful tools and accessories that will make preparing the healthy recipes in this book even easier.

Baking Pan: A baking pan that will fit inside the fryer basket opens a whole new realm of recipe possibilities. It allows you to cook foods in the air fryer that you would traditionally cook in the oven. Frittatas and casseroles can be cooked in a baking pan in the air fryer.

Cooking Rack with Skewers: When cooking meat and vegetable kebobs, the raised rack allows total air circulation around the food, so you get a wonderful, crispy result.

Heat-Resistant Tongs: Tongs are used to turn food during cooking and remove it from the fryer basket. It is important to have tongs that have silicone tips, so they don't scratch the fryer basket.

Meat Thermometer: Cooking meat to the proper internal temperature is important to avoid food-borne illnesses, and it also takes any guesswork out of knowing when the meat is done.

Oil Spray Bottle: You can buy many different types of misters and spray bottles that allow you to spray a light coating of olive oil or avocado oil on foods and into the fryer basket. Just make sure whatever you buy is non-aerosol.

Parchment Liners: Liners help keep food from sticking to the fryer basket. These are extremely helpful when preparing seafood. Air fryer–specific liners work best because they have holes that allow the air to continue to circulate around the food despite the liner.

Step-by-Step Air Frying

The ease of using an air fryer is one of the things that makes it an invaluable tool in your weight-loss repertoire. Follow these simple steps, and you'll be an air-frying expert in no time.

1. Always read the manual that comes with your air fryer before using it. Each air fryer brand has slightly different guidelines and suggestions that will help make your air-frying experience better.

2. It is important to wash the basket and crisper plate (if your unit has one) before using it the first time. Use hot, soapy water to wash, rinse, and dry the basket. Do not use abrasive cleaners, steel wool, or scouring pads to clean the fryer basket.

3. Be sure the air intake vent and/or air outlet vents are not blocked while the air fryer is in use. This could cause the unit to overheat.

4. Check your owner's manual to see if your air fryer needs to be preheated before use. Some models recommend a few minutes of preheat time, and others do not require any preheating.

5. When a recipe requires that you cut up the food, make sure to create similar-sized pieces so the food cooks evenly in the air fryer, and always put food in an even, single layer in the fryer basket for the best results.

6. Set the timer and the temperature setting on the air fryer and press start.

7. Check periodically to make sure you're not overcooking, at least when you first make a recipe. You can also open the drawer to shake, toss, or turn food over during cooking. The recipes in this book will let you know when this is required.

8. Remember that the fryer basket will be extremely hot during and after use. Always use oven mitts or hot pads when handling the basket.

9. When finished, do not overturn the air fryer unit to get food out of the basket. Remove the basket from the unit or use heat-safe tongs to remove food from inside the basket.

CLEANING THE AIR FRYER

Before you start your air-frying adventure, it is important to clean the air fryer properly.

Remove any Packaging and Tape. Start off by removing any packaging materials from inside the unit and taking any tape off the unit.

Wash the Basket. Wash the fryer basket in hot, soapy water. If your unit has a removable crisper plate, this also needs to be washed in hot, soapy water. Rinse the items off and dry them thoroughly.

Dishwasher Safety. There are many different brands and styles of air fryers on the market. Always check your owner's guide to find out if your fryer basket is dishwasher safe before washing it in the dishwasher.

Food Residue. If your fryer basket has difficult food residue stuck inside, soak the basket in a sink filled with warm, soapy water.

Heating Element. If the heating element of your air fryer gets dirty and has food particles on it, the best way to clean it is to use a small cleaning brush to remove the food residue.

Main Unit. You cannot soak or immerse the main air fryer unit in water! Keep the unit clean by wiping it down with a damp cloth. Remember to always unplug the unit before wiping it down.

Perfect Air Frying, Every Time

While using the air fryer couldn't be simpler, there are a few tricks and tips to take your fry skills to the next level.

Watch the food. It's important to keep an eye on your food while it cooks, especially when you are first starting out. Food will cook at different speeds depending on the size of your fryer.

Shake the basket. Shaking the fryer basket can really improve the outcome of your food. If you're cooking smaller items like chopped vegetables, French fries, etc., be sure to pause the cooking a few times and shake the basket a little bit. This will help the food get crunchy all the way around and not stick to the basket.

Oil adds crunch. You still need to use a little bit of oil in an air fryer. It doesn't take very much oil to achieve a crunchy result. Spray the fryer basket lightly with olive oil before adding your ingredients to prevent food from sticking to the basket. It is also helpful to spray the food lightly with olive oil to get a crispier texture. The recipes will indicate if this step is necessary.

Use a meat thermometer. Check your meat for doneness with a meat thermometer. This will help you get perfectly cooked meat.

Recipe conversion is easy. It is easy to convert recipes from your conventional oven. Just reduce the temperature of the air fryer by 25°F. Check on the food periodically to avoid overcooking.

Remove the food from the basket. When the food is done cooking, remove it from the fryer basket immediately to prevent the food from becoming overcooked.

Secure lightweight foods. When cooking lightweight food, the circulating air may blow the foods around in the basket. You can alleviate this issue by securing foods with toothpicks or even a pie weight.

Cooking time depends on food size. Smaller ingredients will typically require a shorter cooking time than larger ones.

Troubleshooting

There are some common problems you may encounter when using your air fryer. Read through these troubleshooting tips so you are ready if any issues arise.

My food is burnt. It is very easy to overcook food in an air fryer until you get the hang of it. My best advice is to watch the food very closely for doneness. It is not a problem to open the air fryer and look in the basket a few times throughout cooking.

Food is sticking to the fryer basket. Mist your basket with olive oil before adding ingredients. This will help prevent food from sticking to the basket. You can also use fryer basket parchment liners.

The air fryer is smoking. The most common cause for smoking is if you are cooking foods that are naturally high in fat. Some of the excess fat may be in the bottom of the air fryer during the cooking process. You can reduce the likelihood of smoke by draining the fat out of the bottom of the air fryer part way through the cooking time. Another tip is to put a tablespoon or two of water under the basket. This will reduce any smoke during the cooking process.

My food does not seem crispy. The best way to ensure the food you air fry comes out crispy is to lightly mist the food with olive oil before cooking. Certain foods and recipes can benefit from a light mist of olive oil midway through the cooking time to add the best crunch to the recipe.

My fryer basket is sticky or flaking. If you are using aerosol cooking sprays, they can cause problems with the fryer basket over time. These non-stick cooking sprays can damage the basket. Remember to always use non-aerosol oils for your air fryer.

My air fryer smells like burnt plastic. Some people report that their air fryer has a burnt plastic smell when they first start using it. Typically, this smell will go away after the first few uses. If the smell continues after that, I would advise contacting the manufacturer for a recommendation.

Fry Time: Healthy Foods

One of my favorite parts of air frying is the ease of cooking healthy foods. This fry time table will give you a cheat sheet to refer to when you are experimenting with your favorite healthy foods. The recipes in this cookbook may have different variations from this chart, but the chart is a good jumping off point when you are starting your air fryer journey.

Fresh Food	Quantity	Time	Temperature	Notes
Apple chips	2 apples	8 to 12 mins	350°F	Sliced thin, shake basket
Asparagus	1 bunch	8 to 12 mins	390°F	Trim ends
Broccoli	1 head	10 to 12 mins	390°F	Cut in 1-inch florets
Broccoli, frozen	1 pound	20 mins	390°F	Shake every 5 minutes
Brussels sprouts	1 pound	15 to 20 mins	390°F	Cut in half, stem removed
Carrots	1 pound	13 to 16 mins	390°F	Cut in ½-inch slices
Cauliflower	1 head	15 to 20 mins	390°F	Cut in 1-inch florets
Chickpeas	15 ounces	15 to 20 mins	390°F	Shake every 5 minutes
Corn on the cob	2 ears	6 to 10 mins	360°F	Whole, husks removed
Corn, frozen	2 ears	15 to 18 mins	360°F	
Edamame	2 cups	10 to 15 mins	390°F	Whole, shake halfway
Green beans, fresh	12 ounces	8 to 10 mins	390°F	Trim ends
Green beans, frozen	12 ounces	18 to 20 mins	390°F	Shake every 5 minutes
Mixed vegetables	1 pound	15 to 20 mins	400°F	Cut into ½-inch chunks
Mushrooms	8 ounces	5 to 7 mins	400°F	Cut in 1-inch pieces
Okra, fresh	1 pound	8 to 12 mins	350°F	Cut into ½-inch slices
Okra, frozen	1 pound	20 mins	350°F	Shake every 5 minutes
Potatoes, baby	1 pound	15 to 17 mins	400°F	Whole
Potatoes, russet	1 pound	18 to 20 mins	390°F	Cut in 1-inch wedges
Potatoes, sweet	1 pound	15 to 20 mins	390°F	Cut in 1-inch chunks
Squash	1 pound	12 to 15 mins	400°F	Cut in 1-inch chunks
Zucchini	1 pound	12 to 15 mins	400°F	Cut in 1-inch sticks
Chicken breasts	2 breasts	18 to 22 mins	375°F	Use boneless
Chicken drumsticks	1 pound	18 to 22 mins	370°F	Don't crowd in basket
Chicken tenders	1 pound	8 to 12 mins	360°F	Fresh, hand-breaded
Pork chops	1 pound	13 to 16 mins	375°F	Boneless
Pork tenderloin	1 pound	20 to 25 mins	370°F	Whole
Burger	4 (4-oz) patties	8 to 10 mins	375°F	Lean ground beef or turkey
Meatballs	1 pound	5 to 8 mins	375°F	1-inch meatballs
Rib eye steak	2 (8-oz) steaks	10 to 15 mins	400°F	Bone-in
Sirloin steak	2 (8-oz) steaks	10 to 20 mins	390°F	Whole
Calamari	1 pound	4 to 8 mins	400°F	Cut into rings, hand-breaded
Fish fillets	4 (8-oz) fillets	10 to 12 mins	400°F	Fresh, hand-breaded
Salmon fillets	2 (4-oz) fillets	10 to 13 mins	390°F	Brushed with oil
Scallops	1 pound	5 to 7 mins	400°F	Shake basket during cooking
Shrimp, fresh	1 pound	7 to 10 mins	390°F	Peeled, tails on, tossed in oil
Shrimp, frozen	1 pound	10 to 12 mins	390°F	Peeled, tails on, tossed in oil

BREAKFAST & BRUNCH RECIPES

1. Strip Steak With Japanese Dipping Sauce

Servings:2
Cooking Time: 40 Minutes
Ingredients:
- 2 strip steaks
- Salt and pepper to taste
- 1 tablespoon olive oil
- ½ cup soy sauce
- ½ cup rice wine vinegar
- ¼ cup grated daikon radish

Directions:
1. Preheat the air fryer at 390°F.
2. Place the grill pan accessory in the air fryer.
3. Season the steak with salt and pepper.
4. Brush with oil.
5. Grill for 20 minutes per piece and make sure to flip the beef halfway through the cooking time
6. Prepare the dipping sauce by combining the soy sauce and vinegar.
7. Serve the steak with the sauce and daikon radish.

2. Tofu Scramble

Servings: 3
Cooking Time: 40 Minutes
Ingredients:
- 2 ½ cups red potato, chopped
- 1 tbsp. olive oil
- 1 block tofu, chopped finely
- 1tbsp. olive oil
- 2 tbsp. tamari
- 1 tsp. turmeric powder
- ½ tsp. onion powder
- ½ tsp. garlic powder
- ½ cup onion, chopped
- 4 cups broccoli florets

Directions:
1. Pre-heat the Air Fryer at 400°F.
2. Toss together the potatoes and olive oil.
3. Cook the potatoes in a baking dish for 15 minutes, shaking once during the cooking time to ensure they fry evenly.
4. Combine the tofu, olive oil, turmeric, onion powder, tamari, and garlic powder together, before stirring in the onions, followed by the broccoli.
5. Top the potatoes with the tofu mixture and allow to cook for an additional 15 minutes. Serve warm.

3. Radish Hash Browns

Servings: 4
Cooking Time: 13 Minutes
Ingredients:
- 1 lb radishes, washed and cut off roots
- 1 tbsp olive oil
- 1/2 tsp paprika
- 1/2 tsp onion powder
- 1/2 tsp garlic powder
- 1 medium onion
- 1/4 tsp pepper
- 3/4 tsp sea salt

Directions:
1. Slice onion and radishes using a mandolin slicer.
2. Add sliced onion and radishes in a large mixing bowl and toss with olive oil.
3. Transfer onion and radish slices in air fryer basket and cook at 360 F for 8 minutes. Shake basket twice.
4. Return onion and radish slices in a mixing bowl and toss with seasonings.
5. Again, cook onion and radish slices in air fryer basket for 5 minutes at 400 F. Shake basket halfway through.
6. Serve and enjoy.

4. Strawberry Rhubarb Parfait

Servings: 1
Cooking Time: 1-2 Days
Ingredients:
- 1 package crème fraiche or plain full-fat yogurt (8.5 oz)
- 2 tbsp toasted flakes
- 2 tbsp toasted coconut flakes
- 6 tbsp homemade strawberry and rhubarb jam (4.25 oz)

Directions:
1. Add the jam into a dessert bowl (3 tbsp per serving).
2. Add the crème fraîche and garnish with the toasted and coconut flakes.
3. Serve!

5. Sausage Bake

Servings: 6
Cooking Time: 23 Minutes
Ingredients:
- 2 jalapeno peppers, sliced
- 7 oz ground sausages
- 1 teaspoon dill seeds
- 3 oz Colby Jack Cheese, shredded
- 4 eggs, beaten
- 1 tablespoon cream cheese
- ½ teaspoon salt
- 1 teaspoon butter, softened
- 1 teaspoon olive oil

Directions:
1. Preheat the skillet well and pour the olive oil inside. Then add ground sausages, salt, and cook the mixture for 5-8 minutes over

the medium heat Stir it from time to time. Meanwhile, preheat the air fryer to 400F. Grease the air fryer basket with softened butter and place the cooked ground sausages inside. Flatten the mixture and top with the sliced jalapeno peppers. Then add shredded cheese. In the mixing bowl mix up eggs and cream cheese. Pour the liquid over the cheese. Sprinkle the casserole with dill seeds. The cooking time of the casserole is 16 minutes at 400F. You can increase the cooking time if you prefer the crunchy crust.

6. Prosciutto, Mozzarella & Egg In A Cup

Servings:2
Cooking Time: 20 Minutes
Ingredients:
- 2 prosciutto slices, chopped
- 2 eggs
- 4 tomato slices
- ¼ tsp balsamic vinegar
- 2 tbsp grated mozzarella
- ¼ tsp maple syrup
- 2 tbsp mayonnaise
- Salt and pepper, to taste
- Cooking spray for greasing

Directions:
1. Preheat air fryer to 320 F. Grease 2 large ramekins. Place one bread slice on the bottom of each ramekin. Arrange 2 tomato slices on top of each bread slice. Divide mozzarella between the ramekins.
2. Crack the eggs over the mozzarella. Drizzle with maple syrup and balsamic vinegar. Season with some salt and pepper. Cook for 10 minutes, or until desired. Top with mayonnaise.

7. Mushroom & Tomato Frittata

Servings:2
Cooking Time: 14 Minutes
Ingredients:
- 1 tablespoon olive oil
- 1 bacon slice, chopped
- 6 cherry tomatoes, halved
- 6 fresh mushrooms, sliced
- Salt and freshly ground black pepper, as needed
- 3 eggs
- 1 tablespoon fresh parsley, chopped
- ½ cup Parmesan cheese, grated

Directions:
1. Set the temperature of Air Fryer to 390 degrees F.
2. In a baking dish, mix together the bacon, tomatoes, mushrooms, salt, and black pepper.
3. Arrange the baking dish into an Air Fryer basket.

4. Air Fry for about 6 minutes.
5. Add the eggs in a small bowl and beat them well.
6. Add in the parsley and cheese and mix them well.
7. Remove the baking dish from Air Fryer and top the bacon mixture evenly with egg mixture.
8. Return the baking dish in Air Fryer basket.
9. Air Fry for about 8 minutes.
10. Serve hot.

8. Artichokes And Parsley Frittata

Servings: 4
Cooking Time: 12 Minutes
Ingredients:
- 1 pound artichoke hearts, steamed and chopped
- Salt and black pepper to the taste
- 4 eggs, whisked
- 1 green onion, chopped
- 2 tablespoons parsley, chopped
- Cooking spray

Directions:
1. Grease a pan that fits your air fryer with cooking spray. In a bowl, mix all the other ingredients, whisk well and pour evenly into the pan. Introduce the pan in the air fryer, cook at 390 degrees F for 12 minutes, divide between plates and serve for breakfast.

9. Hot Cups

Servings: 6
Cooking Time: 3 Minutes
Ingredients:
- 6 eggs, beaten
- 2 jalapeno, sliced
- 2 oz bacon, chopped, cooked
- ½ teaspoon salt
- ½ teaspoon chili powder
- Cooking spray

Directions:
1. Spay the silicone egg molds with cooking spray from inside. In the mixing bowl mix up beaten eggs, sliced jalapeno, salt, bacon, and chili powder. Stir the liquid gently and pour in the egg molds. Preheat the air fryer to 400F. Place the molds with the egg mixture in the air fryer. Cook the meal for 3 minutes. Then cool the cooked jalapeno & bacon cups for 2-3 minutes and remove from the silicone molds.

10. Cheesy Frittata

Servings: 6
Cooking Time: 20 Minutes
Ingredients:
- 1 cup almond milk

- Cooking spray
- 9 ounces cream cheese, soft
- 1 cup cheddar cheese, shredded
- 6 spring onions, chopped
- Salt and black pepper to the taste
- 6 eggs, whisked

Directions:
1. Heat up your air fryer with the oil at 350 degrees F and grease it with cooking spray. In a bowl, mix the eggs with the rest of the ingredients, whisk well, pour and spread into the air fryer and cook everything for 20 minutes. Divide everything between plates and serve.

11. Almond Raspberries Bowls

Servings: 4
Cooking Time: 15 Minutes
Ingredients:
- 2 cups almond milk
- ½ cups raspberries
- 1 and ½ cups coconut, shredded
- ½ teaspoon cinnamon powder
- ¼ teaspoon nutmeg, ground
- 2 teaspoons stevia
- Cooking spray

Directions:
1. Grease the air fryer's pan with cooking spray, mix all the ingredients inside, cover and cook at 360 degrees F for 15 minutes. Divide into bowls and serve for breakfast.

12. Cinnamon Toasts

Servings: 4
Cooking Time: 15 Minutes
Ingredients:
- 10 bread slices
- 1 pack salted butter
- 4 tbsp. sugar
- 2 tsp. ground cinnamon
- ½ tsp. vanilla extract

Directions:
1. In a bowl, combine the butter, cinnamon, sugar, and vanilla extract. Spread onto the slices of bread.
2. Set your Air Fryer to 380°F. When warmed up, put the bread inside the fryer and cook for 4 – 5 minutes.

13. Medium Rare Simple Salt And Pepper Steak

Servings:3
Cooking Time: 30 Minutes
Ingredients:
- 1 ½ pounds skirt steak
- Salt and pepper to taste

Directions:
1. Preheat the air fryer at 390°F.
2. Place the grill pan accessory in the air fryer.
3. Season the skirt steak with salt and pepper.
4. Place on the grill pan and cook for 15 minutes per batch.
5. Flip the meat halfway through the cooking time.

14. French Toast With Vanilla Filling

Servings:3
Cooking Time: 15 Minutes
Ingredients:
- 2 eggs
- ¼ cup heavy cream
- ⅓ cup sugar mixed with 1 tsp ground cinnamon
- 6 tbsp caramel
- 1 tsp vanilla extract
- Cooking spray

Directions:
1. In a bowl, whisk eggs and cream. Dip each piece of bread into the egg and cream. Dip the bread into the sugar and cinnamon mixture until well-coated. On a clean board, lay the coated slices and spread three of the slices with about 2 tbsp of caramel each, around the center.
2. Place the remaining three slices on top to form three sandwiches. Spray the air fryer basket with oil. Arrange the sandwiches into the fryer and cook for 10 minutes at 340 F, turning once.

15. Creamy Chives Muffins

Servings: 4
Cooking Time: 12 Minutes
Ingredients:
- 4 slices of ham
- ¼ teaspoon baking powder
- 4 tablespoons coconut flour
- 4 teaspoons heavy cream
- 1 egg, beaten
- 1 teaspoon chives, chopped
- 1 teaspoon olive oil
- ½ teaspoon white pepper

Directions:
1. Preheat the air fryer to 365F. Meanwhile, mix up baking powder, coconut flour, heavy cream, egg, chives, and white pepper. Stir the ingredients until getting a smooth mixture. Finely chop the ham and add it in the muffin liquid. Brush the air fryer muffin molds with olive oil. Then pour the muffin batter in the molds. Place the rack in the air fryer basket and place the molds on it. Cook the muffins for 12 minutes (365F). Cool the muffins to the room temperature and remove them from the molds.

16. Peppers Cups

Servings: 12

Cooking Time: 12 Minutes
Ingredients:
- 6 green bell peppers
- 12 egg
- ½ teaspoon ground black pepper
- ½ teaspoon chili flakes

Directions:
1. Cut the green bell peppers into halves and remove the seeds. Then crack the eggs in every bell pepper half and sprinkle with ground black pepper and chili flakes. After this, preheat the air fryer to 395F. Put the green bell pepper halves in the air fryer (cook for 2-3 halves per one time of cooking). Cook the egg peppers for 4 minutes. Repeat the same steps with remaining egg peppers.

17. Bistro Wedges

Servings: 4
Cooking Time: 20 Minutes
Ingredients:
- 1 lb. fingerling potatoes, cut into wedges
- 1 tsp. extra virgin olive oil
- ½ tsp. garlic powder
- Salt and pepper to taste
- ½ cup raw cashews, soaked in water overnight
- ½ tsp. ground turmeric
- ½ tsp. paprika
- 1 tbsp. nutritional yeast
- 1 tsp. fresh lemon juice
- 2 tbsp. to ¼ cup water

Directions:
1. Pre-heat your Air Fryer at 400°F.
2. In a bowl, toss together the potato wedges, olive oil, garlic powder, and salt and pepper, making sure to coat the potatoes well.
3. Transfer the potatoes to the basket of your fryer and fry for 10 minutes.
4. In the meantime, prepare the cheese sauce. Pulse the cashews, turmeric, paprika, nutritional yeast, lemon juice, and water together in a food processor. Add more water to achieve your desired consistency.
5. When the potatoes are finished cooking, move them to a bowl that is small enough to fit inside the fryer and add the cheese sauce on top. Cook for an additional 3 minutes.

18. Cream Breakfast Tofu

Servings: 4
Cooking Time:35 Minutes
Ingredients:
- 1 block firm tofu; pressed and cubed
- 1 tsp. rice vinegar
- 2 tbsp. soy sauce
- 1 tbsp. potato starch
- 2 tsp. sesame oil

- 1 cup Greek yogurt

Directions:
1. In a bowl; mix tofu cubes with vinegar, soy sauce and oil, toss, and leave aside for 15 minutes.
2. Dip tofu cubes in potato starch, toss, transfer to your air fryer; heat up at 370 °F and cook for 20 minutes shaking halfway. Divide into bowls and serve for breakfast with some Greek yogurt on the side.

19. Perfect Breakfast Frittata(2)

Servings: 2
Cooking Time: 10 Minutes
Ingredients:
- 2 large eggs
- 1 tbsp bell peppers, chopped
- 1 tbsp spring onions, chopped
- 1 sausage patty, chopped
- 1 tbsp butter, melted
- 2 tbsp cheddar cheese
- Pepper
- Salt

Directions:
1. Add sausage patty in air fryer baking dish and cook in air fryer 350 F for 5 minutes.
2. Meanwhile, in a bowl whisk together eggs, pepper, and salt.
3. Add bell peppers, onions and stir well.
4. Pour egg mixture over sausage patty and stir well.
5. Sprinkle with cheese and cook in the air fryer at 350 F for 5 minutes.
6. Serve and enjoy.

20. Coconut Muffins

Servings: 2
Cooking Time: 10 Minutes
Ingredients:
- 1/3 cup almond flour
- 2 tablespoons Erythritol
- ¼ teaspoon baking powder
- 1 teaspoon apple cider vinegar
- 1 tablespoon coconut milk
- 1 tablespoon coconut oil, softened
- 1 teaspoon ground cinnamon
- Cooking spray

Directions:
1. In the mixing bowl mix up almond flour. Erythritol, baking powder, and ground cinnamon. Add apple cider vinegar, coconut milk, and coconut oil. Stir the mixture until smooth. Spray the muffin molds with cooking spray. Scoop the muffin batter in the muffin molds. Spray the surface of every muffin with the help of the spatula. Preheat the air fryer to 365F. Insert the rack in the air fryer. Place the muffins on the rack and cook them for 10 minutes at 365F. Then

cool the cooked muffins well and remove them from the molds.

21. Spinach Balls

Servings: 4
Cooking Time: 20 Minutes
Ingredients:
- 1 carrot, peeled and grated
- 1 package fresh spinach, blanched and chopped
- ½ onion, chopped
- 1 egg, beaten
- ½ tsp. garlic powder
- 1 tsp. garlic, minced
- 1 tsp. salt
- ½ tsp. black pepper
- 1 tbsp. nutritional yeast
- 1 tbsp. flour
- 2 slices bread, toasted

Directions:
1. In a food processor, pulse the toasted bread to form breadcrumbs. Transfer into a shallow dish or bowl.
2. In a bowl, mix together all the other ingredients.
3. Use your hands to shape the mixture into small-sized balls. Roll the balls in the breadcrumbs, ensuring to cover them well.
4. Put in the Air Fryer and cook at 390°F for 10 minutes.

22. Chives Yogurt Eggs

Servings: 4
Cooking Time: 20 Minutes
Ingredients:
- Cooking spray
- Salt and black pepper to the taste
- 1 and ½ cups Greek yogurt
- 4 eggs, whisked
- 1 tablespoon chives, chopped
- 1 tablespoon cilantro, chopped

Directions:
1. In a bowl, mix all the ingredients except the cooking spray and whisk well. Grease a pan that fits the air fryer with the cooking spray, pour the eggs mix, spread well, put the pan into the machine and cook the omelet at 360 degrees F for 20 minutes. Divide between plates and serve for breakfast.

23. Greek Vegetables

Servings: 6
Cooking Time: 35 Minutes
Ingredients:
- 1 eggplant, sliced
- 4 tomatoes, quarters
- 2 onion, chopped
- 1 thyme sprig, chopped
- 1 bay leaf
- 3 tbsp olive oil
- 3 garlic cloves, minced
- 2 bell peppers, chopped
- 1 zucchini, sliced
- Pepper
- Salt

Directions:
1. Add all ingredients into the air fryer baking pan and mix well.
2. Place pan in the air fryer and cook at 300 F for 35 minutes.
3. Serve and enjoy.

24. Trout Frittata

Servings:4
Cooking Time:23 Minutes
Ingredients:
- 1 onion, sliced
- 6 eggs
- 2 hot-smoked trout fillets, chopped
- ¼ cup fresh dill, chopped
- 1 tomato, chopped
- 2 tablespoons olive oil
- ½ tablespoon horseradish sauce
- 2 tablespoons crème fraiche

Directions:
1. Preheat the Air fryer to 325 °F and grease a baking dish lightly.
2. Whisk together eggs with horseradish sauce and crème fraiche in a bowl.
3. Heat olive oil in a pan and add onions.
4. Sauté for about 3 minutes and transfer into a baking dish.
5. Stir in the whisked eggs, trout, tomato and dill.
6. Arrange the baking dish into an air fryer basket and cook for about 20 minutes.
7. Dish out and serve hot.

25. Turkey Egg Casserole

Servings: 6
Cooking Time: 25 Minutes
Ingredients:
- 12 eggs
- 2 tomatoes, chopped
- 1 cup spinach, chopped
- ½ sweet potato, cubed
- 1 tsp chili powder
- 1 tbsp olive oil
- 1 lb ground turkey
- Pepper
- Salt

Directions:
1. In a bowl, whisk eggs with pepper, chili powder, and salt until well combined.
2. Add spinach, sweet potato, tomato, and turkey and stir well.
3. Pour egg mixture into the air fryer baking dish and place in the air fryer.

4. Cook at 350 F for 25 minutes.
5. Serve and enjoy.

26. Parmesan Muffins

Servings: 4
Cooking Time: 15 Minutes
Ingredients:
- 2 eggs, whisked
- Cooking spray
- 1 and ½ cups coconut milk
- 1 tablespoon baking powder
- 4 ounces baby spinach, chopped
- 2 ounces parmesan cheese, grated
- 3 ounces almond flour

Directions:
1. In a bowl, mix all the ingredients except the cooking spray and whisk really well. Grease a muffin pan that fits your air fryer with the cooking spray, divide the muffins mix, introduce the pan in the air fryer, cook at 380 degrees F for 15 minutes, divide between plates and serve.

27. Puffed Egg Tarts

Servings:4
Cooking Time:42 Minutes
Ingredients:
- 1 sheet frozen puff pastry half, thawed and cut into 4 squares
- ¾ cup Monterey Jack cheese, shredded and divided
- 4 large eggs
- 1 tablespoon fresh parsley, minced
- 1 tablespoon olive oil

Directions:
1. Preheat the Air fryer to 390 °F
2. Place 2 pastry squares in the air fryer basket and cook for about 10 minutes.
3. Remove Air fryer basket from the Air fryer and press each square gently with a metal tablespoon to form an indentation.
4. Place 3 tablespoons of cheese in each hole and top with 1 egg each.
5. Return Air fryer basket to Air fryer and cook for about 11 minutes.
6. Remove tarts from the Air fryer basket and sprinkle with half the parsley.
7. Repeat with remaining pastry squares, cheese and eggs.
8. Dish out and serve warm.

28. Scrambled Eggs

Servings: 2
Cooking Time: 6 Minutes
Ingredients:
- 4 eggs
- 1/4 tsp garlic powder
- 1/4 tsp onion powder
- 1 tbsp parmesan cheese
- Pepper
- Salt

Directions:
1. Whisk eggs with garlic powder, onion powder, parmesan cheese, pepper, and salt.
2. Pour egg mixture into the air fryer baking dish.
3. Place dish in the air fryer and cook at 360 F for 2 minutes. Stir quickly and cook for 3-4 minutes more.
4. Stir well and serve.

29. Avocado Eggs

Servings: 4
Cooking Time: 15 Minutes
Ingredients:
- 2 large avocados, sliced
- 1 cup breadcrumbs
- ½ cup flour 2 eggs, beaten
- ¼ tsp. paprika
- Salt and pepper to taste

Directions:
1. Pre-heat your Air Fryer at 400°F for 5 minutes.
2. Sprinkle some salt and pepper on the slices of avocado. Optionally, you can enhance the flavor with a half-tsp. of dried oregano.
3. Lightly coat the avocados with flour. Dredge them in the eggs, before covering with breadcrumbs. Transfer to the fryer and cook for 6 minutes.

30. Cheddar Hash Browns

Servings:4
Cooking Time: 25 Minutes
Ingredients:
- 1 brown onion, chopped
- 3 garlic cloves, chopped
- ½ cup grated cheddar cheese
- 1 egg, lightly beaten
- Salt and black pepper
- 3 tbsp finely thyme sprigs
- Cooking spray

Directions:
1. In a bowl, mix with hands potatoes, onion, garlic, cheese, egg, salt, black pepper, and thyme. Spray the fryer with cooking spray.
2. Press the hash brown mixture into the basket and cook for 9 minutes at 400 F., shaking once halfway through cooking. When ready, ensure the hash browns are golden and crispy.

31. Pumpkin & Yogurt Bread

Servings:4
Cooking Time: 15 Minutes
Ingredients:
- 2 large eggs
- 8 tablespoons pumpkin puree

- 6 tablespoons banana flour
- 4 tablespoons honey
- 4 tablespoons plain Greek yogurt
- 2 tablespoons vanilla essence
- Pinch of ground nutmeg
- 6 tablespoons oats

Directions:
1. Take a bowl, add in all the ingredients except oats and with a hand mixer, mix until smooth.
2. Add the oats and mix them well using a fork.
3. Set the temperature of Air Fryer to 360 degrees F. Grease and flour a loaf pan.
4. Place the mixture evenly into the prepared pan.
5. Arrange the loaf pan into an Air Fryer basket.
6. Air Fry for about 15 minutes or until a toothpick inserted in the center comes out clean.
7. Remove the pans from Air Fryer and place onto a wire rack for about 5 minutes.
8. Carefully, take out the bread from pan and put onto a wire rack to cool for about 5-10 minutes before slicing.
9. Cut the bread into desired size slices and serve.

32. Egg & Mushroom Scramble

Servings:2
Cooking Time: 10 Minutes
Ingredients:
- 4 eggs
- Salt and freshly ground black pepper, as needed
- 2 tablespoons unsalted butter
- ½ cup fresh mushrooms, finely chopped
- 2 tablespoons Parmesan cheese, shredded

Directions:
1. Set the temperature of Air Fryer to 285 degrees F.
2. In a bowl, mix together the eggs, salt, and black pepper.
3. In a baking pan, melt the butter and tilt the pan to spread the butter in the bottom.
4. Add the beaten eggs and Air Fry for about 4-5 minutes
5. Add in the mushrooms and cheese and cook for 5 minutes, stirring occasionally.
6. Serve hot.

33. Tomatoes Frittata

Servings: 4
Cooking Time: 20 Minutes
Ingredients:
- 4 eggs, whisked
- 1 pound cherry tomatoes, halved
- 1 tablespoon parsley, chopped
- Cooking spray

- 1 tablespoon cheddar, grated
- Salt and black pepper to the taste

Directions:
1. Put the tomatoes in the air fryer's basket, cook at 360 degrees F for 5 minutes and transfer them to the baking pan that fits the machine greased with cooking spray. In a bowl, mix the eggs with the remaining ingredients, whisk, pour over the tomatoes an cook at 360 degrees F for 15 minutes. Serve right away for breakfast.

34. American Donuts

Servings: 6
Cooking Time: 1 Hour 20 Minutes
Ingredients:
- 1 cup flour
- ¼ cup sugar
- 1 tsp. baking powder
- ½ tsp. salt
- ¼ tsp. cinnamon
- 1 tbsp. coconut oil, melted
- 2 tbsp. aquafaba or liquid from canned chickpeas
- ¼ cup milk

Directions:
1. Put the sugar, flour and baking powder in a bowl and combine. Mix in the salt and cinnamon.
2. In a separate bowl, combine the aquafaba, milk and coconut oil.
3. Slowly pour the dry ingredients into the wet ingredients and combine well to create a sticky dough.
4. Refrigerate for at least an hour.
5. Pre-heat your Air Fryer at 370°F.
6. Using your hands, shape the dough into several small balls and place each one inside the fryer. Cook for 10 minutes, refraining from shaking the basket as they cook.
7. Lightly dust the balls with sugar and cinnamon and serve with a hot cup of coffee.

35. Simple Pumpkin Oatmeal

Servings: 4
Cooking Time: 20 Minutes
Ingredients:
- 1½ cups milk
- ½ cup pumpkin puree
- 1 teaspoon pumpkin pie spice
- 3 tablespoons sugar
- ½ cup steel cut oats

Directions:
1. In your air fryer's pan, mix all ingredients.
2. Stir, cover, and cook at 360 degrees F for 20 minutes.
3. Divide into bowls and serve.

36. Breakfast Casserole

Servings: 4
Cooking Time: 28 Minutes
Ingredients:

- 2 eggs
- 4 egg whites
- 4 tsp pine nuts, minced
- 2/3 cup chicken broth
- 1 lb Italian sausage
- 1/4 cup roasted red pepper, sliced
- 1/4 cup pesto sauce
- 2/3 cup parmesan cheese, grated
- 1/8 tsp pepper
- 1/4 tsp sea salt

Directions:

1. Preheat the air fryer to 370 F.
2. Spray air fryer pan with cooking spray and set aside.
3. Heat another pan over medium heat. Add sausage in a pan and cook until golden brown.
4. Once cooked then drain excess oil and spread it into the prepared pan.
5. Whisk remaining ingredients except pine nuts in a bowl and pour over sausage.
6. Place pan in the air fryer and cook for 25-28 minutes.
7. Top with pine nuts and serve.

37. Choco Bread

Servings: 12
Cooking Time: 30 Minutes
Ingredients:

- 1 tbsp. flax egg [1 tbsp. flax meal + 3 tbsp. water]
- 1 cup zucchini, shredded and squeezed
- ½ cup sunflower oil
- ½ cup maple syrup
- 1 tsp. vanilla extract
- 1 tsp. apple cider vinegar
- ½ cup milk
- 1 cup flour
- 1 tsp. baking soda
- ½ cup unsweetened cocoa powder
- ¼ tsp. salt
- ⅓ cup chocolate chips

Directions:

1. Pre-heat your Air Fryer to 350°F.
2. Take a baking dish small enough to fit inside the fryer and line it with parchment paper.
3. Mix together the flax meal, zucchini, sunflower oil, maple, vanilla, apple cider vinegar and milk in a bowl.
4. Incorporate the flour, cocoa powder, salt and baking soda, stirring all the time to combine everything well.
5. Finally, throw in the chocolate chips.

6. Transfer the batter to the baking dish and cook in the fryer for 15 minutes. Make sure to test with a toothpick before serving by sticking it in the center. The bread is ready when the toothpick comes out clean.

38. Chocolate Banana Bread

Servings:10
Cooking Time: 20 Minutes
Ingredients:

- 2 cups flour
- ½ teaspoon baking soda
- ½ teaspoon baking powder
- ½ teaspoon salt
- ¾ cup sugar
- 1/3 cup butter, softened
- 3 eggs
- 1 tablespoon vanilla extract
- 1 cup milk
- ½ cup bananas, peeled and mashed
- 1 cup chocolate chips

Directions:

1. Take a bowl and mix together the flour, baking soda, baking powder, and salt.
2. In another large bowl, add the butter, and sugar. Beat until light and fluffy.
3. Now, add in the eggs, and vanilla extract. Beat until well combined.
4. Add the flour mixture and mix until well combined.
5. Add in the milk, and mashed bananas and mix them well.
6. Gently, fold in the chocolate chips.
7. Set the temperature of Air Fryer to 360 degrees F. Grease a loaf pan.
8. Place the mixture evenly into the prepared pan.
9. Arrange the loaf pan into an Air Fryer basket.
10. Air Fry for about 20 minutes or until a toothpick inserted in the center comes out clean.
11. Remove from Air Fryer and place the pan onto a wire rack for about 10-15 minutes.
12. Carefully, take out the bread from pan and put onto a wire rack until it is completely cool before slicing.
13. Cut the bread into desired size slices and serve.

39. Orange-flavored Cupcakes

Servings:5
Cooking Time: 25 Minutes
Ingredients:

- 1 cup natural yogurt
- Sugar to taste
- 1 orange, juiced
- 1 tbsp orange zest
- 7 oz cream cheese

- Cake:
- 2 lemons, quartered
- ½ cup flour + extra for basing
- ¼ tsp salt
- 2 tbsp sugar
- 1 tsp baking powder
- 1 tsp vanilla extract
- 2 eggs
- ½ cup softened butter
- 2 tbsp milk

Directions:

1. In a bowl, add the yogurt and cream cheese. Mix until smooth. Add the orange juice and zest; mix well. Gradually add the sweetener to your taste while stirring until smooth. Make sure the frost is not runny. Set aside.
2. For cupcakes: Place the lemon quarters in a food processor and process it until pureed. Add the baking powder, softened butter, milk, eggs, vanilla extract, sugar, and salt. Process again until smooth.
3. Preheat the air fryer to 400 F. Flour the bottom of 10 cupcake cases and spoon the batter into the cases ¾ way up. Place them in the air fryer and bake for 7 minutes. Once ready, remove and let cool. Design the cupcakes with the frosting.

40. Cinnamon French Toast Sticks

Servings:3
Cooking Time: 15 Minutes
Ingredients:

- 3 eggs
- Salt and pepper to taste
- 1 ½ tbsp butter
- ⅛ tsp cinnamon powder
- A pinch nutmeg powder
- A pinch clove powder
- Cooking spray

Directions:

1. Preheat the air fryer to 350 F. In a bowl, add clove powder, eggs, nutmeg powder, and cinnamon powder. Beat well using a whisk. Season with salt and pepper. Use a bread knife to apply butter on both sides of the bread slices and cut them into 3 or 4 strips.
2. Dip each strip in the egg mixture and arrange them in one layer in the fryer's basket. Cook for 2 minutes. Once ready, pull out the fryer basket and spray the toasts with cooking spray. Flip the toasts and spray the other side with cooking spray. Slide the basket back to the fryer and cook for 4 minutes. Once the toasts are golden brown, remove to a serving platte. Dust with cinnamon and serve.

41. Sausage Solo

Servings:4

Cooking Time:22 Minutes
Ingredients:

- 6 eggs
- 4 cooked sausages, sliced
- 2 bread slices, cut into sticks
- ½ cup mozzarella cheese, grated
- ½ cup cream

Directions:

1. Preheat the Air fryer to 355 °F and grease 4 ramekins lightly.
2. Whisk together eggs and cream in a bowl and beat well.
3. Transfer the egg mixture into ramekins and arrange the bread sticks and sausage slices around the edges.
4. Top with mozzarella cheese evenly and place the ramekins in Air fryer basket.
5. Cook for about 22 minutes and dish out to serve warm.

42. Grilled Bbq Sausages

Servings:3
Cooking Time: 30 Minutes
Ingredients:

- 6 sausage links
- ½ cup prepared BBQ sauce

Directions:

1. Preheat the air fryer at 390°F.
2. Place the grill pan accessory in the air fryer.
3. Place the sausage links and grill for 30 minutes.
4. Flip halfway through the cooking time.
5. Before serving brush with prepared BBQ sauce.

43. Chicken And Broccoli Quiche

Servings:8
Cooking Time:12 Minutes
Ingredients:

- 1 frozen ready-made pie crust
- 1 egg
- 1/3 cup cheddar cheese, grated
- ¼ cup boiled broccoli, chopped
- ¼ cup cooked chicken, chopped
- ½ tablespoon olive oil
- 3 tablespoons whipping cream
- Salt and black pepper, to taste

Directions:

1. Preheat the Air fryer to 390 °F and grease 2 small pie pans with olive oil.
2. Whisk egg with whipping cream, cheese, salt and black pepper in a bowl.
3. Cut 2 (5-inch) rounds from the pie crust and arrange in each pie pan.
4. Press in the bottom and sides gently and pour the egg mixture over pie crust.
5. Top evenly with chicken and broccoli and place the pie pans into an Air Fryer basket.

6. Cook for about 12 minutes and dish out to serve hot.

44. Date Bread

Servings:10
Cooking Time: 22 Minutes
Ingredients:
- 2½ cup dates, pitted and chopped
- ¼ cup butter
- 1 cup hot water
- 1½ cups flour
- ½ cup brown sugar
- 1 teaspoon baking powder
- 1 teaspoon baking soda
- ½ teaspoon salt
- 1 egg

Directions:
1. In a large bowl, add the dates, butter and top with the hot water.
2. Set aside for about 5 minutes.
3. In a separate bowl, mix together the flour, brown sugar, baking powder, baking soda, and salt.
4. In the same bowl of dates, mix well the flour mixture, and egg.
5. Set the temperature of air fryer to 340 degrees F. Grease an air fryer non-stick pan.
6. Place the mixture into the prepared pan.
7. Arrange the pan into an air fryer basket.
8. Air fry for about 22 minutes or until a toothpick inserted in the center comes out clean.
9. Remove from air fryer and place the pan onto a wire rack for about 10-15 minutes.
10. Carefully, take out the bread from pan and put onto a wire rack until it is completely cool before slicing.
11. Cut the bread into desired size slices and serve.

45. Beans Oatmeal

Servings: 2
Cooking Time: 15 Minutes
Ingredients:
- 1 cup steel cut oats
- 2 tablespoons canned kidney beans, drained
- 2 red bell peppers, chopped
- 4 tablespoons heavy cream
- Salt and black pepper to taste
- ¼ teaspoon cumin, ground

Directions:
1. Heat up your air fryer at 360 degrees F and add all ingredients; stir.
2. Cover and cook for 15 minutes.
3. Divide into bowls, serve, and enjoy!

46. Spanish Style Frittata

Servings:2
Cooking Time:11 Minutes

Ingredients:
- ½ cup frozen corn
- ½ of chorizo sausage, sliced
- 1 potato, boiled, peeled and cubed
- 2 tablespoons feta cheese, crumbled
- 3 jumbo eggs
- 1 tablespoon olive oil
- Salt and black pepper, to taste

Directions:
1. Preheat the Air fryer at 355 °F and grease the baking pan with olive oil.
2. Add chorizo sausage, corn and potato and cook for about 6 minutes.
3. Whisk together eggs, salt and black pepper in a small bowl.
4. Pour eggs over the sausage mixture and top with feta cheese.
5. Place in the Air fryer and cook for about 5 minutes till desired doneness.

47. Veg Frittata

Servings: 2
Cooking Time: 35 Minutes
Ingredients:
- ¼ cup milk
- 1 zucchini
- ½ bunch asparagus
- ½ cup mushrooms
- ½ cup spinach or baby spinach
- ½ cup red onion, sliced
- 4 eggs
- ½ tbsp. olive oil
- 5 tbsp. feta cheese, crumbled
- 4 tbsp. cheddar, grated
- ¼ bunch chives, minced
- Sea salt and pepper to taste

Directions:
1. In a bowl, mix together the eggs, milk, salt and pepper.
2. Cut up the zucchini, asparagus, mushrooms and red onion into slices. Shred the spinach using your hands.
3. Over a medium heat, stir-fry the vegetables for 5 – 7 minutes with the olive oil in a non-stick pan.
4. Place some parchment paper in the base of a baking tin. Pour in the vegetables, followed by the egg mixture. Top with the feta and grated cheddar.
5. Set the Air Fryer at 320°F and allow to warm for five minutes.
6. Transfer the baking tin to the fryer and allow to cook for 15 minutes. Take care when removing the frittata from the Air Fryer and leave to cool for 5 minutes.
7. Top with the minced chives and serve.

48. Parmesan Breakfast Casserole

Servings: 3

Cooking Time: 20 Minutes
Ingredients:
- 5 eggs
- 2 tbsp heavy cream
- 3 tbsp chunky tomato sauce
- 2 tbsp parmesan cheese, grated

Directions:
1. Preheat the air fryer to 325 F.
2. In mixing bowl, combine together cream and eggs.
3. Add cheese and tomato sauce and mix well.
4. Spray air fryer baking dish with cooking spray.
5. Pour mixture into baking dish and place in the air fryer basket.
6. Cook for 20 minutes.
7. Serve and enjoy.

49. Banana And Hazelnut Muffins

Servings:6
Cooking Time: 40 Minutes
Ingredients:
- ½ cup honey
- 2 eggs, lightly beaten
- 4 ripe bananas, mashed
- 1 tsp vanilla extract
- 2 cups flour
- 1 tsp baking powder
- ½ tsp baking soda
- 1 tsp ground cinnamon
- ½ cup chopped hazelnuts
- ½ cup dark chocolate chips

Directions:
1. Spray 10-hole muffin with oil spray. In a bowl, whisk butter, honey, eggs, bananas, and vanilla, until well-combine. Sift in flour, baking powder, baking soda, and cinnamon without overmixing.
2. Stir in the hazelnuts and chocolate into the mixture. Pour the mixture into the muffin holes and place in the air fryer. Cook for 30 minutes at 350 F, checking them at the around 20-minute mark.

50. Spiced Baked Eggs

Servings: 2
Cooking Time: 3 Minutes
Ingredients:
- 2 eggs
- 1 teaspoon mascarpone
- ¼ teaspoon ground nutmeg
- ¼ teaspoon dried basil
- ¼ teaspoon dried oregano
- ¼ teaspoon dried cilantro
- ¼ teaspoon ground turmeric
- ¼ teaspoon onion powder
- ¼ teaspoon salt

Directions:

1. Crack the eggs in the mixing bowl and whisk them well. After this, add mascarpone and stir until you get a homogenous mixture. Then add all spices and mix up the liquid gently. Pour it in the silicone egg molds and transfer in the air fryer basket. Cook the egg cups for 3 minutes at 400F.

51. Breakfast Zucchini

Servings:4
Cooking Time:35 Minutes
Ingredients:
- 4 zucchinis, diced into 1-inch pieces, drained
- 2 small bell pepper, chopped medium
- 2 small onion, chopped medium
- Cooking oil spray
- Pinch salt and black pepper

Directions:
1. Preheat the Air fryer to 350 °F and grease the Air fryer basket with cooking spray.
2. Season the zucchini with salt and black pepper and place in the Air fryer basket.
3. Select Roasting mode and cook for about 20 minutes, stirring occasionally.
4. Add onion and bell pepper and cook for 5 more minutes.
5. Remove from the Air fryer and mix well to serve warm.

52. Tomatoes Casserole

Servings: 4
Cooking Time: 15 Minutes
Ingredients:
- 4 eggs, whisked
- 1 teaspoon olive oil
- 3 ounces Swiss chard, chopped
- 1 cup tomatoes, cubed
- Salt and black pepper to the taste

Directions:
1. In a bowl, mix the eggs with the rest of the ingredients except the oil and whisk well. Grease a pan that fits the fryer with the oil, pour the swish chard mix and cook at 359 degrees F for 15 minutes. Divide between plates and serve for breakfast.

53. Grilled Beef Steak With Herby Marinade

Servings:2
Cooking Time: 40 Minutes
Ingredients:
- 2 porterhouse steaks
- Salt and pepper to taste
- ¼ cup fish sauce
- 2 tablespoons marjoram
- 2 tablespoons thyme
- 2 tablespoons sage

Directions:

1. Place all ingredients in a Ziploc bag and allow to marinate in the fridge for at least 2 hours.
2. Preheat the air fryer at 390°F.
3. Place the grill pan accessory in the air fryer.
4. Grill for 20 minutes per batch.
5. Flip every 10 minutes for even grilling.

54. Spinach Frittata(1)

Servings: 1
Cooking Time: 8 Minutes
Ingredients:

- 3 eggs
- 1 cup spinach, chopped
- 1 small onion, minced
- 2 tbsp mozzarella cheese, grated
- Pepper
- Salt

Directions:

1. Preheat the air fryer to 350 F.
2. Spray air fryer pan with cooking spray.
3. In a bowl, whisk eggs with remaining ingredients until well combined.
4. Pour egg mixture into the prepared pan and place pan in the air fryer basket.
5. Cook frittata for 8 minutes or until set.
6. Serve and enjoy.

55. Potato And Spinach Omelet

Servings:4
Cooking Time: 35 Minutes
Ingredients:

- 2 cups spinach, chopped
- 5 eggs, lightly beaten
- ¼ cup heavy cream
- 1 cup grated mozzarella cheese
- ½ cup parsley, chopped
- Fresh thyme, chopped
- Salt and pepper to taste

Directions:

1. Spray the air fryer's basket with oil. Arrange the potatoes inside.
2. In a bowl, whisk eggs, cream, spinach, mozzarella, parsley, thyme, salt and pepper, and pour over the potatoes. Cook for 16 minutes at 400 F, until nice and golden.

56. Pounded Flank Steak With Tomato Salsa

Servings:4
Cooking Time: 40 Minutes
Ingredients:

- 1 ½ pounds flank steak, pounded
- Salt and pepper to taste
- 2 cups chopped tomatoes
- ¼ cup chopped cilantro
- 1 red onion, chopped
- 1 teaspoon coriander powder

Directions:

1. Preheat the air fryer at 390°F.
2. Place the grill pan accessory in the air fryer.
3. Season the flank steak with salt and pepper.
4. Grill for 20 minutes per batch and make sure to flip the beef halfway through the cooking time.
5. Meanwhile, prepare the salsa by mixing in a bowl the tomatoes, cilantro, onions, and coriander. Season with more salt and pepper to taste.

57. Special Shrimp Sandwiches

Servings: 4
Cooking Time:15 Minutes
Ingredients:

- 1 ¼ cups cheddar; shredded
- 2 tbsp. green onions; chopped.
- 4 whole wheat bread slices
- 6 oz. canned tiny shrimp; drained
- 3 tbsp. mayonnaise
- 2 tbsp. butter; soft

Directions:

1. In a bowl; mix shrimp with cheese, green onion and mayo and stir well.
2. Spread this on half of the bread slices; top with the other bread slices, cut into halves diagonally and spread butter on top.
3. Place sandwiches in your air fryer and cook at 350 °F, for 5 minutes. Divide shrimp sandwiches on plates and serve them for breakfast.

58. Sweet Jalapeño Cornbread

Servings:10
Cooking Time: 18 Minutes
Ingredients:

- 1 cup flour
- 1 cup yellow cornmeal
- ½ cup white sugar
- 2 teaspoons baking powder
- ½ teaspoon baking soda
- 1 teaspoon salt
- 2 large eggs
- ¾ cup sour cream
- ½ cup buttermilk
- 3 tablespoons butter, melted
- 2 tablespoons vegetable oil
- ¼ cup pepper jack cheese, grated
- ½ of jalapeño pepper, finely chopped

Directions:

1. In a bowl, mix together the flour, cornmeal, sugar, baking powder, baking soda, and salt.
2. In another large bowl, mix well the eggs, sour cream, buttermilk, butter, and oil.
3. Then, add in the flour mixture and mix until well combined.
4. Add the cheese, and jalapeño and stir to combine.

5. Set the temperature of Air Fryer to 300 degrees F. Grease a round cake pan.
6. Put the mixture evenly into the prepared pan.
7. Arrange the cake pan into an Air Fryer basket.
8. Air Fry for about 18 minutes or until a toothpick inserted in the center comes out clean, turning the pan once halfway through.
9. Remove from Air Fryer and place the pan onto a wire rack for about 10-15 minutes.
10. Carefully, take out the bread from pan and put onto a wire rack until it is completely cool before slicing.
11. Cut the bread into desired size slices and serve.

59. Roasted Pepper Salad

Servings: 4
Cooking Time: 10 Minutes
Ingredients:
- 4 bell peppers
- 2 oz rocket leaves
- 2 tbsp olive oil
- 4 tbsp heavy cream
- 1 lettuce head, torn
- 1 tbsp fresh lime juice
- Pepper
- Salt

Directions:
1. Add bell peppers into the air fryer basket and cook for 10 minutes at 400 F.
2. Remove peppers from air fryer and let it cool for 5 minutes.
3. Peel cooked peppers and cut into strips and place into the large bowl.
4. Add remaining ingredients into the bowl and toss well.
5. Serve and enjoy.

60. White Filling Coconut And Oat Cookies

Servings:4
Cooking Time: 30 Minutes
Ingredients:

- 1 tsp vanilla extract
- 3 oz sugar
- ½ cup oats
- 1 small egg, beaten
- ¼ cup coconut flakes
- Filling:
- 1 oz white chocolate, melted
- 2 oz butter
- 4 oz powdered sugar
- 1 tsp vanilla extract

Directions:
1. Beat all the cookie ingredients, with an electric mixer, except the flour. When smooth, fold in the flour. Drop spoonfuls of the batter onto a prepared cookie sheet. Cook in the air fryer at 350 F for 18 minutes; then let cool.
2. Meanwhile, prepare the filling by beating all ingredients together; spread the filling on half of the cookies. Top with the other halves to make cookie sandwiches.

61. Bacon And Egg Bite Cups

Servings:4
Cooking Time:15 Minutes
Ingredients:
- 6 large eggs
- ½ cup red peppers, chopped
- ¼ cup fresh spinach, chopped
- ¾ cup mozzarella cheese, shredded
- 3 slices bacon, cooked and crumbled
- 2 tablespoons heavy whipping cream
- Salt and black pepper, to taste

Directions:
1. Preheat the Air fryer to 300 °F and grease 4 silicone molds.
2. Whisk together eggs with cream, salt and black pepper in a large bowl until combined.
3. Stir in rest of the ingredients and transfer the mixture into silicone molds.
4. Place in the Air fryer and cook for about 15 minutes.
5. Dish out and serve warm.

62. Mozzarella Burger

Servings: 2
Cooking Time: 12 Minutes
Ingredients:
- 4 sausage patties
- 1 teaspoon butter, softened
- ½ teaspoon ground black pepper
- ¼ teaspoon salt
- 1 oz Mozzarella, chopped
- 4 bacon slices
- Cooking spray

Directions:
1. Sprinkle the sausage patties with ground black pepper and salt. Then put the cheese and butter on the patties. Make the balls from the sausage patties with the help of the fingertips. After this, roll them in the bacon. Preheat the air fryer to 390F. Put the bacon bombs in the air fryer and spray them with the cooking spray. Cook the bombs for 12 minutes – for 6 minutes from each side.

63. Tuna Bake

Servings: 6
Cooking Time: 15 Minutes
Ingredients:
- 2 spring onions, diced
- 1 pound smoked tuna, boneless
- ¼ cup ricotta cheese
- 3 oz celery stalk, diced
- ½ teaspoon celery seeds
- 1 tablespoon cream cheese
- ¼ teaspoon salt
- ½ teaspoon ground paprika
- 2 tablespoons lemon juice
- 1 tablespoon ghee
- 4 oz Edam cheese, shredded

Directions:
1. Mix up celery seeds, cream cheese, ground paprika, lemon juice, and ricotta cheese. Then shred the tuna until it is smooth and add it in the cream cheese mixture. Add onion and stir the mass with the help of the spoon. Grease the air fryer pan with ghee and put the tuna mixture inside. Flatten its surface gently with the help of the spoon and top with Edam cheese. Preheat the air fryer to 360F. Place the pan with tuna melt in the air fryer and cook it for 15 minutes.

64. Tasty Stuffed Meatballs

Servings: 4
Cooking Time:20 Minutes
Ingredients:
- 1/3 cup bread crumbs
- 1/2 tsp. marjoram; dried
- 3 tbsp. milk
- 1 tbsp. ketchup
- 1 egg
- 1 lb. lean beef; ground
- 20 cheddar cheese cubes
- 1 tbsp. olive oil
- Salt and black pepper to the taste

Directions:
1. In a bowl; mix bread crumbs with ketchup, milk, marjoram, salt, pepper and egg and whisk well.
2. Add beef; stir and shape 20 meatballs out of this mix.
3. Shape each meatball around a cheese cube, drizzle the oil over them and rub.
4. Place all meatballs in your preheated air fryer and cook at 390 °F, for 10 minutes. Serve them for lunch with a side salad.

65. Prosciutto & Potato Salad

Servings: 8
Cooking Time: 15 Minutes
Ingredients:
- 4 lb. potatoes, boiled and cubed
- 15 slices prosciutto, diced
- 15 oz. sour cream
- 2 cups shredded cheddar cheese
- 2 tbsp. mayonnaise
- 1 tsp. salt
- 1 tsp. black pepper
- 1 tsp. dried basil

Directions:
1. Pre-heat the Air Fryer to 350°F.
2. Place the potatoes, prosciutto, and cheddar in a baking dish. Put it in the Air Fryer and allow to cook for 7 minutes.
3. In a separate bowl, mix together the sour cream, mayonnaise, salt, pepper, and basil using a whisk.
4. Coat the salad with the dressing and serve.

66. Eggplant Sandwich

Servings: 2
Cooking Time: 7 Minutes
Ingredients:
- 1 large eggplant
- ½ cup mozzarella, shredded
- 1 tablespoon fresh basil, chopped
- 1 teaspoon minced garlic
- 1 teaspoon salt
- 1 tablespoon nut oil
- 1 tomato

Directions:
1. Slice the tomato on 4 slices. Then slice along the eggplant on 4 slices. Then rub every eggplant slice with salt, minced garlic, and

brush with nut oil. Preheat the air fryer to 400F. Put the eggplant slices in one layer and cook for 2 minutes at 400F. Then flip the vegetables on another side and cook for 2 minutes more. Transfer the cooked eggplant slices on the plate. Sprinkle 2 eggplant slices with basil and mozzarella. Then add 2 tomato slices on 2 eggplant slices. Cover the tomato slices with the remaining 2 eggplant slices and put in the air fryer basket. Cook the sandwich for 3 minutes at 400F.

67. Balsamic Cauliflower Stew

Servings: 4
Cooking Time: 20 Minutes
Ingredients:
- 1 and ½ cups zucchinis, sliced
- 1 tablespoon olive oil
- Salt and black pepper to the taste
- 1 tablespoon balsamic vinegar
- 1 cauliflower head, florets separated
- 2 green onions, chopped
- 1 handful parsley leaves, chopped
- ½ cup keto tomato sauce

Directions:
1. In a pan that fits your air fryer, mix the zucchinis with the rest of the ingredients except the parsley, toss, introduce the pan in the air fryer and cook at 380 degrees F for 20 minutes. Divide into bowls and serve for lunch with parsley sprinkled on top.

68. Quinoa And Spinach Pesto Mix

Servings: 4
Cooking Time: 15 Minutes
Ingredients:
- 1 cup quinoa, cooked
- 3 tablespoons chicken stock
- ¾ cup jarred spinach pesto
- 1 green apple, chopped
- ¼ cup celery, chopped
- Salt and black pepper to taste

Directions:
1. Mix all the ingredients in a pan that fits your air fryer; toss.
2. Place the pan in your fryer and cook at 370 degrees F for 15 minutes.
3. Divide into bowls and serve right away.

69. Monkey Salad

Servings: 1
Cooking Time: 10 Minutes
Ingredients:
- 2 tbsp butter
- 1 cup unsweetened coconut flakes
- 1 cup raw, unsalted cashews
- 1 cup raw, unsalted s
- 1 cup 90% dark chocolate shavings

Directions:
1. In a skillet, melt the butter on a medium heat.
2. Add the coconut flakes and sauté until lightly browned for 4 minutes.
3. Add the cashews and s and sauté for 3 minutes. Remove from the heat and sprinkle with dark chocolate shavings.
4. Serve!

70. Zucchini Casserole

Servings: 4
Cooking Time: 30 Minutes
Ingredients:
- 1 cup ground chicken
- ½ cup ground pork
- 2 oz celery stalk, chopped
- 1 zucchini, grated
- 1 tablespoon coconut oil, melted
- ½ teaspoon salt
- 1 teaspoon ground black pepper
- ½ teaspoon chili flakes
- 1 teaspoon dried dill
- ½ teaspoon dried parsley
- ½ cup beef broth

Directions:
1. In the mixing bowl mix up ground chicken, ground pork, celery stalk, and salt. Add ground black pepper, chili flakes, dried dill, and dried parsley. Stir the meat mixture until homogenous. Then brush the air fryer pan with coconut oil and put ½ part of all grated zucchini. Then spread it with all ground pork mixture. Sprinkle the meat with remaining grated zucchini and cover with foil. Preheat the air fryer to 375F. Place the pan with casserole in the air fryer and cook it for 25 minutes. When the time is finished, remove the foil and cook the casserole for 5 minutes more.

71. Chicken Fillets & Brie

Servings: 4
Cooking Time: 40 Minutes
Ingredients:
- 4 slices turkey, cured
- 2 large chicken fillets
- 4 slices brie cheese
- 1 tbsp. chives, chopped
- Salt and pepper to taste

Directions:
1. Pre-heat Air Fryer to 360°F. Slice each chicken fillet in half and sprinkle on salt and pepper. Coat with the brie and chives.
2. Wrap the turkey around the chicken and secure with toothpick.
3. Cook for 15 minutes until a brown color is achieved.

72. Steak And Cabbage

Servings: 4
Cooking Time:20 Minutes
Ingredients:
- 1/2 lb. sirloin steak; cut into strips
- 2 green onions; chopped.
- 2 garlic cloves; minced
- 2 tsp. cornstarch
- 1 tbsp. peanut oil
- 2 cups green cabbage; chopped
- 1 yellow bell pepper; chopped
- Salt and black pepper to the taste

Directions:
1. In a bowl; mix cabbage with salt, pepper and peanut oil; toss, transfer to air fryer's basket, cook at 370 °F, for 4 minutes and transfer to a bowl.
2. Add steak strips to your air fryer; also add green onions, bell pepper, garlic, salt and pepper, toss and cook for 5 minutes. Add over cabbage; toss, divide among plates and serve for lunch.

73. Mediterranean Vegetables

Servings: 4
Cooking Time: 30 Minutes
Ingredients:
- 1 cup cherry tomatoes, halved
- 1 large zucchini, sliced
- 1 green pepper, sliced
- 1 parsnip, sliced
- 1 carrot, sliced
- 1 tsp. mixed herbs
- 1 tsp. mustard
- 1 tsp. garlic puree
- 6 tbsp. olive oil
- Salt and pepper to taste

Directions:
1. Pre-heat the Air Fryer at 400°F.
2. Combine all the ingredients in a bowl, making sure to coat the vegetables well.
3. Transfer to the fryer and cook for 6 minutes, ensuring the vegetables are tender and browned.

74. Cheese Pies

Servings: 4
Cooking Time: 4 Minutes
Ingredients:
- 8 wonton wraps
- 1 egg, beaten
- 1 cup cottage cheese
- 1 tablespoon Erythritol
- ½ teaspoon vanilla extract
- 1 egg white, whisked
- Cooking spray

Directions:
1. Mix up cottage cheese and Erythritol. Then add vanilla extract and egg. Stir the mixture well with the help of the fork. After this, put the cottage cheese mixture on the wonton wraps and fold them in the shape of pies. Then brush the pies with whisked egg white. Preheat the air fryer to 375F. Then put the cottage cheese pies in the air fryer and spray them with the cooking spray. Cook the meal for 2 minutes from each side.

75. Cauliflower Steak

Servings: 2
Cooking Time: 30 Minutes
Ingredients:
- 1 cauliflower, sliced into two
- 1 tbsp. olive oil
- 2 tbsp. onion, chopped
- ¼ tsp. vegetable stock powder
- ¼ cup milk
- Salt and pepper to taste

Directions:
1. Place the cauliflower in a bowl of salted water and allow to absorb for at least 2 hours.
2. Pre-heat the Air Fryer to 400°F.
3. Rinse off the cauliflower, put inside the fryer and cook for 15 minutes.
4. In the meantime, fry the onions over medium heat, stirring constantly, until they turn translucent. Pour in the vegetable stock powder and milk. Bring to a boil and then lower the heat.
5. Let the sauce reduce and add in salt and pepper.
6. Plate up the cauliflower steak and top with the sauce.

76. Chicken Lunch Recipe

Servings: 6
Cooking Time:30 Minutes
Ingredients:
- 1 bunch kale; chopped
- 1 cup chicken; shredded
- 3 carrots; chopped
- 1 cup shiitake mushrooms; roughly sliced
- 1/4 cup chicken stock
- Salt and black pepper to the taste

Directions:
1. In a blender, mix stock with kale, pulse a few times and pour into a pan that fits your air fryer. Add chicken, mushrooms, carrots, salt and pepper to the taste; toss, introduce in your air fryer and cook at 350 °F, for 18 minutes.

77. French Green Beans

Servings: 4
Cooking Time: 20 Minutes

Ingredients:
- 1 ½ lb. French green beans, stems removed and blanched
- 1 tbsp. salt
- ½ lb. shallots, peeled and cut into quarters
- ½ tsp. ground white pepper
- 2 tbsp. olive oil
- ¼ cup slivered s, toasted

Directions:
1. Pre-heat the Air Fryer at 400°F.
2. Coat the vegetables with the rest of the ingredients in a bowl.
3. Transfer to the basket of your fryer and cook for 10 minutes, making sure the green beans achieve a light brown color.

78. Mac & Cheese

Servings: 2
Cooking Time: 15 Minutes
Ingredients:
- 1 cup cooked macaroni
- ½ cup warm milk
- 1 tbsp. parmesan cheese
- 1 cup grated cheddar cheese
- Salt and pepper, to taste

Directions:
1. Pre-heat the Air Fryer to 350°F.
2. In a baking dish, mix together all of the ingredients, except for Parmesan.
3. Put the dish inside the Air Fryer and allow to cook for 10 minutes.
4. Add the Parmesan cheese on top and serve.

79. Duck Fat Ribeye

Servings: 1
Cooking Time: 20 Minutes
Ingredients:
- One 16-oz ribeye steak (1 - 1 ¼ inch thick)
- 1 tbsp duck fat (or other high smoke point oil like peanut oil)
- ½ tbsp butter
- ½ tsp thyme, chopped
- Salt and pepper to taste

Directions:
1. Preheat a skillet in your fryer at 400°F/200°C.
2. Season the steaks with the oil, salt and pepper. Remove the skillet from the fryer once pre-heated.
3. Put the skillet on your stove top burner on a medium heat and drizzle in the oil.
4. Sear the steak for 1-4 minutes, depending on if you like it rare, medium or well done.
5. Turn over the steak and place in your fryer for 6 minutes.
6. Take out the steak from your fryer and place it back on the stove top on low heat.
7. Toss in the butter and thyme and cook for 3 minutes, basting as you go along.

8. Rest for 5 minutes and serve.

80. Sriracha Cauliflower

Servings: 4
Cooking Time: 25 Minutes
Ingredients:
- ¼ cup vegan butter, melted
- ¼ cup sriracha sauce
- 4 cups cauliflower florets
- 1 cup bread crumbs
- 1 tsp. salt

Directions:
1. Mix together the sriracha and vegan butter in a bowl and pour this mixture over the cauliflower, taking care to cover each floret entirely.
2. In a separate bowl, combine the bread crumbs and salt.
3. Dip the cauliflower florets in the bread crumbs, coating each one well. Cook in the Air Fryer for 17 minutes in a 375°F pre-heated Air Fryer.

81. Cashew & Chicken Manchurian

Servings: 6
Cooking Time: 30 Minutes
Ingredients:
- 1 cup chicken boneless
- 1 spring onions, chopped
- 1 onion, chopped
- 3 green chili
- 6 cashew nuts
- 1 tsp. ginger, chopped
- ½ tsp. garlic, chopped
- 1 Egg
- 2 tbsp. flour
- 1 tbsp. cornstarch
- 1 tsp. soy sauce
- 2 tsp. chili paste
- 1 tsp. pepper
- Pinch MSG
- sugar as needed
- 1 tbsp. oil

Directions:
1. Pre-heat your Air Fryer at 360°F
2. Toss together the chicken, egg, salt and pepper to coat well.
3. Combine the cornstarch and flour and use this to cover the chicken.
4. Cook in the fryer for 10 minutes.
5. In the meantime, toast the nuts in a frying pan. Add in the onions and cook until they turn translucent. Combine with the remaining ingredients to create the sauce.
6. Finally, add in the chicken. When piping hot, garnish with the spring onions and serve.

82. Cauliflower Cheese Tater Tots

Servings: 12

Cooking Time: 25 Minutes

Ingredients:

- 1 lb. cauliflower, steamed and chopped
- ½ cup nutritional yeast
- 1 tbsp. oats
- 1 flax egg [1 tbsp. desiccated coconuts + 3 tbsp. flaxseed meal
- + 3 tbsp. water]
- 1 onion, chopped
- 1 tsp. garlic, minced
- 1 tsp. parsley, chopped
- 1 tsp. oregano, chopped
- 1 tsp. chives, chopped
- Salt and pepper to taste
- ½ cup bread crumbs

Directions:

1. Pre-heat the Air Fryer at 390°F.
2. Drain any excess water out of the cauliflower by wringing it with a paper towel.
3. In a bowl, combine the cauliflower with the remaining ingredients, save the bread crumbs. Using your hands, shape the mixture into several small balls.
4. Coat the balls in the bread crumbs and transfer to the basket of your fryer. Allow to cook for 6 minutes, after which you should raise the temperature to 400°F and then leave to cook for an additional 10 minutes.

83. Okra Stew

Servings: 4
Cooking Time: 20 Minutes

Ingredients:

- 1 cup okra
- 4 zucchinis, roughly cubed
- 1 teaspoon oregano, dried
- 2 green bell peppers, cut into strips
- 2 garlic cloves, minced
- Salt and black pepper to the taste
- 7 ounces keto tomato sauce
- 2 tablespoons olive oil
- 2 tablespoons cilantro, chopped

Directions:

1. In a pan that fits your air fryer, combine all the ingredients for the stew, toss, introduce the pan in the air fryer, cook the stew at 350 degrees F for 20 minutes, divide into bowls, and serve.

84. Pasta Salad

Servings: 8
Cooking Time: 2 Hours 25 Minutes

Ingredients:

- 4 tomatoes, medium and cut in eighths
- 3 eggplants, small
- 3 zucchinis, medium sized
- 2 bell peppers, any color
- 4 cups large pasta, uncooked in any shape
- 1 cup cherry tomatoes, sliced
- ½ cup Italian dressing, fat-free
- 8 tbsp. parmesan, grated
- 2 tbsp. extra virgin olive oil
- 2 tsp. pink Himalayan salt
- 1 tsp. basil, dried
- High quality cooking spray

Directions:

1. Wash and dry the eggplant. Cut off the stem and throw it away. Do not peel the eggplant. Cut it into half-inch-thick round slices.
2. Coat the eggplant slices with 1 tbsp. of extra virgin olive oil, and transfer to the Air Fryer basket.
3. Cook the eggplant for 40 minutes at 350°F. Once it is tender and cooked through, remove from the fryer and set to one side.
4. Wash and dry the zucchini. Cut off the stem and throw it away. Do not peel the zucchini. Cut the zucchini into half-inch-thick round slices.
5. Combine with the olive oil to coat, and put it in the Air Fryer basket.
6. Cook the zucchini for about 25 minutes at 350°F. Once it is tender and cooked through, remove from the fryer and set to one side.
7. Wash the tomatoes and cut them into eight equal slices. Transfer them to the fryer basket and spritz lightly with high quality cooking spray. Cook the tomatoes for 30 minutes at 350°F. Once they have shrunk and are beginning to turn brown, set them to one side.
8. Cook the pasta and drain it. Rinse with cold water and set it aside to cool.
9. Wash, dry and halve the bell peppers. Remove the stems and seeds.
10. Wash and halve the cherry tomatoes.
11. In a large bowl, mix together the bell peppers and cherry tomatoes. Stir in the roasted vegetables, cooked pasta, pink Himalayan salt, dressing, chopped basil leaves, and grated parmesan, ensuring to incorporate everything well.
12. Let the salad cool and marinate in the refrigerator.
13. Serve the salad cold or at room temperature.

85. Spiced Salmon And Cilantro Croquettes

Servings: 4
Cooking Time: 8 Minutes

Ingredients:

- 1-pound smoked salmon, boneless and flaked
- 1 egg, beaten
- 1 tablespoon almond flour
- ½ teaspoon ground black pepper
- ¼ teaspoon ground cumin

- ½ teaspoon ground nutmeg
- 1 tablespoon fresh cilantro, chopped
- 1 teaspoon avocado oil

Directions:

1. Put the salmon in the bowl and churn it with the help of the fork until you get the smooth mass. Then add an egg, almond flour, ground black pepper, cumin, nutmeg, and cilantro. Stir the ingredients until they are smooth. Preheat the air fryer to 365F. Wet your hands and make the croquettes. Then place them in the air fryer in one layer and sprinkle with avocado oil. Cook the croquettes for 5 minutes. Then flip them on another side and cook for 3 minutes more.

86. Bacon Chops

Servings: 2
Cooking Time: 20 Minutes
Ingredients:

- 2 pork chops (I prefer bone-in, but boneless chops work great as well)
- 1 bag shredded brussels sprouts
- 4 slices of bacon
- Worcestershire sauce
- Lemon juice (optional)

Directions:

1. Place the pork chops on a baking sheet with the Worcestershire sauce inside a preheated grill for 5 minutes.
2. Turnover and cook for another 5 minutes. Put to the side when done.
3. Cook the chopped bacon in a large pan until browned. Add the shredded brussels sprouts and cook together.
4. Stir the brussels sprouts with the bacon and grease and cook for 5 minutes until the bacon is crisp.

87. Salmon Salad

Servings: 4
Cooking Time: 8 Minutes
Ingredients:

- 4 salmon fillets, boneless
- 2 tablespoons olive oil
- Salt and black pepper to the taste
- 3 cups kale leaves, shredded
- 2 teaspoons balsamic vinegar

Directions:

1. Put the fish in your air fryer's basket, season with salt and pepper, drizzle half of the oil over them, cook at 400 degrees F for 4 minutes on each side, cool down and cut into medium cubes. In a bowl, mix the kale with salt, pepper, vinegar, the rest of the oil and the salmon, toss gently and serve for lunch.

88. Italian Lamb Chops

Servings: 2
Cooking Time: 20 Minutes
Ingredients:

- 2 lamp chops
- 2 tsp. Italian herbs
- 2 avocados
- ½ cup mayonnaise
- 1 tbsp. lemon juice

Directions:

1. Season the lamb chops with the Italian herbs, then set aside for five minutes.
2. Pre-heat the fryer at 400°F and place the rack inside.
3. Put the chops on the rack and allow to cook for twelve minutes.
4. In the meantime, halve the avocados and open to remove the pits. Spoon the flesh into a blender.
5. Add in the mayonnaise and lemon juice and pulse until a smooth consistency is achieved.
6. Take care when removing the chops from the fryer, then plate up and serve with the avocado mayo.

89. Quinoa And Spinach Salad

Servings: 4
Cooking Time: 15 Minutes
Ingredients:

- 1½ cups quinoa, cooked
- 1 red bell pepper, chopped
- 3 celery stalks, chopped
- Salt and black pepper to taste
- 4 cups spinach, torn
- 2 tomatoes, chopped
- ½ cup chicken stock
- ½ cup black olives, pitted and chopped
- ½ cup feta cheese, crumbled
- ⅓ cup basil pesto
- ¼ cup almonds, sliced

Directions:

1. In a pan that fits your air fryer, combine the quinoa, bell peppers, celery, salt, pepper, spinach, tomatoes, chicken stock, olives, and basil pesto.
2. Sprinkle the almonds and the cheese on top, and then place the pan in the air fryer and cook at 380 degrees F for 15 minutes.
3. Divide between plates and serve.

90. Meatballs, Tomato Sauce

Servings: 4
Cooking Time:245 Minutes
Ingredients:

- 1 lb. lean beef; ground
- 3 green onions; chopped.
- 2 garlic cloves; minced
- 1 egg yolk
- 1/4 cup bread crumbs

- 1 tbsp. olive oil
- 16 oz. tomato sauce
- 2 tbsp. mustard
- Salt and black pepper to the taste

Directions:
1. In a bowl; mix beef with onion, garlic, egg yolk, bread crumbs, salt and pepper; stir well and shape medium meatballs out of this mix.
2. Grease meatballs with the oil, place them in your air fryer and cook them at 400 °F, for 10 minutes.
3. In a bowl; mix tomato sauce with mustard, whisk, add over meatballs; toss them and cook at 400 °F, for 5 minutes more. Divide meatballs and sauce on plates and serve for lunch.

91. Easy Zoodles & Turkey Balls

Servings: 2
Cooking Time: 35 Minutes
Ingredients:
- 1 zucchini, cut into spirals
- 1 can vodka pasta sauce
- 1 package frozen Armour Turkey meatballs

Directions:
1. Cook the meatballs and sauce on a high heat for 25 minutes, stirring occasionally.
2. Wash the zucchini and put through a vegetable spiral maker.
3. Boil the water and blanch the raw zoodles for 60 seconds. Remove and drain.
4. Combine the zoodles and prepared saucy meatballs.
5. Serve!

92. Buffalo Chicken Salad

Servings: 1
Cooking Time: 40 Minutes
Ingredients:
- 3 cups salad of your choice
- 1 chicken breast
- 1/2 cup shredded cheese of your choice
- Buffalo wing sauce of your choice
- Ranch or blue cheese dressing

Directions:
1. Preheat your fryer to 400°F/200°C.
2. Douse the chicken breast in the buffalo wing sauce and bake for 25 minutes. In the last 5 minutes, throw the cheese on the wings until it melts.
3. When cooked, remove from the fryer and slice into pieces.
4. Place on a bed of lettuce.
5. Pour the salad dressing of your choice on top.
6. Serve!

93. Coconut Chicken

Servings: 4
Cooking Time: 20 Minutes
Ingredients:
- 4 chicken breasts, skinless, boneless and cubed
- Salt and black pepper to the taste
- ¼ cup coconut cream
- 1 teaspoon olive oil
- 1 and ½ teaspoon sweet paprika

Directions:
1. Grease a pan that fits your air fryer with the oil, mix all the ingredients inside, introduce the pan in the fryer and cook at 370 degrees F for 17 minutes. Divide between plates and serve for lunch.

94. Chicken Rolls

Servings: 4
Cooking Time: 18 Minutes
Ingredients:
- 2 large zucchini
- ½ cup Cheddar cheese, shredded
- 1-pound chicken breast, skinless, boneless
- 1 teaspoon dried oregano
- ½ teaspoon olive oil
- 1 teaspoon salt
- 2 spring onions, chopped
- 1 teaspoon ground paprika
- ½ teaspoon ground turmeric
- ½ cup keto tomato sauce

Directions:
1. Preheat the skillet well and pour the olive oil inside. Put the onions in it and sprinkle with salt, ground paprika, and ground turmeric. Cook the onion for 5 minutes over the medium-high heat. Stir it from time to time. Meanwhile, shred the chicken. Add it in the skillet. Then add oregano. Stir well and cook the mixture for 2 minutes. After this, remove the skillet from the heat. Cut the zucchini into halves (lengthwise). Then make the zucchini slices with the help of the vegetable peeler. Put 3 zucchini slices on the chopping board overlapping each of them. Then spread the surface of them with the shredded chicken mixture. Roll the zucchini carefully in the shape of the roll. Repeat the same steps with remaining zucchini and shredded chicken mixture. Line the air fryer pan with parchment and put the enchilada rolls inside. Sprinkle them with tomato sauce Preheat the air fryer to 350F. Top the zucchini rolls (enchiladas) with Cheddar cheese and put in the air fryer basket. Cook the meal for 10 minutes.

95. Mexican Pizza

Servings: 4

Cooking Time: 15 Minutes

Ingredients:
- ¾ cup refried beans
- 1 cup salsa
- 12 frozen beef meatballs, pre-cooked
- 2 jalapeno peppers, sliced
- 6 bread
- 1 cup pepper Jack cheese, shredded
- 1 cup Colby cheese, shredded

Directions:
1. Pre-heat the Air Fryer for 4 minutes at 370°F.
2. In a bowl, mix together the salsa, meatball, jalapeno pepper and beans.
3. Place a spoonful of this mixture on top of each pita bread, along with a topping of pepper Jack and Colby cheese.
4. Bake in the fryer for 10 minutes. Serve hot.

96. Cheesy Calzone

Servings: 2
Cooking Time: 8 Minutes
Ingredients:
- 2 tablespoons almond flour
- 2 tablespoons flax meal
- 1 tablespoon coconut oil, softened
- ¼ teaspoon salt
- ¼ teaspoon baking powder
- 2 ham slices, chopped
- 1 oz Parmesan, grated
- 1 egg yolk, whisked
- 1 tablespoon spinach, chopped
- Cooking spray

Directions:
1. Make calzone dough: mix up almond flour, flax meal, coconut oil, salt, and baking powder. Knead the dough until soft and smooth. Then roll it up with the help of the rolling pin and cut into halves. Fill every dough half with chopped ham, grated Parmesan, and spinach. Fold the dough in the shape of calzones and secure the edges. Then brush calzones with the whisked egg yolk. Preheat the air fryer basket to 350F. Place the calzones in the air fryer basket and spray them with cooking spray. Cook them for 8 minutes or until they are light brown. Flip the calzones on another side after 4 minutes of cooking.

97. Lamb Ribs

Servings: 4
Cooking Time: 25 Minutes
Ingredients:
- 1 lb. lamb ribs
- 2 tbsp. mustard
- 1 tsp. rosemary, chopped
- Salt and pepper
- ¼ cup mint leaves, chopped

- 1 cup Green yogurt

Directions:
1. Pre-heat the fryer at 350°F.
2. Use a brush to apply the mustard to the lamb ribs, and season with rosemary, as well as salt and pepper as desired.
3. Cook the ribs in the fryer for eighteen minutes.
4. Meanwhile, combine together the mint leaves and yogurt in a bowl.
5. Remove the lamb ribs from the fryer when cooked and serve with the mint yogurt. Enjoy!

98. Sprouts And Chicken Casserole

Servings: 2
Cooking Time: 25 Minutes
Ingredients:
- 1 cup Brussels sprouts
- ½ teaspoon salt
- ½ cup ground chicken
- ½ teaspoon ground black pepper
- 1 tablespoon coconut cream
- 1 teaspoon chili powder
- 1 tablespoon butter, melted
- ½ teaspoon ground paprika

Directions:
1. Mix up ground chicken, ground black pepper, chili powder, ground paprika, and coconut cream. Add salt and stir the mixture. After this, grease the air fryer casserole mold with butter. Put Brussels sprouts in the casserole mold and flatten them in one layer. Then top the vegetables with ground chicken mixture. Cover the casserole with baking paper and secure the edges. Preheat the air fryer to 365F. Put the casserole mold in the air fryer basket and cook it for 25 minutes.

99. Smoked Chicken Mix

Servings: 4
Cooking Time: 25 Minutes
Ingredients:
- 1 and ½ pound chicken breasts, skinless, boneless and cubed
- Salt and black pepper to the taste
- ½ cup chicken stock
- 2 teaspoons smoked paprika
- ½ teaspoon basil, dried

Directions:
1. In a pan that fits the air fryer, combine all the ingredients, toss, introduce the pan in the fryer and cook at 390 degrees F for 25 minutes. Divide between plates and serve for lunch with a side salad.

100. Cayenne Zucchini Mix

Servings: 2

Cooking Time: 16 Minutes
Ingredients:
- 2 zucchini
- ½ cup Monterey jack cheese, shredded
- ¼ cup ground chicken
- 1 teaspoon salt
- ½ teaspoon cayenne pepper
- 1 teaspoon olive oil

Directions:
1. Trim the zucchini and cut it into the Hasselback. In the mixing bowl mix up ground chicken, cheese, salt, and cayenne pepper. The fill the zucchini with chicken mixture and sprinkle with olive oil. Preheat the air fryer to 400F. Put the Hasselback zucchini in the air fryer and cook for 16 minutes at 400F.

101.Fried Potatoes

Servings: 1
Cooking Time: 55 Minutes
Ingredients:
- 1 medium russet potatoes, scrubbed and peeled
- 1 tsp. olive oil
- ¼ tsp. onion powder
- 1/8 tsp. salt
- A dollop of vegan butter
- A dollop of vegan cream cheese
- 1 tbsp. Kalamata olives
- 1 tbsp. chives, chopped

Directions:
1. Pre-heat the Air Fryer at 400°F.
2. In a bowl, coat the potatoes with the onion powder, salt, olive oil, and vegan butter.
3. Transfer to the fryer and allow to cook for 40 minutes, turning the potatoes over at the halfway point.
4. Take care when removing the potatoes from the fryer and enjoy with the vegan cream cheese, Kalamata olives and chives on top, plus any other vegan sides you desire.

102.Tomato Cod Bake

Servings: 4
Cooking Time: 12 Minutes
Ingredients:
- 3 tablespoons butter, melted
- 2 tablespoons parsley, chopped
- ¼ cup keto tomato sauce
- 8 cherry tomatoes, halved
- 2 cod fillets, boneless, skinless and cubed
- Salt and black pepper to the taste

Directions:
1. In a baking pan that fits the air fryer, combine all the ingredients, toss, put the pan in the machine and cook the mix at 390 degrees F for 12 minutes. Divide the mix into bowls and serve for lunch.

103.Shrimp And Mushroom Pie

Servings: 4
Cooking Time: 15 Minutes
Ingredients:
- 10 oz shrimps, peeled
- ½ cup Cheddar cheese, shredded
- 3 tablespoons cream cheese
- 2 eggs, beaten
- ¼ cup cremini mushrooms, sliced
- ½ teaspoon salt
- ½ teaspoon ground black pepper
- ½ teaspoon seafood seasonings
- 1 teaspoon nut oil

Directions:
1. Mix up shrimps and seafood seasonings. Then brush the air fryer round pan with nut oil and put the shrimps inside. Flatten them gently with the help of the fork. After this, in the mixing bowl mix up shredded Cheddar cheese, cream cheese, mushrooms, salt, and ground black pepper. Add eggs and stir the mixture until homogenous. Pour the mixture over the shrimps and flatten the pie gently with the help of the fork or spoon. Preheat the air fryer to 365F. Put the pan with the pie in the air fryer. Cook the shrimp pie for 15 minutes.

104.Chicken, Eggs And Lettuce Salad

Servings: 3
Cooking Time: 8 Minutes
Ingredients:
- 3 spring onions, sliced
- 8 oz chicken fillet, roughly chopped
- 1 bacon slice, cooked, crumbled
- 2 cherry tomatoes, halved
- ¼ avocado, chopped
- 2 eggs, hard-boiled, peeled, chopped
- 1 cup lettuce, roughly chopped
- 1 tablespoon sesame oil
- ½ teaspoon lemon juice
- ½ teaspoon avocado oil
- ½ teaspoon ground black pepper
- ½ teaspoon salt
- 1 egg, beaten
- 2 tablespoons coconut flakes

Directions:
1. Sprinkle the chopped chicken fillets with salt and ground black pepper. Then dip the chicken in the egg and after this, coat in the coconut flakes. Preheat the air fryer to 385F. Place the chicken fillets inside and sprinkle them with avocado oil. Cook the chicken pieces for 8 minutes. Shake them after 4 minutes of cooking. After this, in the mixing bowl mix up spring onions, bacon, cherry tomatoes, hard-boiled eggs, lettuce, and lemon juice. Add sesame oil and shake the

salad well. When the chicken is cooked, add it in the cobb salad and mix up gently with the help of the wooden spatulas.

105.Lemon Chicken Mix

Servings: 3
Cooking Time: 15 Minutes
Ingredients:
- 4 chicken thighs, skinless, boneless
- 1 tablespoon lemon juice
- 1 teaspoon ground paprika
- ½ teaspoon salt
- ½ teaspoon ground black pepper
- 1 tablespoon sesame oil
- ½ teaspoon dried parsley
- ½ teaspoon keto tomato sauce

Directions:
1. Cut the chicken thighs into halves and put them in the bowl. Add lemon juice, ground paprika, salt, ground black pepper, sesame oil, parsley, and tomato sauce. Mix up the chicken with the help of the fingertips and leave for 10-15 minutes to marinate. Then string the meat on the wooden skewers and put in the preheated to 375F air fryer. Cook the tavuk shish for 10 minutes at 375F. Then flip the meal on another side and cook for 5 minutes more.

106.Cast-iron Cheesy Chicken

Servings: 4
Cooking Time: 10 Minutes
Ingredients:
- 4 chicken breasts
- 4 bacon strips
- 4 oz ranch dressing
- 2 green onions
- 4 oz cheddar cheese

Directions:
1. Pour the oil into a skillet and heat on high. Add the chicken breasts and fry both sides until piping hot.
2. Fry the bacon and crumble it into bits.
3. Dice the green onions.
4. Put the chicken in a baking dish and top with soy sauce.
5. Toss in the ranch, bacon, green onions and top with cheese.
6. Cook until the cheese is browned, for around 4 minutes.
7. Serve.

107.Taco Stuffed Peppers

Servings: 4
Cooking Time: 30 Minutes
Ingredients:
- 1 lb. ground beef
- 1 tbsp. taco seasoning mix
- 1 can diced tomatoes and green chilis
- 4 green bell peppers
- 1 cup shredded Monterey jack cheese, divided

Directions:
1. Set a skillet over a high heat and cook the ground beef for seven to ten minutes. Make sure it is cooked through and brown all over. Drain the fat.
2. Stir in the taco seasoning mix, as well as the diced tomatoes and green chilis. Allow the mixture to cook for a further three to five minutes.
3. In the meantime, slice the tops off the green peppers and remove the seeds and membranes.
4. When the meat mixture is fully cooked, spoon equal amounts of it into the peppers and top with the Monterey jack cheese. Then place the peppers into your fryer.
5. Cook at 350°F for fifteen minutes.
6. The peppers are ready when they are soft, and the cheese is bubbling and brown. Serve warm and enjoy!

108.Thanksgiving Sprouts

Servings: 6
Cooking Time: 20 Minutes
Ingredients:
- 1 ½ lb. Brussels sprouts, cleaned and trimmed
- 3 tbsp. olive oil
- 1 tsp. salt
- 1 tsp. black pepper

Directions:
1. Pre-heat the Air Fryer to 375°F. Cover the basket with aluminum foil and coat with a light brushing of oil.
2. In a mixing bowl, combine all ingredients, coating the sprouts well.
3. Put in the fryer basket and cook for 10 minutes. Shake the Air Fryer basket throughout the duration to ensure even cooking.

109.Cheddar Bacon Burst

Servings: 8
Cooking Time: 90 Minutes
Ingredients:
- 30 slices bacon
- 2 ½ cups cheddar cheese
- 4-5 cups raw spinach
- 1-2 tbsp Tones Southwest Chipotle Seasoning
- 2 tsp Mrs. Dash Table Seasoning

Directions:
1. Preheat your fryer to 375°F/190°C.
2. Weave the bacon into 15 vertical pieces & 12 horizontal pieces. Cut the extra 3 in half to fill in the rest, horizontally.

3. Season the bacon.
4. Add the cheese to the bacon.
5. Add the spinach and press down to compress.
6. Tightly roll up the woven bacon.
7. Line a baking sheet with kitchen foil and add plenty of salt to it.
8. Put the bacon on top of a cooling rack and put that on top of your baking sheet.
9. Bake for 60-70 minutes.
10. Let cool for 10-15 minutes before
11. Slice and enjoy!

110.Chicken & Veggies

Servings: 4
Cooking Time: 30 Minutes
Ingredients:
- 8 chicken thighs
- 5 oz. mushrooms, sliced
- 1 red onion, diced
- Fresh black pepper, to taste
- 10 medium asparagus
- ½ cup carrots, diced
- ¼ cup balsamic vinegar
- 2 red bell peppers, diced
- ½ tsp. sugar
- 2 tbsp. extra-virgin olive oil
- 1 ½ tbsp. fresh rosemary
- 2 cloves garlic, chopped
- ½ tbsp. dried oregano
- 1 tsp. kosher salt
- 2 fresh sage, chopped

Directions:
1. Pre-heat the Air Fryer to 400°F.
2. Grease the inside of a baking tray with the oil.
3. Season the chicken with salt and pepper.
4. Put all of the vegetables in a large bowl and throw in the oregano, garlic, sugar, mushrooms, vinegar, and sage. Combine everything well before transferring to the baking tray.
5. Put the chicken thighs in the baking tray. Cook in the Air Fryer for about 20 minutes.
6. Serve hot.

111.Chicken And Arugula Salad

Servings: 2
Cooking Time: 12 Minutes
Ingredients:
- 2 bacon slices, cooked, chopped
- 2 cups arugula, chopped
- 10 oz chicken breast, skinless, boneless
- 1 teaspoon ground black pepper
- ½ teaspoon salt
- 1 teaspoon avocado oil
- ½ teaspoon ground cumin
- ½ teaspoon ground paprika
- 1 tablespoon olive oil

- ¼ teaspoon minced garlic
- 1 teaspoon fresh cilantro, chopped

Directions:
1. Rub the chicken breast with ground black pepper, salt, ground cumin, ground paprika, and avocado oil. Then preheat the air fryer to 365F. Put the chicken breast in the preheated air fryer and cook for 12 minutes. Meanwhile, in the salad bowl mix up chopped bacon, arugula, and fresh cilantro. In the shallow bowl mix up minced garlic and olive oil. Chop the cooked chicken breasts and add in the salad mixture. Sprinkle the salad with garlic oil and shake well.

112.Italian Style Eggplant Sandwich

Servings: 4
Cooking Time:26 Minutes
Ingredients:
- 1 eggplant; sliced
- 2 tsp. parsley; dried
- 1/2 cup breadcrumbs
- 1/2 tsp. Italian seasoning
- 1/2 tsp. garlic powder
- 1/2 tsp. onion powder
- 2 tbsp. milk
- 4 bread slices
- Cooking spray
- 1/2 cup mayonnaise
- 3/4 cup tomato sauce
- 2 cups mozzarella cheese; grated
- Salt and black pepper to the taste

Directions:
1. Season eggplant slices with salt and pepper, leave aside for 10 minutes and then pat dry them well.
2. In a bowl; mix parsley with breadcrumbs, Italian seasoning, onion and garlic powder, salt and black pepper and stir.
3. In another bowl; mix milk with mayo and whisk well.
4. Brush eggplant slices with mayo mix, dip them in breadcrumbs, place them in your air fryer's basket, spray with cooking oil and cook them at 400 °F, for 15 minutes; flipping them after 8 minutes.
5. Brush each bread slice with olive oil and arrange 2 on a working surface.
6. Add mozzarella and parmesan on each, add baked eggplant slices; spread tomato sauce and basil and top with the other bread slices, greased side down. Divide sandwiches on plates; cut them in halves and serve for lunch.

113.Baby Back Ribs

Servings: 2
Cooking Time: 45 Minutes

Ingredients:
- 2 tsp. red pepper flakes
- ¾ ground ginger
- 3 cloves minced garlic
- Salt and pepper
- 2 baby back ribs

Directions:
1. Pre-heat your fryer at 350°F.
2. Combine the red pepper flakes, ginger, garlic, salt and pepper in a bowl, making sure to mix well. Massage the mixture into the baby back ribs.
3. Cook the ribs in the fryer for thirty minutes.
4. Take care when taking the rubs out of the fryer. Place them on a serving dish and enjoy with a low-carb barbecue sauce of your choosing.

114.Seafood Bowls

Servings: 4
Cooking Time: 12 Minutes
Ingredients:
- 2 salmon fillets, boneless, skinless and cubed
- 8 ounces shrimp, peeled and deveined
- Salt and black pepper to the taste
- 5 garlic cloves, minced
- 1 teaspoon sweet paprika
- 2 tablespoons olive oil

Directions:
1. In a pan that fits the air fryer, combine all the ingredients, toss, cover and cook at 370 degrees F for 12 minutes. Divide into bowls and serve for lunch.

115.Lunch Baby Carrots Mix

Servings: 4
Cooking Time: 15 Minutes
Ingredients:
- 16 ounces baby carrots
- Salt and black pepper to taste
- 2 tablespoons butter, melted
- 4 ounces chicken stock
- 2 tablespoons dill, chopped

Directions:
1. In a pan that fits your air fryer, mix all the ingredients and toss.
2. Place the pan in the fryer and cook at 380 degrees F for 15 minutes.
3. Divide between bowls and serve.

116.Garlic Pork Stew

Servings: 4
Cooking Time: 30 Minutes
Ingredients:
- 1 and ½ pounds pork stew meat, cubed
- 1 red cabbage, shredded
- 1 tablespoon olive oil
- Salt and black pepper to the taste

- 2 chili peppers, chopped
- 4 garlic cloves, minced
- ½ cup veggie stock
- ¼ cup keto tomato sauce

Directions:
1. Heat up a pan that fits the air fryer with the oil over medium heat, add the meat, chili peppers and the garlic, stir and brown for 5 minutes. Add the rest of the ingredients, toss, introduce the pan in the fryer and cook at 380 degrees F for 20 minutes. Divide the into bowls and serve for lunch.

117.Jarlsberg Lunch Omelet

Servings: 2
Cooking Time: 10 Minutes
Ingredients:
- 4 medium mushrooms, sliced, 2 oz
- 1 green onion, sliced
- 2 eggs, beaten
- 1 oz Jarlsberg or Swiss cheese, shredded
- 1 oz ham, diced

Directions:
1. In a skillet, cook the mushrooms and green onion until tender.
2. Add the eggs and mix well.
3. Sprinkle with salt and top with the mushroom mixture, cheese and the ham.
4. When the egg is set, fold the plain side of the omelet on the filled side.
5. Turn off the heat and let it stand until the cheese has melted.
6. Serve!

118.Lunch Green Beans Casserole

Servings: 4
Cooking Time: 20 Minutes
Ingredients:
- 1 teaspoon olive oil
- 3 cups green beans, trimmed and halved
- 2 red chilies, chopped
- ½ teaspoon black mustard seeds
- ½ cup yellow onion, chopped
- ¼ teaspoon fenugreek seeds
- ½ teaspoon turmeric powder
- Salt and black pepper to taste
- 2 tomatoes, chopped
- 3 garlic cloves, minced
- 2 teaspoons tamarind paste
- 2 teaspoons coriander powder
- 1 tablespoon cilantro, chopped

Directions:
1. Use the oil to grease a heat-proof dish that fits your air fryer, then add all the ingredients and toss.
2. Place the dish in the fryer and cook at 370 degrees F for 20 minutes.
3. Divide between plates, serve, and enjoy.

119.Lamb And Leeks

Servings: 4
Cooking Time: 30 Minutes
Ingredients:
- 1 pound lamb shoulder, trimmed and cubed
- 2 tablespoons olive oil
- 3 garlic cloves, minced
- 4 baby leeks, halved
- 1 cup okra
- 1 pound tomatoes, peeled and chopped
- Salt and black pepper to the taste
- 2 tablespoons tarragon, chopped

Directions:
1. Heat up a pan that fits your air fryer with the oil over medium-high heat, add the lamb, garlic, salt and pepper, toss and brown for 5 minutes. Add the remaining ingredients except the tarragon, toss, introduce the pan in the fryer and cook at 400 degrees F for 25 minutes. Divide everything into bowls and serve for lunch.

120.Pancetta Salad

Servings: 3
Cooking Time: 10 Minutes
Ingredients:
- 2 cups iceberg lettuce, chopped
- 6 oz pancetta, chopped
- ½ teaspoon ground black pepper
- ½ teaspoon olive oil
- 3 oz Parmesan, grated

Directions:
1. Mix up pancetta, ground black pepper, and olive oil. Preheat the air fryer to 365F. Put the chopped pancetta in the air fryer and cook for 10 minutes Shake the pancetta every 3 minutes to avoid burning. Meanwhile, in the salad bowl combine iceberg lettuce with grated parmesan. Then add cooked pancetta and mix up the salad.

121.Mashed Garlic Turnips

Servings: 2
Cooking Time: 10 Minutes
Ingredients:
- 3 cups diced turnip
- 2 cloves garlic, minced
- ¼ cup heavy cream
- 3 tbsp melted butter
- Salt and pepper to season

Directions:
1. Boil the turnips until tender.
2. Drain and mash the turnips.
3. Add the cream, butter, salt, pepper and garlic. Combine well.
4. Serve!

122.Paprika Turkey Mix

Servings: 4
Cooking Time: 20 Minutes
Ingredients:
- 1 turkey breast, boneless, skinless and cubed
- 2 teaspoons olive oil
- ½ teaspoon sweet paprika
- Salt and black pepper to the taste
- 2 cups bok choy, torn and steamed
- 1 tablespoon balsamic vinegar

Directions:
1. In a bowl, mix the turkey with the oil, paprika, salt and pepper, toss, transfer them to your Air Fryer's basket and cook at 350 degrees F for 20 minutes. In a salad, mix the turkey with all the other ingredients, toss and serve for lunch.

VEGETABLE & SIDE DISHES

123.Fava Beans Mix

Servings: 4
Cooking Time: 15 Minutes
Ingredients:
- 3 pounds fava beans, shelled
- 1 teaspoon olive oil
- Salt and black pepper to taste
- 4 ounces bacon, cooked and crumbled
- ½ cup white wine
- 1 tablespoon parsley, chopped

Directions:
1. Place all of the ingredients into a pan that fits your air fryer and mix well.
2. Put the pan in the air fryer and cook at 380 degrees F for 15 minutes.
3. Divide between plates and serve as a side dish.

124.Fried Green Beans With Pecorino Romano

Servings: 3
Cooking Time: 15 Minutes
Ingredients:
- 2 tablespoons buttermilk
- 1 egg
- 4 tablespoons cornmeal
- 4 tablespoons tortilla chips, crushed
- 4 tablespoons Pecorino Romano cheese, finely grated
- Coarse salt and crushed black pepper, to taste
- 1 teaspoon smoked paprika
- 12 ounces green beans, trimmed

Directions:
1. In a shallow bowl, whisk together the buttermilk and egg.
2. In a separate bowl, combine the cornmeal, tortilla chips, Pecorino Romano cheese, salt, black pepper, and paprika.
3. Dip the green beans in the egg mixture, then, in the cornmeal/cheese mixture. Place the green beans in the lightly greased cooking basket.
4. Cook in the preheated Air Fryer at 390 degrees F for 4 minutes. Shake the basket and cook for a further 3 minutes.
5. Taste, adjust the seasonings, and serve with the dipping sauce if desired. Bon appétit!

125.Tomato Bites With Creamy Parmesan Sauce

Servings: 4
Cooking Time: 20 Minutes
Ingredients:
- For the Sauce:
- 1/2 cup Parmigiano-Reggiano cheese, grated
- 4 tablespoons pecans, chopped
- 1 teaspoon garlic puree
- 1/2 teaspoon fine sea salt
- 1/3 cup extra-virgin olive oil
- For the Tomato Bites:
- 2 large-sized Roma tomatoes, cut into thin slices and pat them dry
- 8 ounces Halloumi cheese, cut into thin slices
- 1/3 cup onions, sliced
- 1 teaspoon dried basil
- 1/4 teaspoon red pepper flakes, crushed
- 1/8 teaspoon sea salt

Directions:
1. Start by preheating your Air Fryer to 385 degrees F.
2. Make the sauce by mixing all ingredients, except the extra-virgin olive oil, in your food processor.
3. While the machine is running, slowly and gradually pour in the olive oil; puree until everything is well - blended.
4. Now, spread 1 teaspoon of the sauce over the top of each tomato slice. Place a slice of Halloumi cheese on each tomato slice. Top with onion slices. Sprinkle with basil, red pepper, and sea salt.
5. Transfer the assembled bites to the Air Fryer cooking basket. Drizzle with a nonstick cooking spray and cook for approximately 13 minutes.
6. Arrange these bites on a nice serving platter, garnish with the remaining sauce and serve at room temperature. Bon appétit!

126.Simple Tomatoes And Bell Pepper Sauce Recipe

Servings: 4
Cooking Time:25 Minutes
Ingredients:
- 2 red bell peppers; chopped
- 2 garlic cloves; minced
- 2 tbsp. olive oil
- 1 tbsp. balsamic vinegar
- 1 lb. cherry tomatoes; halved
- 1 tsp. rosemary; dried
- 3 bay leaves
- Salt and black pepper to the taste

Directions:
1. In a bowl mix tomatoes with garlic, salt, black pepper, rosemary, bay leaves, half of the oil and half of the vinegar, toss to coat, introduce in your air fryer and roast them at 320 °F, for 15 minutes

2. Meanwhile; in your food processor, mix bell peppers with a pinch of sea salt, black pepper, the rest of the oil and the rest of the vinegar and blend very well.
3. Divide roasted tomatoes on plates, drizzle the bell peppers sauce over them and serve

127.Spicy Cabbage

Servings: 4
Cooking Time: 12 Minutes
Ingredients:
- 1 green cabbage head, shredded
- 1 tablespoon olive oil
- 1 teaspoon cayenne pepper
- A pinch of salt and black pepper
- 2 teaspoons sweet paprika

Directions:
1. Mix all of the ingredients in a pan that fits your fryer.
2. Place the pan in the fryer and cook at 320 degrees F for 12 minutes.
3. Divide between plates and serve right away.

128.Easy Celery Root Mix

Servings: 4
Cooking Time: 15 Minutes
Ingredients:
- 2 cups celery root, roughly cubed
- A pinch of salt and black pepper
- ½ tablespoon butter, melted

Directions:
1. Put all of the ingredients in your air fryer and toss.
2. Cook at 350 degrees F for 15 minutes.
3. Divide between plates and serve.

129.Tender Eggplant Fries

Servings:2
Cooking Time: 20 Minutes
Ingredients:
- 1 tsp olive oil
- 1 tsp soy sauce
- Salt to taste

Directions:
1. Preheat your air fryer to 400 F. Make a marinade of 1 tsp oil, soy sauce and salt. Mix well. Add in the eggplant slices and let stand for 5 minutes. Place the prepared eggplant slices in your air fryer's cooking basket and cook for 5 minutes. Serve with a drizzle of maple syrup.

130.Radishes And Spring Onions Mix

Servings: 4
Cooking Time: 15 Minutes
Ingredients:
- 20 radishes, halved
- 1 tablespoon olive oil
- 3 green onions, chopped

- Salt and black pepper to the taste
- 3 teaspoons black sesame seeds
- 2 tablespoons olive oil

Directions:
1. In a bowl, mix all the ingredients and toss well. Put the radishes in your air fryer's basket, cook at 400 degrees F for 15 minutes, divide between plates and serve as a side dish.

131.Bacon & Asparagus Spears

Servings:4
Cooking Time: 25 Minutes
Ingredients:
- 4 bacon slices
- 1 tbsp olive oil
- 1 tbsp sesame oil
- 1 tbsp brown sugar
- 1 garlic clove, crushed

Directions:
1. Preheat your air fryer to 380 F. In a bowl, mix the oils, sugar and crushed garlic. Separate the asparagus into 4 bunches (5 spears in 1 bunch) and wrap each bunch with a bacon slice. Coat the bunches with the sugar and oil mix. Place the bunches in your air fryer's cooking basket and cook for 8 minutes.

132.Cream Cheese Zucchini

Servings: 4
Cooking Time: 15 Minutes
Ingredients:
- 1 pound zucchinis, cut into wedges
- 1 cup cream cheese, soft
- 1 green onion, sliced
- 1 teaspoon garlic powder
- 2 tablespoons basil, chopped
- A pinch of salt and black pepper
- 1 tablespoon butter, melted

Directions:
1. In a pan that fits your air fryer, mix the zucchinis with all the other ingredients, toss, introduce in the air fryer and cook at 370 degrees F for 15 minutes. Divide between plates and serve as a side dish.

133.Lemon Asparagus

Servings: 4
Cooking Time: 12 Minutes
Ingredients:
- 1 pound asparagus, trimmed
- A pinch of salt and black pepper
- 2 tablespoons olive oil
- 3 garlic cloves, minced
- 3 tablespoons parmesan, grated
- Juice of 1 lemon

Directions:

1. In a bowl, mix the asparagus with the rest of the ingredients and toss. Put the asparagus in your air fryer's basket and cook at 390 degrees F for 12 minutes. Divide between plates and serve.

134.Smoked Asparagus

Servings: 4
Cooking Time: 20 Minutes
Ingredients:
- 1 pound asparagus stalks
- Salt and black pepper to the taste
- ¼ cup olive oil+ 1 teaspoon
- 1 tablespoon smoked paprika
- 2 tablespoons balsamic vinegar
- 1 tablespoon lime juice

Directions:
1. In a bowl, mix the asparagus with salt, pepper and 1 teaspoon oil, toss, transfer to your air fryer's basket and cook at 370 degrees F for 20 minutes. Meanwhile, in a bowl, mix all the other ingredients and whisk them well. Divide the asparagus between plates, drizzle the balsamic vinaigrette all over and serve as a side dish.

135.Tasty Herb Tomatoes

Servings: 4
Cooking Time: 15 Minutes
Ingredients:
- 2 large tomatoes, halved
- 1 tbsp olive oil
- 1/2 tsp thyme, chopped
- 2 garlic cloves, minced
- Pepper
- Salt

Directions:
1. Add all ingredients into the bowl and toss well.
2. Transfer tomatoes into the air fryer basket and cook at 390 F for 15 minutes.
3. Serve and enjoy.

136.Garlic Lemony Asparagus

Servings: 4
Cooking Time: 15 Minutes
Ingredients:
- 1 bunch asparagus, trimmed
- Salt and black pepper to the taste
- 4 tablespoons olive oil
- 4 garlic cloves, minced
- Juice of ½ lemon
- 3 tablespoons parmesan, grated

Directions:
1. In a bowl, mix the asparagus with all the ingredients except the parmesan, toss, transfer it to your air fryer's basket and cook at 400 degrees F for 15 minutes.

Divide between plates, sprinkle the parmesan on top and serve as a side dish.

137.Cheesy Rutabaga

Servings: 2
Cooking Time: 8 Minutes
Ingredients:
- 6 oz rutabaga, chopped
- 2 oz Jarlsberg cheese, grated
- 1 tablespoon butter
- ½ teaspoon dried parsley
- ½ teaspoon salt
- ½ teaspoon minced garlic
- 3 tablespoons heavy cream

Directions:
1. In the mixing bowl mix up a rutabaga, dried parsley, salt, and minced garlic. Then add heavy cream and mix up the vegetables well. After this, preheat the air fryer to 375F. Put the rutabaga mixture in the air fryer and cook it for 6 minutes. Then stir it well and top with grated cheese. Cook the meal for 2 minutes more. Transfer the cooked rutabaga in the plates and top with butter.

138.Carrot Crisps

Servings:2
Cooking Time: 20 Minutes
Ingredients:
- Salt to taste

Directions:
1. Put the carrot strips in a bowl and season with salt to taste. Grease the fryer basket lightly with cooking spray, and add the carrot strips. Cook at 350 F for 10 minutes, stirring once halfway through.

139.Roasted Rhubarb

Servings: 4
Cooking Time: 15 Minutes
Ingredients:
- 1 pound rhubarb, cut in chunks
- 2 teaspoons olive oil
- 2 tablespoons orange zest
- ½ cup walnuts, chopped
- ½ teaspoon sugar

Directions:
1. In your air fryer, mix all the listed ingredients, and toss.
2. Cook at 380 degrees F for 15 minutes.
3. Divide the rhubarb between plates and serve as a side dish.

140.Chicken Wings With Alfredo Sauce

Servings:4
Cooking Time: 60 Minutes
Ingredients:
- Salt to taste
- ½ cup Alfredo sauce

Directions:
1. Preheat the air fryer to 370°F.
2. Season the wings with salt. Arrange them in the air fryer, without touching. Cook in batches if needed, for 20 minutes, until no longer pink in the center. Increase the temperature to 390 F and cook for 5 minutes more. Remove to a big bowl and coat well with the sauce to serve.

141.Broccoli And Scallions Sauce

Servings: 4
Cooking Time: 15 Minutes
Ingredients:
- 1 broccoli head, florets separated
- Salt and black pepper to the taste
- ½ cup keto tomato sauce
- 1 tablespoon sweet paprika
- ¼ cup scallions, chopped
- 1 tablespoon olive oil

Directions:
1. In a pan that fits the air fryer, combine the broccoli with the rest of the ingredients, toss, put the pan in the fryer and cook at 380 degrees F for 15 minutes. Divide between plates and serve.

142.Quick Cheese Sticks

Servings:12
Cooking Time: 5 Minutes
Ingredients:
- 2 tbsp butter, melted
- 2 cups panko crumbs

Directions:
1. With a knife, cut the cheese into equal sized sticks. Brush each stick with melted butter and dip into panko crumbs. Arrange the cheese sticks in a single layer on the fryer basket. Cook at 390 F for 10 minutes. Flip them halfway through, to brown evenly; serve warm.

143.Calamari With Olives

Servings:3
Cooking Time: 25 Minutes
Ingredients:
- ½ piece cilantro, chopped
- 2 strips chili pepper, chopped
- 1 tbsp olive oil
- 1 cup pimiento-stuffed green olives, sliced
- Salt and black pepper to taste

Directions:
1. In a bowl, add rings, chili pepper, salt, pepper, oil, and cilantor. Marinate for 10 minutes. Pour the calamari into a baking dish. Place in the fryer basket and cook for 15 minutes stirring every 5 minutes at 400 F. Serve warm with olives.

144.Mozzarella Green Beans

Servings: 4
Cooking Time: 6 Minutes
Ingredients:
- 1 cup green beans, trimmed
- 2 oz Mozzarella, shredded
- 1 teaspoon butter
- ½ teaspoon chili flakes
- ¼ cup beef broth

Directions:
1. Sprinkle the green beans with chili flakes and put in the air fryer baking pan. Add beef broth and butter. Then top the vegetables with shredded Mozzarella. Preheat the air fryer to 400F. Put the pan with green beans in the air fryer and cook the meal for 6 minutes.

145.Homemade Peanut Corn Nuts

Servings:4
Cooking Time: 30 Minutes
Ingredients:
- 3 tbsp peanut oil
- 2 tbsp old bay seasoning
- Salt to taste

Directions:
1. Preheat the Air Fryer to 390 F.
2. Pat dry hominy and season with salt and old bay seasoning. Drizzle with oil and toss to coat. Spread in the air fryer basket. Cook for 14 minutes. Slide out the basket and shake; cook for another 10 minutes until crispy. Remove to a towel-lined plate to soak up the excess fat. Leave to cool before serving.

146.Turmeric Zucchini Patties

Servings: 4
Cooking Time: 10 Minutes
Ingredients:
- 2 zucchinis, trimmed, grated
- 1 egg yolk
- ½ teaspoon salt
- 1 teaspoon ground turmeric
- ½ teaspoon ground paprika
- 1 teaspoon cream cheese
- 3 tablespoons flax meal
- 1 teaspoon sesame oil

Directions:
1. Squeeze the juice from the zucchinis and put them in the big bowl. Add egg yolk, salt, ground turmeric, ground paprika, flax meal, and cream cheese. Stir the mixture well with the help of the spoon. Then make medium size patties from the zucchini mixture. Preheat the air fryer to 385F. Brush the air fryer basket with sesame oil and put the patties inside. Cook them for 5 minutes from each side.

147.Zucchini Parmesan Crisps

Servings: 4
Cooking Time: 20 Minutes
Ingredients:
- 1 pound zucchini, peeled and sliced
- 1 egg, lightly beaten
- 1 cup parmesan cheese, preferably freshly grated

Directions:
1. Pat the zucchini dry with a kitchen towel.
2. In a mixing dish, thoroughly combine the egg and cheese. Then, coat the zucchini slices with the breadcrumb mixture.
3. Cook in the preheated Air Fryer at 400 degrees F for 9 minutes, shaking the basket halfway through the cooking time.
4. Work in batches until the chips is golden brown. Bon appétit!

148.Fried Yellow Beans With Blue Cheese And Pecans

Servings: 3
Cooking Time: 15 Minutes
Ingredients:
- 3/4 pound wax yellow beans, cleaned
- 2 tablespoons peanut oil
- 4 tablespoons Romano cheese, grated
- Sea salt and ground black pepper, to taste
- 1/2 teaspoon red pepper flakes, crushed
- 2 tablespoons pecans, sliced
- 1/3 cup blue cheese, crumbled

Directions:
1. Toss the wax beans with the peanut oil, Romano cheese, salt, black pepper, and red pepper.
2. Place the wax beans in the lightly greased cooking basket.
3. Cook in the preheated Air Fryer at 400 degrees F for 5 minutes. Shake the basket once or twice.
4. Add the pecans and cook for 3 minutes more or until lightly toasted. Serve topped with blue cheese and enjoy!

149.Spinach Salad

Servings: 4
Cooking Time: 10 Minutes
Ingredients:
- 1 pound baby spinach
- Salt and black pepper to the taste
- 1 tablespoon mustard
- Cooking spray
- ¼ cup apple cider vinegar
- 1 tablespoon chives, chopped

Directions:
1. Grease a pan that fits your air fryer with cooking spray, combine all the ingredients, introduce the pan in the fryer and cook at

350 degrees F for 10 minutes. Divide between plates and serve as a side dish.

150.Air-fried Chickpeas With Herbs

Servings:4
Cooking Time: 20 Minutes
Ingredients:
- 2 tbsp olive oil
- 1 tsp dried rosemary
- ½ tsp dried thyme
- ¼ tsp dried sage
- ¼ tsp salt

Directions:
1. In a bowl, mix together chickpeas, oil, rosemary, thyme, sage, and salt. Transfer them to the air fryer and spread in an even layer. Cook 14 minutes at 380 F, shaking once, halfway through cooking.

151.Creamy Brussels Sprouts Side Dish

Servings: 8
Cooking Time:35 Minutes
Ingredients:
- 3 lbs. Brussels sprouts; halved
- A drizzle of olive oil
- 1 lb. bacon; chopped
- 4 tbsp. butter
- 3 shallots; chopped
- 1 cup milk
- 2 cups heavy cream
- 1/4 tsp. nutmeg; ground
- 3 tbsp. prepared horseradish
- Salt and black pepper to the taste

Directions:
1. Preheated you air fryer at 370 degrees F; add oil, bacon, salt and pepper and Brussels sprouts and toss.
2. Add butter, shallots, heavy cream, milk, nutmeg and horseradish; toss again and cook for 25 minutes. Divide among plates and serve as a side dish.

152.Cheese Eggplant Bites

Servings: 5
Cooking Time: 12 Minutes
Ingredients:
- 1 egg
- 1 eggplant, sliced
- 1/4 cup parmesan cheese, grated
- 1/2 tbsp dried thyme
- 1/4 cup almond flour
- 1/2 cup cheese, grated
- 1/2 tbsp dried rosemary
- Pepper
- Salt

Directions:
1. Spray air fryer basket with cooking spray.
2. Place sliced eggplants into the air fryer basket season with pepper and salt.

3. Cook eggplant at 390 F for 6 minutes.
4. In a small bowl, mix together almond flour, dried rosemary, dried thyme, and grated cheese.
5. Remove from eggplant slices from air fryer and brush with beaten egg. Sprinkle with almond flour mixture and cook until cheese is melted, about 4-6 minutes more.
6. Serve and enjoy.

153.Parmesan Artichoke Hearts

Servings:4
Cooking Time: 15 Minutes
Ingredients:
- 1 egg
- ¼ cup flour
- ¼ Parmesan cheese, grated
- ⅓ cup panko breadcrumbs
- 1 tsp garlic powder
- Salt and black pepper to taste

Directions:
1. Preheat the Air fryer to 390 F. Grease the air fryer basket with cooking spray.
2. Pat dry the artichokes with paper towels and cut them into wedges. In a bowl, whisk the egg white with salt. In another bowl, combine Parmesan cheese, breadcrumbs, and garlic powder. In a third pour the flour; mix with salt and pepper.
3. Dip the artichokes in the flour, followed by a dip in the egg, and finally coat with breadcrumb mixture. Place in your air fryer's cooking basket and cook for 10 minutes, flipping once. Let cool before serving.

154.Fried Squash Croquettes

Servings: 4
Cooking Time: 22 Minutes
Ingredients:
- 1/3 cup all-purpose flour
- 1/3 teaspoon freshly ground black pepper, or more to taste
- 1/3 teaspoon dried sage
- 4 cloves garlic, minced
- 1 ½ tablespoons olive oil
- 1/3 butternut squash, peeled and grated
- 2 eggs, well whisked
- 1 teaspoon fine sea salt
- A pinch of ground allspice

Directions:
1. Thoroughly combine all ingredients in a mixing bowl.
2. Preheat your Air Fryer to 345 degrees and set the timer for 17 minutes; cook until your fritters are browned; serve right away.

155.Grilled Cheese

Servings: 2

Cooking Time: 25 Minutes
Ingredients:
- 4 slices bread
- ½ cup sharp cheddar cheese
- ¼ cup butter, melted

Directions:
1. Pre-heat the Air Fryer at 360°F.
2. Put cheese and butter in separate bowls.
3. Apply the butter to each side of the bread slices with a brush.
4. Spread the cheese across two of the slices of bread and make two sandwiches. Transfer both to the fryer.
5. Cook for 5 – 7 minutes or until a golden brown color is achieved and the cheese is melted.

156.Turmeric Tofu

Servings: 2
Cooking Time: 9 Minutes
Ingredients:
- 6 oz tofu, cubed
- 1 teaspoon avocado oil
- 1 teaspoon apple cider vinegar
- 1 garlic clove, diced
- ¼ teaspoon ground turmeric
- ¼ teaspoon ground paprika
- ½ teaspoon dried cilantro
- ¼ teaspoon lemon zest, grated

Directions:
1. In the bowl mix up avocado oil, apple cider vinegar, diced garlic, ground turmeric, paprika, cilantro, and lime zest. Coat the tofu cubes in the oil mixture. Preheat the air fryer to 400F. Put the tofu cubes in the air fryer and cook them for 9 minutes. Shake the tofu cubes from time to time during cooking.

157.Garlic Bread

Servings: 4
Cooking Time: 8 Minutes
Ingredients:
- 1 oz Mozzarella, shredded
- 2 tablespoons almond flour
- 1 teaspoon cream cheese
- ¼ teaspoon garlic powder
- ¼ teaspoon baking powder
- 1 egg, beaten
- 1 teaspoon coconut oil, melted
- ¼ teaspoon minced garlic
- 1 teaspoon dried dill
- 1 oz Provolone cheese, grated

Directions:
1. In the mixing bowl mix up Mozzarella, almond flour, cream cheese, garlic powder, baking powder, egg, minced garlic, dried dill, and Provolone cheese. When the mixture is homogenous, transfer it on the baking

paper and spread it in the shape of the bread. Sprinkle the garlic bread with coconut oil. Preheat the air fryer to 400F. Transfer the baking paper with garlic bread in the air fryer and cook for 8 minutes or until it is light brown. When the garlic bread is cooked, cut it on 4 servings and place it in the serving plates.

158.Coconut Broccoli

Servings: 4
Cooking Time: 30 Minutes
Ingredients:
- 3 tablespoons ghee, melted
- 15 ounces coconut cream
- 2 eggs, whisked
- 2 cups cheddar, grated
- 1 cup parmesan, grated
- 1 tablespoon mustard
- 1 pound broccoli florets
- A pinch of salt and black pepper
- 1 tablespoon parsley, chopped

Directions:
1. Grease a baking pan that fits the air fryer with the ghee and arrange the broccoli on the bottom. Add the cream, mustard, salt, pepper and the eggs and toss. Sprinkle the cheese on top, put the pan in the air fryer and cook at 380 degrees F for 30 minutes. Divide between plates and serve.

159.Ginger Paneer

Servings: 4
Cooking Time: 6 Minutes
Ingredients:
- 1 cup paneer, cubed
- 1 tomato
- 2 spring onions, chopped
- ½ teaspoon ground coriander
- 1 tablespoon lemon juice
- ½ teaspoon fresh cilantro, chopped
- 1 tablespoon mustard oil
- ¼ teaspoon ginger paste
- ½ teaspoon minced garlic
- ½ teaspoon red chili powder
- ¼ teaspoon garam masala powder
- ¼ teaspoon salt

Directions:
1. Chop the tomato on 4 cubes. Then chop the onion on 4 cubes too. Sprinkle the paneer with ground coriander, lemon juice, cilantro, mustard oil, ginger paste, minced garlic, red chili powder, garam masala, and salt. Massage the paneer cubes with the help of the fingertips to coat them well. After this, string the paneer cubes, tomato, and onion on the skewers. Preheat the air fryer to 385F. Place the paneer tikka skewers in the

air fryer basket and cook them for 3 minutes from each side.

160.Awesome Cheese Sticks

Servings:6
Cooking Time: 15 Minutes
Ingredients:
- 12 sticks mozzarella cheese
- ¼ cup flour
- 2 cups breadcrumbs
- 2 whole eggs
- ¼ cup Parmesan cheese, grated

Directions:
1. Preheat air fryer to 350 F. Pour breadcrumbs in a bowl. Beat the eggs in a separate bowl. In a third bowl, mix Parmesan and flour. Dip each cheese stick the in flour mixture, then in eggs and finally in breadcrumbs. Put in air fryer's basket and cook for 7 minutes, turning once.

161.Asparagus Salad With Boiled Eggs

Servings: 4
Cooking Time: 10 Minutes + Chilling Time
Ingredients:
- 1/4 cup olive oil
- 1 pound asparagus, trimmed
- 1 cup cherry tomatoes, halved
- 1/4 cup balsamic vinegar
- 2 garlic cloves, minced
- 2 scallion stalks, chopped
- 1/2 teaspoon oregano
- Coarse sea salt and ground black pepper, to your liking
- 2 hard-boiled eggs, sliced

Directions:
1. Start by preheating your Air Fryer to 400 degrees F. Brush the cooking basket with 1 tablespoon of olive oil.
2. Add the asparagus and cherry tomatoes to the cooking basket. Drizzle 1 tablespoon of olive oil all over your veggies.
3. Cook for 5 minutes, shaking the basket halfway through the cooking time. Let it cool slightly.
4. Toss with the remaining olive oil, balsamic vinegar, garlic, scallions, oregano, salt, and black pepper.
5. Afterwards, add the hard-boiled eggs on the top of your salad and serve.

162.Bacon Cabbage

Servings: 2
Cooking Time: 12 Minutes
Ingredients:
- 8 oz Chinese cabbage, roughly chopped
- 2 oz bacon, chopped
- 1 tablespoon sunflower oil
- ½ teaspoon onion powder

- ½ teaspoon salt

Directions:
1. Cook the bacon at 400F for 10 minutes. Stir it from time to time. Then sprinkle it with onion powder and salt. Add Chinese cabbage and shake the mixture well. Cook it for 2 minutes. Then add sunflower oil, stir the meal and place in the serving plates.

163.Green Beans And Tomato Sauce

Servings: 4
Cooking Time: 15 Minutes
Ingredients:
- ½ pound green beans, trimmed and halved
- 1 cup black olives, pitted and halved
- ¼ cup bacon, cooked and crumbled
- 1 tablespoon olive oil
- ¼ cup keto tomato sauce

Directions:
1. In a pan that fits the air fryer, combine all the ingredients, toss, put the pan in the air fryer and cook at 380 degrees F for 15 minutes. Divide between plates and serve.

164.Crunchy Chicken Egg Rolls

Servings:6
Cooking Time: 30 Minutes
Ingredients:
- 2 garlic cloves, minced
- ¼ cup soy sauce
- 2 tsp grated fresh ginger
- 1 pound ground chicken
- 2 cups white cabbage, shredded
- 1 onion, chopped
- 1 egg, beaten
- 12 egg roll wrappers

Directions:
1. Heat olive oil in a pan over medium heat and add garlic, onion, and ginger, and ground chicken. Cook for 5 minutes until the chicken is no longer pink. Pour in soy sauce and cabbage and continue cooking for 5-6 minutes until the cabbage is tender, stirring occasionally. Fill each wrapper with chicken mixture, arranging the mixture just below the center of the wrappers.
2. Fold in both sides and tightly roll-up. Use the beaten egg to seal the edges. Place the rolls into a greased air fryer basket, spray them with cooking spray and cook for 12 minutes at 370 F, turning once halfway through. Let cool and serve.

165.Cheesy Zucchini Tots

Servings: 4
Cooking Time: 6 Minutes
Ingredients:
- 1 zucchini, grated
- ½ cup Mozzarella, shredded
- 1 egg, beaten
- 2 tablespoons almond flour
- ½ teaspoon ground black pepper
- 1 teaspoon coconut oil, melted

Directions:
1. Mix up grated zucchini, shredded Mozzarella, egg, almond flour, and ground black pepper. Then make the small zucchini tots with the help of the fingertips. Preheat the air fryer to 385F. Place the zucchini tots in the air fryer basket and cook for 3 minutes from each side or until the zucchini tots are golden brown.

166.Green Beans And Potatoes Recipe

Servings: 5
Cooking Time:25 Minutes
Ingredients:
- 2 lbs. green beans
- 6 new potatoes; halved
- Salt and black pepper to the taste
- 6 bacon slices; cooked and chopped.
- A drizzle of olive oil

Directions:
1. In a bowl; mix green beans with potatoes, salt, pepper and oil, toss, transfer to your air fryer and cook at 390 °F, for 15 minutes. Divide among plates and serve with bacon sprinkled on top

167.Garlic Tomatoes Recipe

Servings: 4
Cooking Time:25 Minutes
Ingredients:
- 4 garlic cloves; crushed
- 1 lb. mixed cherry tomatoes
- 3 thyme springs; chopped.
- 1/4 cup olive oil
- Salt and black pepper to the taste

Directions:
1. In a bowl; mix tomatoes with salt, black pepper, garlic, olive oil and thyme, toss to coat, introduce in your air fryer and cook at 360 °F, for 15 minutes. Divide tomatoes mix on plates and serve

168.Lime Kale And Bell Peppers Bowls

Servings: 4
Cooking Time: 10 Minutes
Ingredients:
- 2 cups kale, torn
- A pinch of salt and black pepper
- 1 and ½ cups avocado, peeled, pitted and cubed
- 1 cup red bell pepper, sliced
- ¼ cup olive oil
- 1 tablespoon mustard
- 2 tablespoons lime juice
- 1 tablespoon white vinegar

Directions:

1. In a pan that fits the air fryer, combine the kale with salt, pepper, avocado and half of the oil, toss, put in your air fryer and cook at 360 degrees F for 10 minutes. In a bowl, combine the kale mix with the rest of the ingredients, toss and serve.

169.Air-fried Brussels Sprouts

Servings:2
Cooking Time: 15 Minutes
Ingredients:

- 1 tbsp butter, melted
- Salt and black pepper to taste
- ¼ tsp cayenne pepper

Directions:

1. In a bowl, mix Brussels sprouts, butter, cayenne pepper, salt, and pepper. Place Brussels sprouts in air fryer basket. Cook for 10 minutes at 380 F. Serve with sautéed onion rings.

170.Herbed Garlic Radishes

Servings: 2
Cooking Time: 15 Minutes
Ingredients:

- 1 lb. radishes
- 2 tbsp. unsalted butter, melted
- ¼ tsp. dried oregano
- ½ tsp. dried parsley
- ½ tsp. garlic powder

Directions:

1. Prepare the radishes by cutting off their tops and bottoms and quartering them.
2. In a bowl, combine the butter, dried oregano, dried parsley, and garlic powder. Toss with the radishes to coat.
3. Transfer the radishes to your air fryer and cook at 350°F for ten minutes, shaking the basket at the halfway point to ensure the radishes cook evenly through. The radishes are ready when they begin to turn brown.

171.Zucchini Sweet Potatoes

Servings: 4
Cooking Time: 20 Minutes
Ingredients:

- 2 large-sized sweet potatoes, peeled and quartered
- 1 medium-sized zucchini, sliced
- 1 Serrano pepper, deveined and thinly sliced
- 1 bell pepper, deveined and thinly sliced
- 1 – 2 carrots, cut into matchsticks
- ¼ cup olive oil
- 1 ½ tbsp. maple syrup
- ½ tsp. porcini powder
- ¼ tsp. mustard powder
- ½ tsp. fennel seeds

- 1 tbsp. garlic powder
- ½ tsp. fine sea salt
- ¼ tsp. ground black pepper
- Tomato ketchup to serve

Directions:

1. Put the sweet potatoes, zucchini, peppers, and the carrot into the basket of your Air Fryer. Coat with a drizzling of olive oil.
2. Pre-heat the fryer at 350°F.
3. Cook the vegetables for 15 minutes.
4. In the meantime, prepare the sauce by vigorously combining the other ingredients, save for the tomato ketchup, with a whisk.
5. Lightly grease a baking dish small enough to fit inside your fryer.
6. Move the cooked vegetables to the baking dish, pour over the sauce and make sure to coat the vegetables well.
7. Raise the temperature to 390°F and cook the vegetables for an additional 5 minutes.
8. Serve warm with a side of ketchup.

172.Lemon Parsley Peppers

Servings: 4
Cooking Time: 15 Minutes
Ingredients:

- 1 and ½ pounds mixed bell peppers, halved and deseeded
- 2 teaspoons lemon zest, grated
- 2 tablespoons balsamic vinegar
- 2 tablespoons lemon juice
- A handful parsley, chopped
- A drizzle of olive oil

Directions:

1. Put the peppers in your air fryer's basket and cook at 350 degrees F for 15 minutes. Peel the bell peppers, mix them with the rest of the ingredients, toss and serve.

173.Lime Green Beans And Sauce

Servings: 4
Cooking Time: 8 Minutes
Ingredients:

- 1 pound green beans, trimmed
- 1 tablespoon lime juice
- A pinch of salt and black pepper
- 2 tablespoons ghee, melted
- 1 teaspoon chili powder

Directions:

1. In a bowl, mix the ghee with the rest of the ingredients except the green beans and whisk really well. Mix the green beans with the lime sauce, toss, put them in your air fryer's basket and cook at 400 degrees F for 8 minutes. Serve right away.

174.Air-frier Baked Potatoes

Servings:4
Cooking Time: 45 Minutes

Ingredients:
- 2 tbsp olive oil
- Salt and ground black pepper to taste

Directions:
1. Rub potatoes with half tbsp of olive oil. Season with salt and pepper, and arrange them on the air fryer. Cook for 40 minutes at 400 F. Let cool slightly, then make a slit on top. Use a fork to fluff the insides of the potatoes. Fill the potato with cheese or garlic mayo.

175.Cheesy Stuffed Mushrooms

Servings:10
Cooking Time: 30 Minutes
Ingredients:
- Olive oil to brush the mushrooms
- 1 cup cooked brown rice
- 1 cup grated Grana Padano cheese
- 1 tsp dried mixed herbs
- Salt and black pepper

Directions:
1. Brush every mushroom with oil and set aside. In a bowl, mix rice, cheese, herbs, salt and pepper. Stuff the mushrooms with the mixture. Arrange the mushrooms in the air fryer and cook for 14 minutes at 360 F. Make sure the mushrooms cooked until golden and the cheese has melted. Serve with herbs.

176.Zucchini Casserole With Cooked Ham

Servings: 4
Cooking Time: 30 Minutes
Ingredients:
- 2 tablespoons butter, melted
- 1 zucchini, diced
- 1 bell pepper, seeded and sliced
- 1 red chili pepper, seeded and minced
- 1 medium-sized leek, sliced
- 3/4 pound ham, cooked and diced
- 5 eggs
- 1 teaspoon cayenne pepper
- Sea salt, to taste
- 1/2 teaspoon ground black pepper
- 1 tablespoon fresh cilantro, chopped

Directions:
1. Start by preheating the Air Fryer to 380 degrees F. Grease the sides and bottom of a baking pan with the melted butter.
2. Place the zucchini, peppers, leeks and ham in the baking pan. Bake in the preheated Air Fryer for 6 minutes.
3. Crack the eggs on top of ham and vegetables; season with the cayenne pepper, salt, and black pepper. Bake for a further 20 minutes or until the whites are completely set.
4. Garnish with fresh cilantro and serve. Bon appétit!

177.Cheesy Onion Rings

Servings:3
Cooking Time: 20 Minutes
Ingredients:
- ¾ cup Parmesan cheese, shredded
- 2 medium eggs, beaten
- 1 tsp garlic powder
- A pinch of salt
- 1 cup flour
- 1 tsp paprika powder

Directions:
1. Add eggs to a bowl. In another bowl, mix cheese, garlic powder, salt, flour, and paprika. Dip onion rings in egg, then in the cheese mixture, in the egg again and finally in the cheese mixture. Add the rings to the basket and cook them for 8 minutes at 350 F. Serve with a cheese or tomato dip.

178.Italian-style Sausage Casserole

Servings: 4
Cooking Time: 20 Minutes
Ingredients:
- 1 pound Italian sausage
- 2 Italian peppers, seeded and sliced
- 1 cup mushrooms, sliced
- 1 shallot, sliced
- 4 cloves garlic
- 1 teaspoon dried basil
- 1 teaspoon dried oregano
- 1/4 teaspoon black pepper
- 1/4 teaspoon cayenne pepper
- Sea salt, to taste
- 2 tablespoons Dijon mustard
- 1 cup chicken broth

Directions:
1. Toss all ingredients in a lightly greased baking pan. Make sure the sausages and vegetables are coated with the oil and seasonings.
2. Bake in the preheated Air Fryer at 380 degrees F for 15 minutes.
3. Divide between individual bowls and serve warm. Bon appétit!

179.Authentic Peperonata Siciliana

Servings: 4
Cooking Time: 25 Minutes
Ingredients:
- 4 tablespoons olive oil
- 4 bell peppers, seeded and sliced
- 1 serrano pepper, seeded and sliced
- 1/2 cup onion, peeled and sliced
- 2 garlic cloves, crushed
- 1 large tomato, pureed
- Sea salt and black pepper
- 1 teaspoon cayenne pepper
- 4 fresh basil leaves

- 8 Sicilian olives green, pitted and sliced

Directions:
1. Brush the sides and bottom of the cooking basket with 1 tablespoon of olive oil. Add the peppers, onions, and garlic to the cooking basket. Cook for 5 minutes or until tender.
2. Add the tomatoes, salt, black pepper, and cayenne pepper; add the remaining tablespoon of olive oil and cook in the preheated Air Fryer at 380 degrees F for 15 minutes, stirring occasionally.
3. Divide between individual bowls and garnish with basil leaves and olives. Bon appétit!

180. Swiss Chard Mix

Servings: 5
Cooking Time: 15 Minutes
Ingredients:
- 7 oz Swiss chard, chopped
- 4 oz Swiss cheese, grated
- 4 teaspoons almond flour
- ½ cup heavy cream
- ½ teaspoon ground black pepper

Directions:
1. Mix up Swiss chard and Swiss cheese. Add almond flour, heavy cream, and ground black pepper. Stir the mixture until homogenous. After this, transfer it in 5 small ramekins. Preheat the air fryer to 365F. Place the ramekins with gratin in the air fryer basket and cook them for 15 minutes.

181. Spicy Buffalo Cauliflower

Servings: 4
Cooking Time: 15 Minutes
Ingredients:
- 8 oz cauliflower florets
- 1 tsp cayenne pepper
- 1 tsp chili powder
- 1 tsp olive oil
- 1 tsp garlic, minced
- 1 tomato, diced
- 6 tbsp almond flour
- 1 tsp black pepper
- 1/2 tsp salt

Directions:
1. Preheat the air fryer to 350 F.
2. Spray air fryer basket with cooking spray.
3. Add tomato, garlic, black pepper, olive oil, cayenne pepper, and chili powder into the blender and blend until smooth.
4. Add cauliflower florets into the bowl. Season with pepper and salt.
5. Pour blended mixture over cauliflower florets and toss well to coat.
6. Coat cauliflower florets with almond flour and place into the air fryer basket and cook for 15 minutes. Shake basket 2-3 times.
7. Serve and enjoy.

182. Collard Greens And Bacon Recipe

Servings: 4
Cooking Time:22 Minutes
Ingredients:
- 1 lb. collard greens
- 1 tbsp. apple cider vinegar
- 2 tbsp. chicken stock
- 3 bacon strips; chopped
- 1/4 cup cherry tomatoes; halved
- Salt and black pepper to the taste

Directions:
1. Heat up a pan that fits your air fryer over medium heat, add bacon; stir and cook 1-2 minutes
2. Add tomatoes, collard greens, vinegar, stock, salt and pepper; stir, introduce in your air fryer and cook at 320 °F, for 10 minutes. Divide among plates and serve

183. Feta Peppers

Servings: 4
Cooking Time: 10 Minutes
Ingredients:
- 5 oz Feta, crumbled
- 8 oz banana pepper, trimmed
- 1 teaspoon sesame oil
- 1 garlic clove, minced
- ½ teaspoon fresh dill, chopped
- 1 teaspoon lemon juice
- ½ teaspoon lime zest, grated

Directions:
1. Clean the seeds from the peppers and cut them into halves. Then sprinkle the peppers with sesame oil and put in the air fryer. Cook them for 10 minutes at 385F. Flip the peppers on another side after 5 minutes of cooking. Meanwhile, mix up minced garlic, fresh dill, lemon juice, and lime zest. Put the cooked banana peppers on the plate and sprinkle with lemon juice mixture. Then top the vegetables with crumbled feta.

VEGAN & VEGETARIAN RECIPES

184.Garden Fresh Veggie Medley

Servings:4
Cooking Time:15 Minutes
Ingredients:
- 2 yellow bell peppers seeded and chopped
- 1 eggplant, chopped
- 1 zucchini, chopped
- 3 tomatoes, chopped
- 2 small onions, chopped
- 2 garlic cloves, minced
- 2 tablespoons herbs de Provence
- 1 tablespoon olive oil
- 1 tablespoon balsamic vinegar
- Salt and black pepper, to taste

Directions:
1. Preheat the Air fryer to 355 °F and grease an Air fryer basket.
2. Mix all the ingredients in a bowl and toss to coat well.
3. Transfer into the Air fryer basket and cook for about 15 minutes.
4. Keep in the Air fryer for about 5 minutes and dish out to serve hot.

185.Air-fried Cauliflower

Servings:4
Cooking Time: 20 Minutes
Ingredients:
- 2 tbsp olive oil
- ½ tsp salt
- ¼ tsp freshly ground black pepper

Directions:
1. In a bowl, toss cauliflower, oil, salt, and black pepper, until the florets are well-coated. Arrange the florets in the air fryer and cook for 8 minutes at 360 F; work in batches if needed. Serve the crispy cauliflower in lettuce wraps with chicken, cheese or mushrooms.

186.Cool Mini Zucchini's

Servings:4
Cooking Time: 25 Minutes
Ingredients:
- 4 large eggs, beaten
- 1 medium zucchini, sliced
- 4 ounces feta cheese, drained and crumbled
- 2 tbsp fresh dill, chopped
- Cooking spray
- Salt and pepper as needed

Directions:
1. Preheat the air fryer to 360 F, and un a bowl, add the beaten eggs and season with salt and pepper.
2. Stir in zucchini, dill and feta cheese. Grease 8 muffin tins with cooking spray. Roll pastry

and arrange them to cover the sides of the muffin tins. Divide the egg mixture evenly between the holes. Place the prepared tins in your air fryer and cook for 15 minutes. Serve and enjoy!

187.Pepper-pineapple With Butter-sugar Glaze

Servings:2
Cooking Time: 10 Minutes
Ingredients:
- 1 medium-sized pineapple, peeled and sliced
- 1 red bell pepper, seeded and julienned
- 1 teaspoon brown sugar
- 2 teaspoons melted butter
- Salt to taste

Directions:
1. Preheat the air fryer to 390°F.
2. Place the grill pan accessory in the air fryer.
3. Mix all ingredients in a Ziploc bag and give a good shake.
4. Dump onto the grill pan and cook for 10 minutes making sure that you flip the pineapples every 5 minutes.

188.Chickpeas & Spinach With Coconut

Servings:4
Cooking Time: 20 Minutes
Ingredients:
- 1 tbsp pepper
- 1 onion, chopped
- 1 tsp salt
- 4 garlic cloves, minced
- 1 can coconut milk
- 1 tbsp ginger, minced
- 1 pound spinach
- ½ cup dried tomatoes, chopped
- 1 can chickpeas
- 1 lemon, juiced
- 1 hot pepper

Directions:
1. Preheat air fryer to 370 F.
2. In a bowl, mix lemon juice, tomatoes, pepper, ginger, coconut milk, garlic, salt, hot pepper and onion. Rinse chickpeas under running water to get rid of all the gunk. Put them in a large bowl. Cover with spinach. Pour the sauce over, and stir in oil. Cook in the air fryer for 15 minutes. Serve warm.

189.Jacket Potatoes

Servings:2
Cooking Time: 15 Minutes
Ingredients:
- 2 potatoes
- 1 tablespoon mozzarella cheese, shredded

- 3 tablespoons sour cream
- 1 tablespoon butter, softened
- 1 teaspoon chives, minced
- Salt and ground black pepper, as required

Directions:
1. Set the temperature of air fryer to 355 degrees F. Grease an air fryer basket.
2. With a fork, prick the potatoes.
3. Arrange potatoes into the prepared air fryer basket.
4. Air fry for about 15 minutes.
5. In a bowl, add the remaining ingredients and mix until well combined.
6. Remove from air fryer and transfer the potatoes onto a platter.
7. Open potatoes from the center and stuff them with cheese mixture.
8. Serve immediately

190.Buttered Carrot-zucchini With Mayo

Servings:4
Cooking Time: 25 Minutes
Ingredients:
- 1 tablespoon grated onion
- 2 tablespoons butter, melted
- 1/2-pound carrots, sliced
- 1-1/2 zucchinis, sliced
- 1/4 cup water
- 1/4 cup mayonnaise
- 1/4 teaspoon prepared horseradish
- 1/4 teaspoon salt
- 1/4 teaspoon ground black pepper
- 1/4 cup Italian bread crumbs

Directions:
1. Lightly grease baking pan of air fryer with cooking spray. Add carrots. For 8 minutes, cook on 360°F. Add zucchini and continue cooking for another 5 minutes.
2. Meanwhile, in a bowl whisk well pepper, salt, horseradish, onion, mayonnaise, and water. Pour into pan of veggies. Toss well to coat.
3. In a small bowl mix melted butter and bread crumbs. Sprinkle over veggies.
4. Cook for 10 minutes at 390°F until tops are lightly browned.
5. Serve and enjoy.

191.Brussels Sprouts With Garlic Aioli

Servings:4
Cooking Time: 25 Minutes
Ingredients:
- Salt and pepper to taste
- 1 ½ tbsp olive oil
- 2 tsp lemon juice
- 1 tsp powdered chili
- 3 cloves garlic
- ¾ cup mayonnaise, whole egg
- 2 cups water

Directions:
1. Place a skillet over medium heat, add the garlic cloves with the peels on it and roast until lightly brown and fragrant. Remove the skillet and place a pot with water over the same heat; bring to a boil. Add in Brussels sprouts and blanch for 3 minutes. Drain and set aside.
2. Preheat air fryer to 350 F. Remove the garlic from the skillet to a plate; peel, crush and set aside. Add olive oil to the skillet and light the fire to medium heat. Stir in the Brussels sprouts, season with pepper and salt; sauté for 2 minutes. Pour the brussels sprouts in the fryer's basket and cook for 5 minutes.
3. In a bowl, add mayonnaise, crushed garlic, lemon juice, powdered chili, pepper and salt; mix well. Remove the brussels sprouts onto a serving bowl and serve with the garlic aioli.

192.Prawn Toast

Servings:2
Cooking Time: 12 Minutes
Ingredients:
- 1 large spring onion, finely sliced
- 3 white bread slices
- ½ cup sweet corn
- 1 egg white, whisked
- 1 tbsp black sesame seeds

Directions:
1. In a bowl, place prawns, corn, spring onion and the sesame seeds. Add the whisked egg and mix the ingredients. Spread the mixture over the bread slices. Place in the prawns in the air fryer's basket and sprinkle oil. Fry the prawns until golden, for 8-10 minutes at 370 F. Serve with ketchup or chili sauce.

193.Spiced Eggplant

Servings:3
Cooking Time:27 Minutes
Ingredients:
- 2 medium eggplants, cubed
- 2 tablespoons butter, melted
- 2 tablespoons Parmesan cheese, shredded
- 1 tablespoon Maggi seasoning sauce
- 1 teaspoon sumac
- 1 teaspoon garlic powder
- 1 teaspoon onion powder
- Salt and ground black pepper, as required
- 1 tablespoon fresh lemon juice

Directions:
1. Preheat the Air fryer to 320 °F and grease an Air fryer basket.
2. Mix the eggplant cubes, butter, seasoning sauce and spices in a bowl and toss to coat well.

3. Arrange the eggplant cubes in the Air fryer basket and cook for about 15 minutes.
4. Dish out in a bowl and set the Air fryer to 350 °F.
5. Cook for about 12 minutes, tossing once in between.
6. Dish out in a bowl and sprinkle with lemon juice and Parmesan cheese to serve.

194. Roasted Brussels Sprouts

Servings:4
Cooking Time: 25 Minutes
Ingredients:
- ½ tsp garlic, chopped
- 2 tbsp olive oil
- Salt and black pepper to taste

Directions:
1. Wash the Brussels sprouts thoroughly under cold water and trim off the outer leaves, keeping only the head of the sprouts. In a bowl, mix oil, garlic, salt, and pepper. Add sprouts to this mixture and let rest for 5 minutes. Place the coated sprouts in your air fryer's cooking basket and cook for 15 minutes.

195. Cauliflower Rice With Tofu

Servings:4
Cooking Time: 30 Minutes
Ingredients:
- ½ block tofu
- ½ cup diced onion
- 2 tbsp soy sauce
- 1 tsp turmeric
- 1 cup diced carrot
- Cauliflower:
- 3 cups cauliflower rice (pulsed in a food processor)
- 2 tbsp soy sauce
- ½ cup chopped broccoli
- 2 garlic cloves, minced
- 1 ½ tsp toasted sesame oil
- 1 tbsp minced ginger
- ½ cup frozen peas
- 1 tbsp rice vinegar

Directions:
1. Preheat the air fryer to 370 F, crumble the tofu and combine it with all tofu ingredients. Place in a baking dish and air fry for 10 minutes. Place all cauliflower ingredients in a large bowl; mix to combine.
2. Add the cauliflower mixture to the tofu and stir to combine; cook for 12 minutes. Serve and enjoy.

196. Cheddar, Squash 'n Zucchini Casserole

Servings:4
Cooking Time: 30 Minutes
Ingredients:
- 1 egg
- 5 saltine crackers, or as needed, crushed
- 2 tablespoons bread crumbs
- 1/2-pound yellow squash, sliced
- 1/2-pound zucchini, sliced
- 1/2 cup shredded Cheddar cheese
- 1-1/2 teaspoons white sugar
- 1/2 teaspoon salt
- 1/4 onion, diced
- 1/4 cup biscuit baking mix
- 1/4 cup butter

Directions:
1. Lightly grease baking pan of air fryer with cooking spray. Add onion, zucchini, and yellow squash. Cover pan with foil and for 15 minutes, cook on 360°F or until tender.
2. Stir in salt, sugar, egg, butter, baking mix, and cheddar cheese. Mix well. Fold in crushed crackers. Top with bread crumbs.
3. Cook for 15 minutes at 390°F until tops are lightly browned.
4. Serve and enjoy.

197. Barbecue Roasted Almonds

Servings: 6
Cooking Time: 20 Minutes
Ingredients:
- 1 ½ cups raw almonds
- Sea salt and ground black pepper, to taste
- 1/4 teaspoon garlic powder
- 1/4 teaspoon mustard powder
- 1/2 teaspoon cumin powder
- 1/4 teaspoon smoked paprika
- 1 tablespoon olive oil

Directions:
1. Toss all ingredients in a mixing bowl.
2. Line the Air Fryer basket with baking parchment. Spread out the coated almonds in a single layer in the basket.
3. Roast at 350 degrees F for 6 to 8 minutes, shaking the basket once or twice. Work in batches. Enjoy!

198. Marinated Tofu Bowl With Pearl Onions

Servings: 4
Cooking Time: 1 Hour 20 Minutes
Ingredients:
- 16 ounces firm tofu, pressed and cut into 1-inch pieces
- 2 tablespoons vegan Worcestershire sauce
- 1 tablespoon apple cider vinegar
- 1 tablespoon maple syrup
- 1/2 teaspoon shallot powder
- 1/2 teaspoon porcini powder
- 1/2 teaspoon garlic powder
- 2 tablespoons peanut oil
- 1 cup pearl onions, peeled

Directions:
1. Place the tofu, Worcestershire sauce, vinegar, maple syrup, shallot powder, porcini powder, and garlic powder in a ceramic dish. Let it marinate in your refrigerator for 1 hour.
2. Transfer the tofu to the lightly greased Air Fryer basket. Add the peanut oil and pearl onions; toss to combine.
3. Cook the tofu with the pearl onions in the preheated Air Fryer at 380 degrees F for 6 minutes; pause and brush with the reserved marinade; cook for a further 5 minutes.
4. Serve immediately. Bon appétit!

199.Cheesy Stuffed Peppers

Servings:4
Cooking Time: 40 Minutes
Ingredients:
- Salt and pepper to taste
- ½ cup olive oil
- 1 red onion, chopped
- 1 large tomato, chopped
- ½ cup crumbled Goat cheese
- 3 cups cauliflower, chopped
- 2 tbsp grated Parmesan cheese
- 2 tbsp chopped basil
- 1 tbsp lemon zest

Directions:
1. Preheat the air fryer to 350 F, and cut the peppers a quarter way from the head down and lengthwise. Remove the membrane and seeds. Season the peppers with pepper, salt, and drizzle olive oil over. Place the pepper bottoms in the fryer's basket and cook for 5 minutes at 350 F to soften a little bit.
2. In a mixing bowl, add tomatoes, goat cheese, lemon zest, basil, and cauliflower and season with salt and pepper; mix well. Remove the bottoms from the air fryer to a flat surface and spoon the cheese mixture into them. Sprinkle with Parmesan cheese and return to the basket; cook for 15 minutes.

200.Cheese Stuffed Zucchini With Scallions

Servings: 4
Cooking Time: 20 Minutes
Ingredients:
- 1 large zucchini, cut into four pieces
- 2 tablespoons olive oil
- 1 cup Ricotta cheese, room temperature
- 2 tablespoons scallions, chopped
- 1 heaping tablespoon fresh parsley, roughly chopped
- 1 heaping tablespoon coriander, minced
- 2 ounces Cheddar cheese, preferably freshly grated

- 1 teaspoon celery seeds
- 1/2 teaspoon salt
- 1/2 teaspoon garlic pepper

Directions:
1. Cook your zucchini in the Air Fryer cooking basket for approximately 10 minutes at 350 degrees F. Check for doneness and cook for 2-3 minutes longer if needed.
2. Meanwhile, make the stuffing by mixing the other items.
3. When your zucchini is thoroughly cooked, open them up. Divide the stuffing among all zucchini pieces and bake an additional 5 minutes.

201.Winter Squash And Tomato Bake

Servings: 4
Cooking Time: 30 Minutes
Ingredients:
- Cashew Cream:
- 1/2 cup sunflower seeds, soaked overnight, rinsed and drained
- 1/4 cup lime juice
- Sea salt, to taste
- 2 teaspoons nutritional yeast
- 1 tablespoon tahini
- 1/2 cup water
- Squash:
- 1 pound winter squash, peeled and sliced
- 2 tablespoons olive oil
- Sea salt and ground black pepper, to taste
- Sauce:
- 2 tablespoons olive oil
- 2 ripe tomatoes, crushed
- 6 ounces spinach, torn into small pieces
- 2 garlic cloves, minced
- 1 cup vegetable broth
- 1/2 teaspoon dried rosemary
- 1/2 teaspoon dried basil

Directions:
1. Mix the ingredients for the cashew cream in your food processor until creamy and uniform. Reserve.
2. Place the squash slices in the lightly greased casserole dish. Add the olive oil, salt, and black pepper.
3. Mix all the ingredients for the sauce. Pour the sauce over the vegetables. Bake in the preheated Air Fryer at 390 degrees F for 15 minutes.
4. Top with the cashew cream and bake an additional 5 minutes or until everything is thoroughly heated.
5. Transfer to a wire rack to cool slightly before sling and serving.

202.Parmesan Asparagus

Servings:3
Cooking Time:10 Minutes

Ingredients:
- 1 pound fresh asparagus, trimmed
- 1 tablespoon Parmesan cheese, grated
- 1 tablespoon butter, melted
- 1 teaspoon garlic powder
- Salt and black pepper, to taste

Directions:
1. Preheat the Air fryer to 400 °F and grease an Air fryer basket.
2. Mix the asparagus, cheese, butter, garlic powder, salt, and black pepper in a bowl and toss to coat well.
3. Arrange the asparagus into the Air fryer basket and cook for about 10 minutes.
4. Dish out in a serving plate and serve hot.

203.Italian Seasoned Easy Pasta Chips

Servings:2
Cooking Time:10 Minutes
Ingredients:
- ½ teaspoon salt
- 1 ½ teaspoon Italian seasoning blend
- 1 tablespoon nutritional yeast
- 1 tablespoon olive oil
- 2 cups whole wheat bowtie pasta

Directions:
1. Place the baking dish accessory in the air fryer.
2. Give a good stir.
3. Close the air fryer and cook for 10 minutes at 390°F.

204.Thai Zucchini Balls

Servings: 4
Cooking Time: 30 Minutes
Ingredients:
- 1 pound zucchini, grated
- 1 tablespoon orange juice
- 1/2 teaspoon ground cinnamon
- 1/4 teaspoon ground cloves
- 1/2 cup almond meal
- 1 teaspoon baking powder
- 1 cup coconut flakes

Directions:
1. In a mixing bowl, thoroughly combine all ingredients, except for coconut flakes.
2. Roll the balls in the coconut flakes.
3. Bake in the preheated Air Fryer at 360 degrees F for 15 minutes or until thoroughly cooked and crispy.
4. Repeat the process until you run out of ingredients. Bon appétit!

205.Crispy Air-fried Tofu

Servings:4
Cooking Time: 25 Minutes
Ingredients:
- 2 tbsp olive oil
- ½ cup flour
- ½ cup crushed cornflakes
- Salt and black pepper to taste
- Cooking spray

Directions:
1. Sprinkle oil over tofu and massage gently until well-coated. On a plate, mix flour, cornflakes, salt, and black pepper. Dip each strip into the mixture to coat, spray with oil and arrange the strips in your air fryer lined with baking paper. Cook for 14 minutes at 360 F, turning once halfway through.

206.Crunchy Eggplant Rounds

Servings: 4
Cooking Time: 45 Minutes
Ingredients:
- 1 (1-pound) eggplant, sliced
- 1/2 cup flax meal
- 1/2 cup rice flour
- Coarse sea salt and ground black pepper, to taste
- 1 teaspoon paprika
- 1 cup water
- 1 cup cornbread crumbs, crushed
- 1/2 cup vegan parmesan

Directions:
1. Toss the eggplant with 1 tablespoon of salt and let it stand for 30 minutes. Drain and rinse well.
2. Mix the flax meal, rice flour, salt, black pepper, and paprika in a bowl. Then, pour in the water and whisk to combine well.
3. In another shallow bowl, mix the cornbread crumbs and vegan parmesan.
4. Dip the eggplant slices in the flour mixture, then in the crumb mixture; press to coat on all sides. Transfer to the lightly greased Air Fryer basket.
5. Cook at 370 degrees F for 6 minutes. Turn each slice over and cook an additional 5 minutes.
6. Serve garnished with spicy ketchup if desired. Bon appétit!

207.Feisty Baby Carrots

Servings:4
Cooking Time: 20 Minutes
Ingredients:
- 1 tsp dried dill
- 1 tbsp olive oil
- 1 tbsp honey
- Salt and pepper to taste

Directions:
1. Preheat air fryer to 350 F. In a bowl, mix oil, carrots and honey; stir to coat. Season with dill, pepper and salt. Place the prepared carrots in your air fryer's cooking basket and cook for 12 minutes.

208.Herby Zucchini 'n Eggplant Bake

Servings:4
Cooking Time: 25 Minutes
Ingredients:
- ½ lemon, juiced
- 1 fennel bulb, sliced crosswise
- 1 sprig flat-leaf parsley
- 1 sprig mint
- 1 sprig of basil
- 1 tablespoon coriander powder
- 1 teaspoon capers
- 2 eggplants, sliced crosswise
- 2 red onions, chopped
- 2 red peppers, sliced crosswise
- 2 teaspoons herb de Provence
- 3 large zucchinis, sliced crosswise
- 4 cloves of garlic, minced
- 4 large tomatoes, chopped
- 5 tablespoons olive oil
- salt and pepper to taste

Directions:
1. In a blender, combine basil, parsley, mint, coriander, capers and lemon juice. Season with salt and pepper to taste. Pulse until well combined.
2. Preheat the air fryer to 400°F.
3. Toss the eggplant, onions, garlic, peppers, fennel, and zucchini with olive oil.
4. In a baking dish that can fit in the air fryer, arrange the vegetables and pour over the tomatoes and the herb puree. Season with more salt and pepper and sprinkle with herbs de Provence.
5. Place inside the air fryer and cook for 25 minutes.

209.The Best Falafel Ever

Servings: 2
Cooking Time: 20 Minutes
Ingredients:
- 1 cup dried chickpeas, soaked overnight
- 1 small-sized onion, chopped
- 2 cloves garlic, minced
- 2 tablespoons fresh cilantro leaves, chopped
- 1 tablespoon flour
- 1/2 teaspoon baking powder
- 1 teaspoon cumin powder
- A pinch of ground cardamom
- Sea salt and ground black pepper, to taste

Directions:
1. Pulse all the ingredients in your food processor until the chickpeas are ground.
2. Form the falafel mixture into balls and place them in the lightly greased Air Fryer basket.
3. Cook at 380 degrees F for about 15 minutes, shaking the basket occasionally to ensure even cooking.

4. Serve in pita bread with toppings of your choice. Enjoy!

210.Low-calorie Beets Dish

Servings:2
Cooking Time: 20 Minutes
Ingredients:
- ⅓ cup balsamic vinegar
- 1 tbsp olive oil
- 1 tbsp honey
- Salt and pepper to taste
- 2 springs rosemary

Directions:
1. In a bowl, mix rosemary, pepper, salt, vinegar and honey. Cover beets with the prepared sauce and then coat with oil. Preheat your air fryer to 400 F, and cook the beets in the air fryer for 10 minutes. Pour the balsamic vinegar in a pan over medium heat; bring to a boil and cook until reduced by half. Drizzle the beets with balsamic glaze, to serve.

211.Mediterranean Falafel With Tzatziki

Servings: 4
Cooking Time: 30 Minutes
Ingredients:
- For the Falafel:
- 2 cups cauliflower, grated
- 1/4 teaspoon baking powder
- 1/3 cup warm water
- 1/2 teaspoon salt
- 1 tablespoon coriander leaves, finely chopped
- 2 tablespoons fresh lemon juice
- Vegan Tzatziki:
- 1 cup plain Greek yogurt
- 2 tablespoons lime juice, freshly squeezed
- 1/4 teaspoon ground black pepper, or more to taste
- 1/3 teaspoon sea salt flakes
- 2 tablespoons extra-virgin olive oil
- 2 tablespoons chopped fresh dill
- 1 clove garlic, pressed
- 1/2 fresh cucumber, grated

Directions:
1. In a bowl, thoroughly combine all the ingredients for the falafel. Allow the mixture to stay for approximately 10 minutes.
2. Now, air-fry at 390 degrees F for 15 minutes; make sure to flip them over halfway through the cooking time.
3. To make Greek tzatziki, blend all ingredients in your food processor.
4. Serve warm falafel with chilled tzatziki. Enjoy!

212.Warm Farro Salad With Roasted Tomatoes

Servings: 2
Cooking Time: 40 Minutes
Ingredients:
- 3/4 cup farro
- 3 cups water
- 1 tablespoon sea salt
- 1 pound cherry tomatoes
- 2 spring onions, chopped
- 2 carrots, grated
- 2 heaping tablespoons fresh parsley leaves
- 2 tablespoons champagne vinegar
- 2 tablespoons white wine
- 2 tablespoons extra-virgin olive oil
- 1 teaspoon red pepper flakes

Directions:
1. Place the farro, water, and salt in a saucepan and bring it to a rapid boil. Turn the heat down to medium-low, and simmer, covered, for 30 minutes or until the farro has softened.
2. Drain well and transfer to an air fryer-safe pan.
3. Meanwhile, place the cherry tomatoes in the lightly greased Air Fryer basket. Roast at 400 degrees F for 4 minutes.
4. Add the roasted tomatoes to the pan with the cooked farro, Toss the salad ingredients with the spring onions, carrots, parsley, vinegar, white wine, and olive oil.
5. Bake at 360 degrees F an additional 5 minutes. Serve garnished with red pepper flakes and enjoy!

213.Veggies Stuffed Eggplants

Servings:5
Cooking Time:14 Minutes
Ingredients:
- 10 small eggplants, halved lengthwise
- 1 onion, chopped
- 1 tomato, chopped
- ¼ cup cottage cheese, chopped
- ½ green bell pepper, seeded and chopped
- 1 tablespoon fresh lime juice
- 1 tablespoon vegetable oil
- ½ teaspoon garlic, chopped
- Salt and ground black pepper, as required
- 2 tablespoons tomato paste

Directions:
1. Preheat the Air fryer to 320 °F and grease an Air fryer basket.
2. Cut a slice from one side of each eggplant lengthwise and scoop out the flesh in a bowl.
3. Drizzle the eggplants with lime juice and arrange in the Air fryer basket.
4. Cook for about 4 minutes and remove from the Air fryer.
5. Heat vegetable oil in a skillet over medium heat and add garlic and onion.
6. Sauté for about 2 minutes and stir in the eggplant flesh, tomato, salt, and black pepper.
7. Sauté for about 3 minutes and add cheese, bell pepper, tomato paste, and cilantro.
8. Cook for about 1 minute and stuff this mixture into the eggplants.
9. Close each eggplant with its cut part and set the Air fryer to 360 °F.
10. Arrange in the Air fryer basket and cook for about 5 minutes.
11. Dish out in a serving plate and serve hot.

214.Mushrooms With Peas

Servings:4
Cooking Time:15 Minutes
Ingredients:
- 16 ounces cremini mushrooms, halved
- ½ cup frozen peas
- ½ cup soy sauce
- 4 tablespoons maple syrup
- 4 tablespoons rice vinegar
- 4 garlic cloves, finely chopped
- 2 teaspoons Chinese five spice powder
- ½ teaspoon ground ginger

Directions:
1. Preheat the Air fryer to 350 °F and grease an Air fryer pan.
2. Mix soy sauce, maple syrup, vinegar, garlic, five spice powder, and ground ginger in a bowl.
3. Arrange the mushrooms in the Air fryer basket and cook for about 10 minutes.
4. Stir in the soy sauce mixture and peas and cook for about 5 more minutes.
5. Dish out the mushroom mixture in plates and serve hot.

215.Cottage And Mayonnaise Stuffed Peppers

Servings: 2
Cooking Time: 20 Minutes
Ingredients:
- 1 red bell pepper, top and seeds removed
- 1 yellow bell pepper, top and seeds removed
- Salt and pepper, to taste
- 1 cup Cottage cheese
- 4 tablespoons mayonnaise
- 2 pickles, chopped

Directions:
1. Arrange the peppers in the lightly greased cooking basket. Cook in the preheated Air Fryer at 400 degrees F for 15 minutes, turning them over halfway through the cooking time.
2. Season with salt and pepper.

3. Then, in a mixing bowl, combine the cream cheese with the mayonnaise and chopped pickles. Stuff the pepper with the cream cheese mixture and serve. Enjoy!

216.Barbecue Tofu With Green Beans

Servings: 3
Cooking Time: 1 Hour
Ingredients:
- 12 ounces super firm tofu, pressed and cubed
- 1/4 cup ketchup
- 1 tablespoon white vinegar
- 1 tablespoon coconut sugar
- 1 tablespoon mustard
- 1/4 teaspoon ground black pepper
- 1/2 teaspoon sea salt
- 1/4 teaspoon smoked paprika
- 1/2 teaspoon freshly grated ginger
- 2 cloves garlic, minced
- 2 tablespoons olive oil
- 1 pound green beans

Directions:
1. Toss the tofu with the ketchup, white vinegar, coconut sugar, mustard, black pepper, sea salt, paprika, ginger, garlic, and olive oil. Let it marinate for 30 minutes.
2. Cook at 360 degrees F for 10 minutes; turn them over and cook for 12 minutes more. Reserve.
3. Place the green beans in the lightly greased Air Fryer basket. Roast at 400 degrees F for 5 minutes. Bon appétit!

217.Couscous Stuffed Tomatoes

Servings:4
Cooking Time:25 Minutes
Ingredients:
- 4 tomatoes, tops and seeds removed
- 1 parsnip, peeled and finely chopped
- 1 cup mushrooms, chopped
- 1½ cups couscous
- 1 teaspoon olive oil
- 1 garlic clove, minced
- 1 tablespoon mirin sauce

Directions:
1. Preheat the Air fryer to 355 °F and grease an Air fryer basket.
2. Heat olive oil in a skillet on low heat and add parsnips, mushrooms and garlic.
3. Cook for about 5 minutes and stir in the mirin sauce and couscous.
4. Stuff the couscous mixture into the tomatoes and arrange into the Air fryer basket.
5. Cook for about 20 minutes and dish out to serve warm.

218.Spicy Tofu

Servings:3
Cooking Time:13 Minutes
Ingredients:
- 1 (14-ounces) block extra-firm tofu, pressed and cut into ¾-inch cubes
- 3 teaspoons cornstarch
- 1½ tablespoons avocado oil
- 1½ teaspoons paprika
- 1 teaspoon onion powder
- 1 teaspoon garlic powder
- Salt and black pepper, to taste

Directions:
1. Preheat the Air fryer to 390 °F and grease an Air fryer basket.
2. Mix the tofu, oil, cornstarch, and spices in a bowl and toss to coat well.
3. Arrange the tofu pieces in the Air fryer basket and cook for about 13 minutes, tossing twice in between.
4. Dish out the tofu onto serving plates and serve hot.

219.Simply Awesome Vegetables

Servings:4
Cooking Time:35 Minutes
Ingredients:
- ½ pound carrots, peeled and sliced
- 1 pound yellow squash, sliced
- 1 pound zucchini, sliced
- 1 tablespoon tarragon leaves, chopped
- 6 teaspoons olive oil, divided
- 1 teaspoon kosher salt
- ½ teaspoon ground white pepper

Directions:
1. Preheat the Air fryer to 400 °F and grease an Air fryer basket.
2. Mix 2 teaspoons olive oil and carrots in a bowl until combined.
3. Transfer into the Air fryer basket and cook for about 5 minutes.
4. Meanwhile, mix remaining 4 teaspoons of olive oil, yellow squash, zucchini, salt and white pepper in a large bowl.
5. Transfer this veggie mixture into the Air fryer basket with carrots.
6. Cook for about 30 minutes and dish out in a bowl.
7. Top with tarragon leaves and mix well to serve.

220.Onion Rings With Spicy Ketchup

Servings: 2
Cooking Time: 30 Minutes
Ingredients:
- 1 onion, sliced into rings
- 1/3 cup all-purpose flour
- 1/2 cup oat milk
- 1 teaspoon curry powder

- 1 teaspoon cayenne pepper
- Salt and ground black pepper, to your liking
- 1/2 cup cornmeal
- 4 tablespoons vegan parmesan
- 1/4 cup spicy ketchup

Directions:
1. Place the onion rings in the bowl with cold water; let them soak approximately 20 minutes; drain the onion rings and pat dry using a kitchen towel.
2. In a shallow bowl, mix the flour, milk, curry powder, cayenne pepper, salt, and black pepper. Mix to combine well.
3. Mix the cornmeal and vegan parmesan in another shallow bowl. Dip the onion rings in the flour/milk mixture; then, dredge in the cornmeal mixture.
4. Spritz the Air Fryer basket with cooking spray; arrange the breaded onion rings in the Air Fryer basket.
5. Cook in the preheated Air Fryer at 400 degrees F for 4 to 5 minutes, turning them over halfway through the cooking time. Serve with spicy ketchup. Bon appétit!

221.Scrumptiously Healthy Chips

Servings:2
Cooking Time: 10 Minutes
Ingredients:
- 1 bunch kale
- 1 teaspoon garlic powder
- 2 tablespoons almond flour
- 2 tablespoons olive oil
- Salt and pepper to taste

Directions:
1. Preheat the air fryer for 5 minutes.
2. In a bowl, combine all ingredients until the kale leaves are coated with the other ingredients.
3. Place in a fryer basket and cook for 10 minutes until crispy.

222.Grilled Olive-tomato With Dill-parsley Oil

Servings:6
Cooking Time: 16 Minutes
Ingredients:
- 1 big block of feta (about 12-oz.), cut into cubes
- 1 tbsp lemon juice
- 1 clove garlic, smashed
- 1 tbsp Chopped fresh dill
- 1 tbsp chopped fresh parsley
- Flaky sea salt
- Freshly ground black pepper
- 12 pitted kalamata olives
- 12 cherry tomatoes
- 1 cucumber, cut into 12 large cubes
- 1/4 cup extra-virgin olive oil

Directions:
1. In a medium bowl, whisk well parsley, dill, garlic, lemon juice, and olive oil. Season with pepper and salt. Add feta cheese and marinate for at least 15 minutes.
2. Thread feta, olives, cherry tomatoes, and cucumber in skewers. Place on skewer rack in air fryer. If needed, cook in batches.
3. Cook for 8 minutes at 390°F.
4. Serve and enjoy.

223.Zucchini Salad

Servings:4
Cooking Time:30 Minutes
Ingredients:
- 1 pound zucchini, cut into rounds
- 5 cups fresh spinach, chopped
- ¼ cup feta cheese, crumbled
- 2 tablespoons olive oil
- 1 teaspoon garlic powder
- Salt and black pepper, as required
- 2 tablespoons fresh lemon juice

Directions:
1. Preheat the Air fryer to 400 °F and grease an Air fryer basket.
2. Mix the zucchini, oil, garlic powder, salt, and black pepper in a bowl and toss to coat well.
3. Arrange the zucchini slices in the Air fryer basket and cook for about 30 minutes, flipping thrice in between.
4. Dish out the zucchini slices in a serving bowl and keep aside to cool.
5. Add spinach, feta cheese, lemon juice, a little bit of salt and black pepper and mix well.
6. Toss to coat well and serve immediately.

224.Potato Filled Bread Rolls

Servings:4
Cooking Time: 25 Minutes
Ingredients:
- 5 large potatoes, boiled and mashed
- ½ tsp turmeric
- 2 green chilies, deseeded and chopped
- 1 medium onion, finely chopped
- ½ tsp mustard seeds
- 1 tbsp olive oil
- 2 sprigs curry leaf
- Salt to taste

Directions:
1. Preheat air fryer to 350 F.
2. Combine olive oil, onion, curry leaves, and mustard seed in a baking dish. Place in the air fryer basket and cook for 5 minutes. Mix the onion mixture with the mashed potatoes, chilies, turmeric, and salt.
3. Divide the mixture into 8 equal pieces. Trim the sides of the bread, and wet with some water. Make sure to get rid of the excess water. Take one wet bread slice in your

palm and place one of the potato pieces in the center. Roll the bread over the filling, sealing the edges. Place the rolls onto a prepared baking dish, and air fry for 12 minutes.

225.Quick Crispy Cheese Lings

Servings:4
Cooking Time: 15 Minutes
Ingredients:
- 1 cup all-purpose flour
- 1 tbsp butter
- 1 tbsp baking powder
- ¼ tsp chili powder
- ¼ tsp salt, to taste
- 2 tbsp water

Directions:
1. In a bowl, mix flour and baking powder. Add in chili powder, salt, butter, cheese and 2 tbsp of water. Make a stiff dough. Knead the dough for a while and sprinkle about a tablespoon of flour on the table. With a rolling pin, roll the dough into ½-inch thickness. Cut into shapes. Cook for 6 minutes at 370 F.

226.Veggie Fajitas With Simple Guacamole

Servings: 4
Cooking Time: 25 Minutes
Ingredients:
- 1 tablespoon canola oil
- 1/2 cup scallions, thinly sliced
- 2 bell peppers, seeded and sliced into strips
- 1 habanero pepper, seeded and minced
- 1 garlic clove, minced
- 4 large Portobello mushrooms, thinly sliced
- 1/4 cup salsa
- 1 tablespoon yellow mustard
- Kosher salt and ground black pepper, to taste
- 1/2 teaspoon Mexican oregano
- 1 medium ripe avocado, peeled, pitted and mashed
- 1 tablespoon fresh lemon juice
- 1/2 teaspoon onion powder
- 1/2 teaspoon garlic powder
- 1 teaspoon red pepper flakes
- 4 (8-inch) flour tortillas

Directions:
1. Brush the sides and bottom of the cooking basket with canola oil. Add the scallions and cook for 1 to 2 minutes or until aromatic.
2. Then, add the peppers, garlic, and mushrooms to the cooking basket. Cook for 2 to 3 minutes or until tender.
3. Stir in the salsa, mustard, salt, black pepper, and oregano. Cook in the preheated Air Fryer at 380 degrees F for 15 minutes, stirring occasionally.
4. In the meantime, make your guacamole by mixing mashed avocado together with the lemon juice, garlic powder, onion powder, and red pepper flakes.
5. Divide between the tortillas and garnish with guacamole. Roll up your tortillas and enjoy!

227.Roasted Chat-masala Spiced Broccoli

Servings:2
Cooking Time:15 Minutes
Ingredients:
- ¼ teaspoon chat masala
- ¼ teaspoons turmeric powder
- ½ teaspoon salt
- 1 tablespoon chickpea flour
- 2 cups broccoli florets
- 2 tablespoons yogurt

Directions:
1. Place all ingredients in a bowl and toss the broccoli florets to combine.
2. Place the baking dish accessory in the air fryer and place the broccoli florets.
3. Close the air fryer and cook for 15 minutes at 330°F.
4. Halfway through the cooking time, give the baking dish a shake.

228.Mediterranean Vegetable Gratin

Servings: 4
Cooking Time: 35 Minutes
Ingredients:
- 1 eggplant, peeled and sliced
- 2 bell peppers, seeded and sliced
- 1 red onion, sliced
- 1 teaspoon fresh garlic, minced
- 4 tablespoons olive oil
- 1 teaspoon mustard
- 1 teaspoon dried oregano
- 1 teaspoon smoked paprika
- Salt and ground black pepper, to taste
- 1 tomato, sliced
- 6 ounces halloumi cheese, sliced lengthways

Directions:
1. Start by preheating your Air Fryer to 370 degrees F. Spritz a baking pan with nonstick cooking spray.
2. Place the eggplant, peppers, onion, and garlic on the bottom of the baking pan. Add the olive oil, mustard, and spices. Transfer to the cooking basket and cook for 14 minutes.
3. Top with the tomatoes and cheese; increase the temperature to 390 degrees F and cook for 5 minutes more until bubbling. Let it sit on a cooling rack for 10 minutes before serving.
4. Bon appétit!

229.Parmesan Broccoli

Servings:2
Cooking Time:20 Minutes
Ingredients:

- 10 ounces frozen broccoli
- 2 tablespoons Parmesan cheese, grated
- 3 tablespoons balsamic vinegar
- 1 tablespoon olive oil
- 1/8 teaspoon cayenne pepper
- Salt and black pepper, as required

Directions:
1. Preheat the Air fryer to 400 °F and grease an Air fryer basket.
2. Mix broccoli, vinegar, oil, cayenne, salt, and black pepper in a bowl and toss to coat well.
3. Arrange broccoli into the Air fryer basket and cook for about 20 minutes.
4. Dish out in a bowl and top with Parmesan cheese to serve.

230.Salted Garlic Zucchini Fries

Servings:6
Cooking Time: 15 Minutes
Ingredients:
- ¼ teaspoon garlic powder
- ½ cup almond flour
- 2 large egg whites, beaten
- 3 medium zucchinis, sliced into fry sticks
- Salt and pepper to taste

Directions:
1. Preheat the air fryer for 5 minutes.
2. Mix all ingredients in a bowl until the zucchini fries are well coated.
3. Place in the air fryer basket.
4. Close and cook for 15 minutes for 425°F.

231.Roasted Broccoli With Salted Garlic

Servings:6
Cooking Time:15 Minutes
Ingredients:
- ½ teaspoon black pepper
- ½ teaspoon lemon juice.
- 1 clove of garlic, minced
- 1 teaspoon salt
- 2 heads broccoli, cut into florets
- 2 teaspoons extra virgin olive oil

Directions:
1. Line the air fryer basket with aluminum foil and brush with oil.
2. Preheat the air fryer to 375°F.
3. Combine all ingredients except the lemon juice in a mixing bowl and place inside the air fryer basket.
4. Cook for 15 minutes.
5. Serve with lemon juice.

232.Stuffed Tomatoes

Servings:4
Cooking Time: 22 Minutes
Ingredients:
- 4 tomatoes
- 1 teaspoon olive oil
- 1 carrot, peeled and finely chopped
- 1 onion, chopped
- 1 cup frozen peas, thawed
- 1 garlic clove, minced

- 2 cups cold cooked rice
- 1 tablespoon soy sauce

Directions:
1. Cut the top of each tomato and scoop out pulp and seeds.
2. In a skillet, heat oil over low heat and sauté the carrot, onion, garlic, and peas for about 2 minutes.
3. Stir in the soy sauce and rice and remove from heat.
4. Set the temperature of air fryer to 355 degrees F. Grease an air fryer basket.
5. Stuff each tomato with the rice mixture.
6. Arrange tomatoes into the prepared air fryer basket.
7. Air fry for about 20 minutes.
8. Remove from air fryer and transfer the tomatoes onto a serving platter.
9. Set aside to cool slightly.
10. Serve warm.

233.Curly Vegan Fries

Servings:2
Cooking Time: 20 Minutes
Ingredients:
- 1 tbsp tomato ketchup
- 2 tbsp olive oil
- Salt and pepper to taste
- 2 tbsp coconut oil

Directions:
1. Preheat your air fryer to 360 F and use a spiralizer to spiralize the potatoes. In a bowl, mix oil, coconut oil, salt and pepper. Cover the potatoes with the oil mixture. Place the potatoes in the cooking basket and cook for 15 minutes. Serve with ketchup and enjoy!

234.Hoisin-glazed Bok Choy

Servings: 4
Cooking Time: 10 Minutes
Ingredients:
- 1 pound baby Bok choy, bottoms removed, leaves separated
- 2 garlic cloves, minced
- 1 teaspoon onion powder
- 1/2 teaspoon sage
- 2 tablespoons hoisin sauce
- 2 tablespoons sesame oil
- 1 tablespoon all-purpose flour

Directions:
1. Place the Bok choy, garlic, onion powder, and sage in the lightly greased Air Fryer basket.
2. Cook in the preheated Air Fryer at 350 degrees F for 3 minutes.
3. In a small mixing dish, whisk the hoisin sauce, sesame oil, and flour. Drizzle the sauce over the Bok choy. Cook for a further 3 minutes. Bon appétit!

235.Easy Fry Portobello Mushroom

Servings:2
Cooking Time: 10 Minutes
Ingredients:
- 1 tablespoon cooking oil
- 1-pound Portobello mushroom, sliced
- Salt and pepper to taste

Directions:
1. Place the grill pan accessory in the air fryer.
2. In a bowl, place all Ingredients and toss to coat and season the mushrooms.
3. Place in the grill pan.
4. Close the air fryer and cook for 10 minutes at 330°F.

236.Sweet 'n Nutty Marinated Cauliflower-tofu

Servings:2
Cooking Time: 20 Minutes
Ingredients:
- ¼ cup brown sugar
- ¼ cup low sodium soy sauce
- ½ teaspoon chili garlic sauce
- 1 package extra firm tofu, pressed to release extra water and cut into cubes
- 1 small head cauliflower, cut into florets
- 1 tablespoon sesame oil
- 2 ½ tablespoons almond butter
- 2 cloves of garlic, minced

Directions:
1. Place the garlic, sesame oil, soy sauce, sugar, chili garlic sauce, and almond butter in a mixing bowl. Whisk until well combined.
2. Place the tofu cubes and cauliflower in the marinade and allow to soak up the sauce for at least 30 minutes.
3. Preheat the air fryer to 400°F. Add tofu and cauliflower. Coo for 20 minutes. Shake basket halfway through cooking time.
4. Meanwhile, place the remaining marinade in a saucepan and bring to a boil over medium heat. Adjust the heat to low once boiling and stir until the sauce thickens.
5. Pour the sauce over the tofu and cauliflower.
6. Serve with rice or noodles.

237.Herb Roasted Potatoes And Peppers

Servings: 4
Cooking Time: 30 Minutes
Ingredients:
- 1 pound russet potatoes, cut into 1-inch chunks
- 2 bell peppers, seeded and cut into 1-inch chunks
- 2 tablespoons olive oil
- 1 teaspoon dried rosemary
- 1 teaspoon dried basil
- 1 teaspoon dried oregano
- 1 teaspoon dried parsley flakes
- Sea salt and ground black pepper, to taste
- 1/2 teaspoon smoked paprika

Directions:
1. Toss all ingredients in the Air Fryer basket.
2. Roast at 400 degrees F for 15 minutes, tossing the basket occasionally. Work in batches.
3. Serve warm and enjoy!

238.Almond Flour Battered Wings

Servings:4
Cooking Time: 25 Minutes
Ingredients:
- ¼ cup butter, melted
- ¾ cup almond flour
- 16 pieces chicken wings
- 2 tablespoons stevia powder
- 4 tablespoons minced garlic
- Salt and pepper to taste

Directions:
1. Preheat the air fryer for 5 minutes.
2. In a mixing bowl, combine the chicken wings, almond flour, stevia powder, and garlic Season with salt and pepper to taste.
3. Place in the air fryer basket and cook for 25 minutes at 400°F.
4. Halfway through the cooking time, make sure that you give the fryer basket a shake.
5. Once cooked, place in a bowl and drizzle with melted butter. Toss to coat.

239.Stuffed Eggplant

Servings: 2
Cooking Time: 35 Minutes
Ingredients:
- large eggplant
- ¼ medium yellow onion, diced
- 2 tbsp. red bell pepper, diced
- 1 cup spinach
- ¼ cup artichoke hearts, chopped

Directions:
1. Cut the eggplant lengthwise into slices and spoon out the flesh, leaving a shell about a half-inch thick. Chop it up and set aside.
2. Set a skillet over a medium heat and spritz with cooking spray. Cook the onions for about three to five minutes to soften. Then add the pepper, spinach, artichokes, and the flesh of eggplant. Fry for a further five minutes, then remove from the heat.
3. Scoop this mixture in equal parts into the eggplant shells and place each one in the fryer.
4. Cook for twenty minutes at 320°F until the eggplant shells are soft. Serve warm.

240.Stuffed Okra

Servings:2
Cooking Time:12 Minutes
Ingredients:
- 8 ounces large okra
- ¼ cup chickpea flour
- ¼ of onion, chopped
- 2 tablespoons coconut, grated freshly

68

- 1 teaspoon garam masala powder
- ½ teaspoon ground turmeric
- ½ teaspoon red chili powder
- ½ teaspoon ground cumin
- Salt, to taste

Directions:
1. Preheat the Air fryer to 390 °F and grease an Air fryer basket.
2. Mix the flour, onion, grated coconut, and spices in a bowl and toss to coat well.
3. Stuff the flour mixture into okra and arrange into the Air fryer basket.
4. Cook for about 12 minutes and dish out in a serving plate.

241.Vegetable Fried Rice

Servings:4
Cooking Time: 15 Minutes
Ingredients:
- 2 tsp melted butter
- 1 cup mushrooms, chopped
- 1 cup peas
- 1 carrot, chopped
- 1 red onion, chopped
- 1 garlic clove, minced
- Salt and black pepper to taste
- 1 tbsp soy sauce
- 2 hard-boiled eggs, grated

Directions:
1. Preheat the Air fryer to 380 F. Brush the bottom of a baking dish with melted butter.
2. In a bowl, combine the rice, mushrooms, carrot, peas, onion, garlic, salt, and pepper. Pour the mixture in the baking dish. Place in the air fryer and cook for 12 minutes. When ready, remove to a serving plate, top with the grated eggs, and drizzle the soy sauce all over to serve.

242.Spicy Veggie Recipe From Thailand

Servings:4
Cooking Time: 15 Minutes
Ingredients:
- 1 ½ cups packed cilantro leaves
- 1 tablespoon black pepper
- 1 tablespoon chili garlic sauce
- 1/3 cup vegetable oil
- 2 pounds vegetable of your choice, sliced into cubes
- 2 tablespoons fish sauce

- 8 cloves of garlic, minced

Directions:
1. Preheat the air fryer to 330°F.
2. Place the grill pan accessory in the air fryer.
3. Place all Ingredients in a mixing bowl and toss to coat all Ingredients.
4. Put in the grill pan and cook for 15 minutes.

243.Turmeric Crispy Chickpeas

Servings:4
Cooking Time: 22 Minutes
Ingredients:
- 1 tbsp butter, melted
- ½ tsp dried rosemary
- ¼ tsp turmeric
- Salt to taste

Directions:
1. Preheat the Air fryer to 380 F.
2. In a bowl, combine together chickpeas, butter, rosemary, turmeric, and salt; toss to coat. Place the prepared chickpeas in your Air Fryer's cooking basket and cook for 6 minutes. Slide out the basket and shake; cook for another 6 minutes until crispy.

244.Favorite Broccoli With Garlic Sauce

Servings: 4
Cooking Time: 19 Minutes
Ingredients:
- 2 tablespoons vegetable oil of choice
- Kosher salt and freshly ground black pepper, to taste
- 1 pound broccoli florets
- For the Dipping Sauce:
- 2 teaspoons dried rosemary, crushed
- 3 garlic cloves, minced
- 1/3 teaspoon dried marjoram, crushed
- 1/4 cup sour cream
- 1/3 cup mayonnaise

Directions:
1. Lightly grease your broccoli with a thin layer of vegetable oil. Season with salt and ground black pepper.
2. Arrange the seasoned broccoli in an Air Fryer cooking basket. Bake at 395 degrees F for 15 minutes, shaking once or twice.
3. In the meantime, prepare the dipping sauce by mixing all the sauce ingredients. Serve warm broccoli with the dipping sauce and enjoy!

POULTRY RECIPES

245.Simple Turkey Breast

Servings:10
Cooking Time:40 Minutes
Ingredients:
- 1 (8-pounds) bone-in turkey breast
- Salt and black pepper, as required
- 2 tablespoons olive oil

Directions:
1. Preheat the Air fryer to 360 °F and grease an Air fryer basket.
2. Season the turkey breast with salt and black pepper and drizzle with oil.
3. Arrange the turkey breast into the Air Fryer basket, skin side down and cook for about 20 minutes.
4. Flip the side and cook for another 20 minutes.
5. Dish out in a platter and cut into desired size slices to serve.

246.Pretzel Crusted Chicken With Spicy Mustard Sauce

Servings: 6
Cooking Time: 20 Minutes
Ingredients:
- 2 eggs
- 1 ½ pound chicken breasts, boneless, skinless, cut into bite-sized chunks
- 1/2 cup crushed pretzels
- 1 teaspoon shallot powder
- 1 teaspoon paprika
- Sea salt and ground black pepper, to taste
- 1/2 cup vegetable broth
- 1 tablespoon cornstarch
- 3 tablespoons Worcestershire sauce
- 3 tablespoons tomato paste
- 1 tablespoon apple cider vinegar
- 2 tablespoons olive oil
- 2 garlic cloves, chopped
- 1 jalapeno pepper, minced
- 1 teaspoon yellow mustard

Directions:
1. Start by preheating your Air Fryer to 390 degrees F.
2. In a mixing dish, whisk the eggs until frothy; toss the chicken chunks into the whisked eggs and coat well.
3. In another dish, combine the crushed pretzels with shallot powder, paprika, salt and pepper. Then, lay the chicken chunks in the pretzel mixture; turn it over until well coated.
4. Place the chicken pieces in the air fryer basket. Cook the chicken for 12 minutes, shaking the basket halfway through.

5. Meanwhile, whisk the vegetable broth with cornstarch, Worcestershire sauce, tomato paste, and apple cider vinegar.
6. Preheat a cast-iron skillet over medium flame. Heat the olive oil and sauté the garlic with jalapeno pepper for 30 to 40 seconds, stirring frequently.
7. Add the cornstarch mixture and let it simmer until the sauce has thickened a little. Now, add the air-fried chicken and mustard; let it simmer for 2 minutes more or until heated through.
8. Serve immediately and enjoy!

247.Easy Hot Chicken Drumsticks

Servings: 6
Cooking Time: 40 Minutes
Ingredients:
- 6 chicken drumsticks
- Sauce:
- 6 ounces hot sauce
- 3 tablespoons olive oil
- 3 tablespoons tamari sauce
- 1 teaspoon dried thyme
- 1/2 teaspoon dried oregano

Directions:
1. Spritz the sides and bottom of the cooking basket with a nonstick cooking spray.
2. Cook the chicken drumsticks at 380 degrees F for 35 minutes, flipping them over halfway through.
3. Meanwhile, heat the hot sauce, olive oil, tamari sauce, thyme, and oregano in a pan over medium-low heat; reserve.
4. Drizzle the sauce over the prepared chicken drumsticks; toss to coat well and serve. Bon appétit!

248.Orange-tequila Glazed Chicken

Servings:6
Cooking Time: 40 Minutes
Ingredients:
- ¼ cup tequila
- 1 shallot, minced
- 1/3 cup orange juice
- 2 tablespoons brown sugar
- 2 tablespoons honey
- 2 tablespoons whole coriander seeds
- 3 cloves of garlic, minced
- 3 pounds chicken breasts
- Salt and pepper to taste

Directions:
1. Place all Ingredients in a Ziploc bag and allow to marinate for at least 2 hours in the fridge.
2. Preheat the air fryer to 390°F.
3. Place the grill pan accessory in the air fryer.

4. Grill the chicken for at least 40 minutes
5. Flip the chicken every 10 minutes for even cooking.
6. Meanwhile, pour the marinade in a saucepan and simmer until the sauce thickens.
7. Brush the chicken with the glaze before serving.

249.Bacon Chicken Mix

Servings: 2
Cooking Time: 25 Minutes
Ingredients:
- 2 chicken legs
- 4 oz bacon, sliced
- ½ teaspoon salt
- ½ teaspoon ground black pepper
- 1 teaspoon sesame oil

Directions:
1. Sprinkle the chicken legs with salt and ground black pepper and wrap in the sliced bacon. After this, preheat the air fryer to 385F. Put the chicken legs in the air fryer and sprinkle with sesame oil. Cook the bacon chicken legs for 25 minutes.

250.Buffalo Chicken Tenders

Servings: 4
Cooking Time: 20 Minutes
Ingredients:
- 1 egg
- 1 cup mozzarella cheese, shredded
- ¼ cup buffalo sauce
- 1 cup cooked chicken, shredded
- ¼ cup feta cheese

Directions:
1. Combine all ingredients (except for the feta). Line the basket of your fryer with a suitably sized piece of parchment paper. Lay the mixture into the fryer and press it into a circle about half an inch thick. Crumble the feta cheese over it.
2. Cook for eight minutes at 400°F. Turn the fryer off and allow the chicken to rest inside before removing with care.
3. Cut the mixture into slices and serve hot.

251.Mouthwatering Turkey Roll

Servings:4
Cooking Time:40 Minutes
Ingredients:
- 1 pound turkey breast fillet, deep slit cut lengthwise with knife
- 3 tablespoons fresh parsley, chopped finely
- 1 small red onion, chopped finely
- 1 garlic clove, crushed
- 1½ teaspoons ground cumin
- 1 teaspoon ground cinnamon
- ½ teaspoon red chili powder

- Salt, to taste
- 2 tablespoons olive oil

Directions:
1. Preheat the Air fryer to 355 °F and grease an Air fryer basket.
2. Mix garlic, parsley, onion, spices and olive oil in a bowl.
3. Coat the open side of fillet with onion mixture and roll the fillet tightly.
4. Coat the outer side of roll with remaining spice mixture and transfer into the Air fryer.
5. Cook for about 40 minutes and dish out to serve warm.

252.Garlic Rosemary Roasted Chicken

Servings:6
Cooking Time: 50 Minutes
Ingredients:
- 1 tsp rosemary
- 2 pounds whole chicken
- 4 cloves of garlic, minced
- Salt and pepper to taste

Directions:
1. Season the whole chicken with garlic, salt, and pepper.
2. Place in the air fryer basket.
3. Cook for 30 minutes at 330°F.
4. Flip the chicken in the other side and cook for another 20 minutes.

253.Crispy Chicken Thighs

Servings: 1
Cooking Time: 35 Minutes
Ingredients:
- 1 lb. chicken thighs
- Salt and pepper
- 2 cups roasted pecans
- 1 cup water
- 1 cup flour

Directions:
1. Pre-heat your fryer to 400°F.
2. Season the chicken with salt and pepper, then set aside.
3. Pulse the roasted pecans in a food processor until a flour-like consistency is achieved.
4. Fill a dish with the water, another with the flour, and a third with the pecans.
5. Coat the thighs with the flour. Mix the remaining flour with the processed pecans.
6. Dredge the thighs in the water and then press into the -pecan mix, ensuring the chicken is completely covered.
7. Cook the chicken in the fryer for twenty-two minutes, with an extra five minutes added if you would like the chicken a darker-brown color. Check the temperature has reached 165°F before serving.

254.Chicken And Apricot Sauce Recipe

Servings: 4
Cooking Time:30 Minutes
Ingredients:
- 1 whole chicken; cut into medium pieces
- 2 tbsp. honey
- 1 tbsp. olive oil
- 1/2 tsp. smoked paprika
- 1/4 cup white wine
- 2 tbsp. white vinegar
- 1/4 cup apricot preserves
- 1 ½ tsp. ginger; grated
- 1/2 tsp. marjoram; dried
- 1/4 cup chicken stock
- Salt and black pepper to the taste

Directions:
1. Season chicken with salt, pepper, marjoram and paprika; toss to coat, add oil, rub well, place in your air fryer and cook at 360 °F, for 10 minutes.
2. Transfer chicken to a pan that fits your air fryer, add stock, wine, vinegar, ginger, apricot preserves and honey; toss, put in your air fryer and cook at 360 °F, for 10 minutes more. Divide chicken and apricot sauce on plates and serve.

255.Bbq Pineapple 'n Teriyaki Glazed Chicken

Servings:4
Cooking Time: 23 Minutes
Ingredients:
- ¼ cup pineapple juice
- ¼ teaspoon pepper
- ½ cup brown sugar
- ½ cup soy sauce
- ½ teaspoon salt
- 1 green bell pepper, cut into 1-inch cubes
- 1 red bell pepper, cut into 1-inch cubes
- 1 red onion, cut into 1-inch cubes
- 1 Tablespoon cornstarch
- 1 Tablespoon water
- 1 yellow red bell pepper, cut into 1-inch cubes
- 2 boneless skinless chicken breasts, cut into 1-inch cubes
- 2 cups fresh pineapple cut into 1-inch cubes
- 2 garlic cloves, minced
- green onions, for garnish

Directions:
1. In a saucepan, bring to a boil salt, pepper, garlic, pineapple juice, soy sauce, and brown sugar. In a small bowl whisk well, cornstarch and water. Slowly stir in to mixture in pan while whisking constantly. Simmer until thickened, around 3 minutes. Save ¼ cup of the sauce for basting and set aside.

2. In shallow dish, mix well chicken and remaining thickened sauce. Toss well to coat. Marinate in the ref for a half hour.
3. Thread bell pepper, onion, pineapple, and chicken pieces in skewers. Place on skewer rack in air fryer.
4. For 10 minutes, cook on 360°F. Halfway through cooking time, turnover skewers and baste with sauce. If needed, cook in batches.
5. Serve and enjoy with a sprinkle of green onions.

256.Honey & Garlic Chicken Breasts

Servings:4
Cooking Time: 22 Minutes
Ingredients:
- 1 tbsp honey
- 2 garlic cloves, minced
- Salt and black pepper to taste
- 1 pound boneless skinless chicken breasts
- 3 tbsp butter, melted

Directions:
1. Preheat the Air fryer to 360 F.
2. In a bowl, combine together mustard, butter, garlic, honey, pepper, and salt; mix well. Rub the chicken with the mixture and place in the greased with cooking spray air fryer basket. Cook for 10 minutes. Slide out the basket and flip; cook for 10 minutes until crispy. Slice before serving.

257.Rosemary Partridge

Servings: 4
Cooking Time: 14 Minutes
Ingredients:
- 10 oz partridges
- 1 teaspoon dried rosemary
- 1 tablespoon butter, melted
- 1 teaspoon salt

Directions:
1. Cut the partridges into the halves and sprinkle with dried rosemary and salt. Then brush them with melted butter. Preheat the air fryer to 385F. Put the partridge halves in the air fryer and cook them for 8 minutes. Then flip the poultry on another side and cook for 6 minutes more.

258.Honey & Garlic Chicken Wings

Servings: 4
Cooking Time: 25 Minutes
Ingredients:
- 16 chicken wings
- ½ tsp. salt
- ¾ cup potato starch
- ¼ cup butter, melted
- 4 cloves garlic, minced
- ¼ cup honey

Directions:
1. Pre-heat your Air Fryer to 370°F.
2. Put the chicken wings in a bowl and cover them well with the potato starch.
3. Spritz a baking dish with cooking spray.
4. Transfer the wings to the dish, place inside the fryer and cook for 5 minutes.
5. In the meantime, mix together the rest of the ingredients with a whisk.
6. Top the chicken with this mixture and allow to cook for another 10 minutes before serving.

259.Hot Chicken Wings

Servings: 4
Cooking Time: 30 Minutes
Ingredients:
- 1 tablespoon olive oil
- 2 pounds chicken wings
- 1 tablespoon lime juice
- 2 teaspoons smoked paprika
- 1 teaspoon red pepper flakes, crushed
- Salt and black pepper to the taste

Directions:
1. In a bowl, mix the chicken wings with all the other ingredients and toss well. Put the chicken wings in your air fryer's basket and cook at 380 degrees F for 15 minutes on each side. Divide between plates and serve with a side salad.

260.Spicy Chicken Legs

Servings:3
Cooking Time:25 Minutes
Ingredients:
- 3 (8-ounces) chicken legs
- 1 cup buttermilk
- 2 cups white flour
- 1 teaspoon garlic powder
- 1 teaspoon onion powder
- 1 teaspoon ground cumin
- 1 teaspoon paprika
- Salt and ground black pepper, as required
- 1 tablespoon olive oil

Directions:
1. Preheat the Air fryer to 360 °F and grease an Air fryer basket.
2. Mix the chicken legs, and buttermilk in a bowl and refrigerate for about 2 hours.
3. Combine the flour and spices in another bowl and dredge the chicken legs into this mixture.
4. Now, dip the chicken into the buttermilk and coat again with the flour mixture.
5. Arrange the chicken legs into the Air fryer basket and drizzle with the oil.
6. Cook for about 25 minutes and dish out in a serving platter to serve hot.

261.Turkey Meatballs

Servings: 4
Cooking Time: 12 Minutes
Ingredients:
- 1 lb ground turkey
- 2 garlic cloves, minced
- ¼ cup carrots, grated
- 1 egg, lightly beaten
- 2 tbsp coconut flour
- 2 green onion, chopped
- ¼ cup celery, chopped
- Pepper
- Salt

Directions:
1. Spray air fryer basket with cooking spray.
2. Preheat the air fryer to 400 F.
3. Add all ingredients into the large bowl and mix until well combined.
4. Make balls from meat mixture and place into the air fryer basket and cook for 12 minutes. Turn halfway through.
5. Serve and enjoy.

262.Mozzarella Turkey Rolls

Servings: 4
Cooking Time: 20 Minutes
Ingredients:
- 4 slices turkey breast
- 1 cup sliced fresh mozzarella
- 1 tomato, sliced
- ½ cup fresh basil
- 4 chive shoots

Directions:
1. Pre-heat your Air Fryer to 390°F.
2. Lay the slices of mozzarella, tomato and basil on top of each turkey slice.
3. Roll the turkey up, enclosing the filling well, and secure by tying a chive shoot around each one.
4. Put in the Air Fryer and cook for 10 minutes. Serve with a salad if desired.

263.Air Fried Chicken Tenderloin

Servings:8
Cooking Time: 15 Minutes
Ingredients:
- ½ cup almond flour
- 1 egg, beaten
- 2 tablespoons coconut oil
- 8 chicken tenderloins
- Salt and pepper to taste

Directions:
1. Preheat the air fryer for 5 minutes.
2. Season the chicken tenderloin with salt and pepper to taste.
3. Soak in beaten eggs then dredge in almond flour.
4. Place in the air fryer and brush with coconut oil.

5. Cook for 15 minutes at 375°F.
6. Halfway through the cooking time, give the fryer basket a shake to cook evenly.

264.Air Fried Crispy Chicken Tenders

Servings:3
Cooking Time:30 Minutes
Ingredients:
- 2 (6-ounces) boneless, skinless chicken breasts, pounded into ½-inch thickness and cut into tenders
- ½ cup all-purpose flour
- 1½ cups panko breadcrumbs
- ¼ cup Parmesan cheese, finely grated
- 2 large eggs
- 1½ teaspoons Worcestershire sauce, divided
- ¾ cup buttermilk
- ½ teaspoon smoked paprika, divided
- Salt and ground black pepper, as required

Directions:
1. Preheat the Air fryer to 400 °F and grease an Air fryer basket.
2. Mix buttermilk, ¾ teaspoon of Worcestershire sauce, ¼ teaspoon of paprika, salt, and black pepper in a bowl.
3. Combine the flour, remaining paprika, salt, and black pepper in another bowl.
4. Whisk the egg and remaining Worcestershire sauce in a third bowl.
5. Mix the panko breadcrumbs and Parmesan cheese in a fourth bowl.
6. Put the chicken tenders into the buttermilk mixture and refrigerate overnight.
7. Remove the chicken tenders from the buttermilk mixture and dredge into the flour mixture.
8. Dip into the egg and coat with the breadcrumb mixture.
9. Arrange half of the chicken tenders into the Air Fryer basket and cook for about 15 minutes, flipping once in between.
10. Repeat with the remaining mixture and dish out to serve hot.

265.Buttery Turkey And Mushroom Sauce

Servings: 4
Cooking Time: 25 Minutes
Ingredients:
- 6 cups leftover turkey meat, skinless, boneless and shredded
- A pinch of salt and black pepper
- 1 tablespoon parsley, chopped
- 1 cup chicken stock
- 3 tablespoons butter, melted
- 1 pound mushrooms, sliced
- 2 spring onions, chopped

Directions:
1. Heat up a pan that fits the air fryer with the butter over medium-high heat, add the mushrooms and sauté for 5 minutes. Add the rest of the ingredients, toss, put the pan in the machine and cook at 370 degrees F for 20 minutes. Divide everything between plates and serve.

266.Chicken And Olives Mix

Servings: 4
Cooking Time: 30 Minutes
Ingredients:
- 8 chicken thighs, boneless and skinless
- A pinch of salt and black pepper
- 2 tablespoons olive oil
- 1 teaspoon oregano, dried
- ½ teaspoon garlic powder
- 1 cup pepperoncini, drained and sliced
- ½ cup black olives, pitted and sliced
- ½ cup kalamata olives, pitted and sliced
- ¼ cup parmesan, grated

Directions:
1. Heat up a pan that fits the air fryer with the oil over medium-high heat, add the chicken and brown for 2 minutes on each side. Add salt, pepper, and all the other ingredients except the parmesan and toss. Put the pan in the air fryer, sprinkle the parmesan on top and cook at 370 degrees F for 25 minutes. Divide the chicken mix between plates and serve.

267.Sweet And Sour Chicken Thighs

Servings:2
Cooking Time:20 Minutes
Ingredients:
- 1 scallion, finely chopped
- 2 (4-ounces) skinless, boneless chicken thighs
- ½ cup corn flour
- 1 garlic clove, minced
- ½ tablespoon soy sauce
- ½ tablespoon rice vinegar
- 1 teaspoon sugar
- Salt and black pepper, as required

Directions:
1. Preheat the Air fryer to 390 °F and grease an Air fryer basket.
2. Mix all the ingredients except chicken and corn flour in a bowl.
3. Place the corn flour in another bowl.
4. Coat the chicken thighs into the marinade and then dredge into the corn flour.
5. Arrange the chicken thighs into the Air Fryer basket, skin side down and cook for about 10 minutes.
6. Set the Air fryer to 355 °F and cook for 10 more minutes.

7. Dish out the chicken thighs onto a serving platter and serve hot.

268.Balsamic Duck And Cranberry Sauce

Servings: 4
Cooking Time: 25 Minutes
Ingredients:
- 4 duck breasts, boneless, skin-on and scored
- A pinch of salt and black pepper
- 1 tablespoon olive oil
- ¼ cup balsamic vinegar
- ½ cup dried cranberries

Directions:
1. Heat up a pan that fits your air fryer with the oil over medium-high heat, add the duck breasts skin side down and cook for 5 minutes. Add the rest of the ingredients, toss, put the pan in the fryer and cook at 380 degrees F for 20 minutes. Divide between plates and serve.

269.Duck Breasts And Raspberry Sauce Recipe

Servings: 4
Cooking Time:25 Minutes
Ingredients:
- 2 duck breasts; skin on and scored
- 1 tbsp. sugar
- 1 tsp. red wine vinegar
- 1/2 cup raspberries
- 1/2 cup water
- 1/2 tsp. cinnamon powder
- Salt and black pepper to the taste
- Cooking spray

Directions:
1. Season duck breasts with salt and pepper, spray them with cooking spray, put in preheated air fryer skin side down and cook at 350 °F, for 10 minutes.
2. Heat up a pan with the water over medium heat, add raspberries, cinnamon, sugar and wine; stir, bring to a simmer, transfer to your blender, puree and return to pan. Add air fryer duck breasts to pan as well; toss to coat, divide among plates and serve right away.

270.Classic Chicken Nuggets

Servings: 4
Cooking Time: 20 Minutes
Ingredients:
- 1 ½ pounds chicken tenderloins, cut into small pieces
- 1/2 teaspoon garlic salt
- 1/2 teaspoon cayenne pepper
- 1/4 teaspoon black pepper, freshly cracked
- 4 tablespoons olive oil

- 2 scoops low-carb unflavored protein powder
- 4 tablespoons Parmesan cheese, freshly grated

Directions:
1. Start by preheating your Air Fryer to 390 degrees F.
2. Season each piece of the chicken with garlic salt, cayenne pepper, and black pepper.
3. In a mixing bowl, thoroughly combine the olive oil with protein powder and parmesan cheese. Dip each piece of chicken in the parmesan mixture.
4. Cook for 8 minutes, working in batches.
5. Later, if you want to warm the chicken nuggets, add them to the basket and cook for 1 minute more. Enjoy!

271.Peppery Turkey Sandwiches

Servings: 4
Cooking Time: 25 Minutes
Ingredients:
- 1 cup leftover turkey, cut into bite-sized chunks
- 2 bell peppers, deveined and chopped
- 1 Serrano pepper, deveined and chopped
- 1 leek, sliced
- ½ cup sour cream
- 1 tsp. hot paprika
- ¾ tsp. kosher salt
- ½ tsp. ground black pepper
- 1 heaping tbsp. fresh cilantro, chopped
- Dash of Tabasco sauce
- 4 hamburger buns

Directions:
1. Combine all of the ingredients except for the hamburger buns, ensuring to coat the turkey well.
2. Place in an Air Fryer baking pan and roast for 20 minutes at 385°F.
3. Top the hamburger buns with the turkey, and serve with mustard or sour cream as desired.

272.Garlic Turkey And Lemon Asparagus

Servings: 4
Cooking Time: 25 Minutes
Ingredients:
- 1 pound turkey breast tenderloins, cut into strips
- 1 pound asparagus, trimmed and cut into medium pieces
- A pinch of salt and black pepper
- 1 tablespoon lemon juice
- 1 teaspoon coconut aminos
- 2 tablespoons olive oil
- 2 garlic cloves, minced
- ¼ cup chicken stock

Directions:

1. Heat up a pan that fits the air fryer with the oil over medium-high heat, add the meat and brown for 2 minutes on each side. Add the rest of the ingredients, toss, put the pan in the machine and cook at 380 degrees F for 20 minutes. Divide everything between plates and serve

273.Duck Legs And Scallions Mix

Servings: 2
Cooking Time: 16 Minutes
Ingredients:
- 2 duck legs
- 1 teaspoon olive oil
- ½ teaspoon ground cumin
- 1 teaspoon salt
- 1 tablespoon scallions, chopped

Directions:
1. In the shallow bowl mix up ground cumin and salt. Then rub the duck legs with the spice mixture. After this, mix up the scallions and olive oil. Sprinkle the duck legs with the scallions mix. Preheat the air fryer to 385F. Put the duck legs in the air fryer and cook them for 8 minutes. Then flip the duck legs on another side and cook for 8 minutes.

274.Chicken And Spinach Salad Recipe

Servings: 2
Cooking Time:22 Minutes
Ingredients:
- 2 chicken breasts; skinless and boneless
- 2 tsp. parsley; dried
- 1/2 tsp. onion powder
- 1 avocado; pitted, peeled and chopped
- 1/4 cup olive oil
- 1 tbsp. tarragon; chopped.
- 2 tsp. sweet paprika
- 1/2 cup lemon juice
- 5 cups baby spinach
- 8 strawberries; sliced
- 1 small red onion; sliced
- 2 tbsp. balsamic vinegar
- Salt and black pepper to the taste

Directions:
1. Put chicken in a bowl, add lemon juice, parsley, onion powder and paprika and toss.
2. Transfer chicken to your air fryer and cook at 360 °F, for 12 minutes.
3. In a bowl, mix spinach, onion, strawberries and avocado and toss.
4. In another bowl, mix oil with vinegar, salt, pepper and tarragon, whisk well, add to the salad and toss. Divide chicken on plates, add spinach salad on the side and serve.

275.Sweet Sriracha Turkey Legs

Servings:2

Cooking Time:35 Minutes
Ingredients:
- 1-pound turkey legs
- 1 tablespoon butter
- 1 tablespoon cilantro
- 1 tablespoon chives
- 1 tablespoon scallions
- 4 tablespoons sriracha sauce
- 1½ tablespoons soy sauce
- ½ lime, juiced

Directions:
1. Preheat the Air fryer on Roasting mode to 360 °F for 3 minutes and grease an Air fryer basket.
2. Arrange the turkey legs in the Air fryer basket and cook for about 30 minutes, flipping several times in between.
3. Mix butter, scallions, sriracha sauce, soy sauce and lime juice in the saucepan and cook for about for 3 minutes until the sauce thickens.
4. Drizzle this sauce over the turkey legs and garnish with cilantro and chives to serve.

276.Chipotle-garlic Smoked Wings

Servings:8
Cooking Time: 30 Minutes
Ingredients:
- ½ cup barbecue sauce
- 1 tablespoon chili powder
- 1 tablespoon garlic powder
- 1 tablespoon liquid smoke seasoning
- 1 teaspoon chipotle chili powder
- 1 teaspoon mustard powder
- 3 tablespoons paprika
- 4 pounds chicken wings
- 4 teaspoons salt

Directions:
1. Place all Ingredients in a Ziploc bag
2. Allow to marinate for at least 2 hours in the fridge.
3. Preheat the air fryer to 390°F.
4. Place the grill pan accessory in the air fryer.
5. Grill the chicken for 30 minutes.
6. Flip the chicken every 10 minutes for even grilling.
7. Meanwhile, pour the marinade in a saucepan and heat over medium flame until the sauce thickens.
8. Before serving the chicken, brush with the glaze.

277.Holiday Colby Turkey Meatloaf

Servings:6
Cooking Time:50 Minutes
Ingredients:
- 1 pound turkey mince
- 1/2 cup scallions, finely chopped
- 2 garlic cloves, finely minced

- 1 teaspoon dried thyme
- 1/2 teaspoon dried basil
- 3/4 cup Colby cheese, shredded
- 3/4 cup crushed saltines
- 1 tablespoon tamari sauce
- Salt and black pepper, to your liking
- 1/4 cup roasted red pepper tomato sauce
- 1 teaspoon brown sugar
- 3/4 tablespoons olive oil
- 1 medium-sized egg, well beaten

Directions:
1. In a nonstick skillet, that is preheated over a moderate heat, sauté the turkey mince, scallions, garlic, thyme, and basil until just tender and fragrant.
2. Then set your Air Fryer to cook at 360 degrees. Combine sautéed mixture with the cheese, saltines and tamari sauce; then form the mixture into a loaf shape.
3. Mix the remaining items and pour them over the meatloaf. Cook in the Air Fryer baking pan for 45 to 47 minutes. Eat warm.

278.Chicken And Veggie Kabobs

Servings:3
Cooking Time:30 Minutes
Ingredients:
- 1 lb. skinless, boneless chicken thighs, cut into cubes
- ½ cup plain Greek yogurt
- 2 small tomatoes, seeded and cut into large chunks
- 1 large red onion, cut into large chunks
- Wooden skewers, presoaked
- 1 tablespoon olive oil
- 2 teaspoons curry powder
- ½ teaspoon smoked paprika
- ¼ teaspoon cayenne pepper
- Salt, to taste

Directions:
1. Preheat the Air fryer to 360 °F and grease an Air fryer pan.
2. Mix the chicken, oil, yogurt, and spices in a large baking dish.
3. Thread chicken cubes, tomatoes and onion onto presoaked wooden skewers.
4. Coat the skewers generously with marinade and refrigerate for about 3 hours.
5. Transfer half of the skewers in the Air fryer pan and cook for about 15 minutes.
6. Repeat with the remaining mixture and dish out to serve warm.

279.Lemongrass Hens

Servings: 4
Cooking Time: 65 Minutes
Ingredients:
- 14 oz hen (chicken)
- 1 teaspoon lemongrass

- 1 teaspoon ground coriander
- 1 oz celery stalk, chopped
- 1 teaspoon dried cilantro
- 3 spring onions, diced
- 2 tablespoons avocado oil
- 2 tablespoons lime juice
- ½ teaspoon lemon zest, grated
- 1 teaspoon salt
- 1 tablespoon apple cider vinegar
- 1 teaspoon chili powder
- ½ teaspoon ground black pepper

Directions:
1. In the mixing bowl mix up lemongrass, ground coriander, dried cilantro, lime juice, lemon zest, salt, apple cider vinegar, and ground black pepper. Then add spring onions and celery stalk. After this, rub the hen with the spice mixture and leave for 10 minutes to marinate. Meanwhile, preheat the air fryer to 375F. Put the hen in the air fryer and cook it for 55 minutes. Then flip it on another side and cook for 10 minutes more.

280.Bacon-wrapped Chicken

Servings: 6
Cooking Time: 20 Minutes
Ingredients:
- 1 chicken breast, cut into 6 pieces
- 6 rashers back bacon
- 1 tbsp. soft cheese

Directions:
1. Put the bacon rashers on a flat surface and cover one side with the soft cheese.
2. Lay the chicken pieces on each bacon rasher. Wrap the bacon around the chicken and use a toothpick stick to hold each one in place. Put them in Air Fryer basket.
3. Air fry at 350°F for 15 minutes.

281.Tasty Southwest Chicken

Servings: 2
Cooking Time: 25 Minutes
Ingredients:
- 1/2 lb chicken breasts, skinless and boneless
- 1/2 tsp chili powder
- 1 tbsp olive oil
- 1 tbsp lime juice
- 1/8 tsp garlic powder
- 1/8 tsp onion powder
- 1/4 tsp cumin
- 1/8 tsp salt

Directions:
1. Add all ingredients into the zip-lock bag and shake well to coat and place in the refrigerator for 1 hour.

2. Add a marinated chicken wing to the air fryer basket and cook at 400 F for 25 minutes. Shake halfway through.
3. Serve and enjoy.

282.Chicken Roast With Pineapple Salsa

Servings:2
Cooking Time: 45 Minutes
Ingredients:
- ¼ cup extra virgin olive oil
- ¼ cup freshly chopped cilantro
- 1 avocado, diced
- 1-pound boneless chicken breasts
- 2 cups canned pineapples
- 2 teaspoons honey
- Juice from 1 lime
- Salt and pepper to taste

Directions:
1. Preheat the air fryer to 390°F.
2. Place the grill pan accessory in the air fryer.
3. Season the chicken breasts with lime juice, olive oil, honey, salt, and pepper.
4. Place on the grill pan and cook for 45 minutes.
5. Flip the chicken every 10 minutes to grill all sides evenly.
6. Once the chicken is cooked, serve with pineapples, cilantro, and avocado.

283.Pizza Spaghetti Casserole

Servings: 4
Cooking Time: 30 Minutes
Ingredients:
- 8 ounces spaghetti
- 1 pound smoked chicken sausage, sliced
- 2 tomatoes, pureed
- 1/2 cup Asiago cheese, shredded
- 1 tablespoon Italian seasoning mix
- 3 tablespoons Romano cheese, grated
- 1 tablespoon fresh basil leaves, chiffonade

Directions:
1. Bring a large pot of lightly salted water to a boil. Cook your spaghetti for 10 minutes or until al dente; drain and reserve, keeping warm.
2. Stir in the chicken sausage, tomato puree, Asiago cheese, and Italian seasoning mix.
3. Then, spritz a baking pan with cooking spray; add the spaghetti mixture to the pan. Bake in the preheated Air Fryer at 325 degrees F for 11 minutes.
4. Top with the grated Romano cheese. Turn the temperature to 390 degrees F and cook an additional 5 minutes or until everything is thoroughly heated and the cheese is melted.
5. Garnish with fresh basil leaves. Bon appétit!

284.Tomato, Cheese 'n Broccoli Quiche

Servings:2
Cooking Time: 24 Minutes
Ingredients:
- ½ cup Cheddar Cheese grated
- ½ cup Whole Milk
- 1 Large Carrot, peeled and diced
- 1 Large Tomato, chopped
- 1 small Broccoli, cut into florets
- 1 Tsp Parsley
- 1 Tsp Thyme
- 2 Large Eggs
- 2 tbsp Feta Cheese
- Salt & Pepper

Directions:
1. Lightly grease baking pan of air fryer with cooking spray.
2. Spread carrots, broccoli, and tomato in baking pan.
3. For 10 minutes, cook on 330°F.
4. Meanwhile, in a medium bowl whisk well eggs and milk. Season generously with pepper and salt. Whisk in parsley and thyme.
5. Remove basket and toss the mixture a bit. Sprinkle cheddar cheese. Pour egg mixture over vegetables and cheese.
6. Cook for another 12 minutes or until set to desired doneness.
7. Sprinkle feta cheese and let it sit for 2 minutes.
8. Serve and enjoy.

285.Poppin' Pop Corn Chicken

Servings: 1
Cooking Time: 20 Minutes
Ingredients:
- 1 lb. skinless, boneless chicken breast
- 1 tsp. chili flakes
- 1 tsp. garlic powder
- ½ cup flour
- 1 tbsp. olive oil cooking spray

Directions:
1. Pre-heat your fryer at 365°F. Spray with olive oil.
2. Cut the chicken breasts into cubes and place in a bowl. Toss with the chili flakes, garlic powder, and additional seasonings to taste and make sure to coat entirely.
3. Add the coconut flour and toss once more.
4. Cook the chicken in the fryer for ten minutes. Turnover and cook for a further five minutes before serving.

286.Easy How-to Hard Boil Egg In Air Fryer

Servings:6
Cooking Time: 15 Minutes
Ingredients:

- 6 eggs

Directions:
1. Preheat the air fryer for 5 minutes.
2. Place the eggs in the air fryer basket.
3. Cook for 15 minutes at 360°F.
4. Remove from the air fryer basket and place in cold water.

287.Non-fattening Breakfast Frittata

Servings:2
Cooking Time: 15 Minutes
Ingredients:
- ¼ cup sliced mushrooms
- ¼ cup sliced tomato
- 1 cup egg whites
- 2 Tbsp chopped fresh chives
- 2 Tbsp skim milk
- Salt and Black pepper, to taste

Directions:
1. Lightly grease baking pan of air fryer with cooking spray.
2. Spread mushrooms and tomato on bottom of pan.
3. In a bowl, whisk well egg whites, milk, chives, pepper and salt. Pour into baking pan.
4. For 15 minutes, cook on 330°F.
5. Remove basket and let it sit for a minute.
6. Serve and enjoy.

288.Cauliflower Stuffed Chicken

Servings:5
Cooking Time: 25 Minutes
Ingredients:
- 1 ½-pound chicken breast, skinless, boneless
- ½ cup cauliflower, shredded
- 1 jalapeno pepper, chopped
- 1 teaspoon ground nutmeg
- 1 teaspoon salt
- ¼ cup Cheddar cheese, shredded
- ½ teaspoon cayenne pepper
- 1 tablespoon cream cheese
- 1 tablespoon sesame oil
- ½ teaspoon dried thyme

Directions:
1. Make the horizontal cut in the chicken breast. In the mixing bowl mix up shredded cauliflower, chopped jalapeno pepper, ground nutmeg, salt, and cayenne pepper. Fill the chicken cut with the shredded cauliflower and secure the cut with toothpicks. Then rub the chicken breast with cream cheese, dried thyme, and sesame oil. Preheat the air fryer to 380F. Put the chicken breast in the air fryer and cook it for 20 minutes. Then sprinkle it with Cheddar cheese and cook for 5 minutes more.

289.Cajun-mustard Turkey Fingers

Servings: 4
Cooking Time: 20 Minutes
Ingredients:
- ½ cup cornmeal mix
- ½ cup flour
- 1 ½ tbsp. Cajun seasoning
- 1 ½ tbsp. whole-grain mustard
- 1 ½ cups buttermilk
- 1 tsp. soy sauce
- ¾ lb. turkey tenderloins, cut into finger-sized strips
- Salt and ground black pepper to taste

Directions:
1. In a bowl, combine the cornmeal, flour, and Cajun seasoning.
2. In a separate bowl, combine the whole-grain mustard, buttermilk and soy sauce.
3. Sprinkle some salt and pepper on the turkey fingers.
4. Dredge each finger in the buttermilk mixture, before coating them completely with the cornmeal mixture.
5. Place the prepared turkey fingers in the Air Fryer baking pan and cook for 15 minutes at 360°F.
6. Serve immediately, with ketchup if desired.

290.Chicken Taquitos With Homemade Guacamole

Servings: 4
Cooking Time: 35 Minutes
Ingredients:
- 1 tablespoon peanut oil
- 1 pound chicken breast
- Seasoned salt and ground black pepper, to taste
- 1 teaspoon chili powder
- 1 teaspoon garlic powder
- 1 teaspoon ground cumin
- 1 cup Colby cheese, shredded
- 8 corn tortillas
- 1/2 cup sour cream
- Guacamole:
- 1 ripe avocado, pitted and peeled
- 1 tomato, crushed
- 1/2 onion, finely chopped
- 1 tablespoon fresh cilantro, chopped
- 1 chili pepper, seeded and minced
- 1 teaspoon fresh garlic, minced
- 1 lime, juiced
- Sea salt and black pepper, to taste

Directions:
1. Start by preheating your Air Fryer to 370 degrees F.
2. Drizzle the peanut oil all over the chicken breast. Then, rub the chicken breast with

salt, black pepper, chili powder, garlic powder, and ground cumin.

3. Cook in the preheated Air Fryer approximately 15 minutes. Turn them over and cook an additional 8 minutes.
4. Then, increase the temperature to 380 degrees F.
5. Divide the roasted chicken and cheese between tortillas. Now, roll up the tortilla and transfer them to the lightly greased cooking basket. Spritz a nonstick cooking spray over the tortillas.
6. Cook approximately 10 minutes, turning them over halfway through.
7. Mash the avocado with a fork and add the remaining ingredients for the guacamole. Serve the chicken taquitos with the guacamole sauce and sour cream. Enjoy!

291.Dill Chicken Quesadilla

Servings:2
Cooking Time: 10 Minutes
Ingredients:
- 2 low carb tortillas
- 7 oz chicken breast, skinless, boneless, boiled
- 1 tablespoon cream cheese
- 1 teaspoon butter, melted
- 1 teaspoon minced garlic
- 1 teaspoon fresh dill, chopped
- ½ teaspoon salt
- 2 oz Monterey Jack cheese, shredded
- Cooking spray

Directions:
1. Shred the chicken breast with the help of the fork and put it in the bowl. Add cream cheese, butter, minced garlic, dill, and salt. Add shredded Monterey jack cheese and stir the shredded chicken. Then put 1 tortilla in the air fryer baking pan. Top it with the shredded chicken mixture and cover with the second corn tortilla. Cook the meal for 5 minutes at 400F.

292.Creamy Duck Strips

Servings: 5
Cooking Time: 17 Minutes
Ingredients:
- 12 oz duck breast, skinless, boneless
- ½ cup coconut flour
- 1/3 cup heavy cream
- 1 teaspoon salt
- 1 teaspoon white pepper

Directions:
1. Cut the duck breast on the small strips (fingers) and sprinkle with salt and white pepper. Then dip the duck fingers in the heavy cream and coat in the coconut flour. Preheat the air fryer to 375F. Put the duck

fingers in the air fryer basket in one layer and cook them for 10 minutes. Then flip the duck fingers on another side and cook them for 7 minutes more.

293.Chicken Kabobs With Salsa Verde

Servings:3
Cooking Time: 35 Minutes
Ingredients:
- Salt to season
- 1 tbsp chili powder
- ¼ cup maple syrup
- ½ cup soy sauce
- 2 red peppers, cut into sticks
- 1 green pepper, cut into sticks
- 7 mushrooms, halved
- 2 tbsp sesame seeds
- Cooking spray
- For the Salsa Verde:
- 1 garlic clove
- 2 tbsp olive oil
- Zest and juice from 1 lime
- A pinch of salt
- ¼ cup fresh parsley, chopped

Directions:
1. In a bowl, put the chicken along with the chili powder, salt, maple syrup, soy sauce, sesame seeds, and spray them with cooking spray. Toss to coat. Start stacking up the ingredients - stick 1 red pepper, then green, a chicken cube, and a mushroom half. Repeat the arrangement until the skewer is full. Repeat the process until all the ingredients are used.
2. Preheat the air fryer to 330 F.
3. Brush the kabobs with soy sauce mixture and place them into the fryer basket. Grease with cooking spray and cook for 20 minutes; flip halfway through. Mix all salsa verde ingredients in your food processor and blend until you obtain a chunky paste. Remove the kabobs and serve with salsa verde.

294.Sticky-sweet Chicken Bbq

Servings:2
Cooking Time: 40 Minutes
Ingredients:
- ½ cup balsamic vinegar
- ½ cup soy sauce
- 1-pound chicken drumsticks
- 2 cloves of garlic, minced
- 2 green onion, sliced thinly
- 2 tablespoons sesame seeds
- 3 tablespoons honey

Directions:
1. In a Ziploc bag, combine the soy sauce, balsamic vinegar, honey, garlic, and chicken.

Allow to marinate in the fridge for at least 30 minutes.
2. Preheat the air fryer to 330°F.
3. Place the grill pan accessory in the air fryer.
4. Place on the grill and cook for 30 to 40 minutes. Make sure to flip the chicken every 10 minutes to cook evenly.
5. Meanwhile, use the remaining marinade and put it in a saucepan. Simmer until the sauce thickens.
6. Once the chicken is cooked, brush with the thickened marinade and garnish with sesame seeds and green onions.

295.Chives, Eggs 'n Ham Casserole

Servings:4
Cooking Time: 15 Minutes
Ingredients:
- 1 egg, whole
- 2 tablespoons butter, unsalted
- 2 tablespoons coconut cream
- 2 teaspoon fresh chives, chopped
- 3 uncured ham, chopped
- 4 large eggs, beaten
- Salt and pepper to taste

Directions:
1. Preheat the air fryer for 5 minutes.
2. In a mixing bowl, combine the beaten eggs, coconut cream, butter, and chives. Season with salt and pepper to taste.
3. Pour into a baking dish that will fit in the air fryer and sprinkle ham on top.
4. Crack 1 egg on top.
5. Place in the air fryer.
6. Cook for 15 minutes at 350°F.

296.Strawberry Turkey

Servings: 2
Cooking Time: 50 Minutes
Ingredients:
- 2 lb. turkey breast
- 1 tbsp. olive oil
- Salt and pepper
- 1 cup fresh strawberries

Directions:
1. Pre-heat your fryer to 375°F.
2. Massage the turkey breast with olive oil, before seasoning with a generous amount of salt and pepper.
3. Cook the turkey in the fryer for fifteen minutes. Flip the turkey and cook for a further fifteen minutes.
4. During these last fifteen minutes, blend the strawberries in a food processor until a smooth consistency has been achieved.
5. Heap the strawberries over the turkey, then cook for a final seven minutes and enjoy.

297.Copycat Kfc Chicken Strips

Servings:8
Cooking Time: 20 Minutes
Ingredients:
- 1 chicken breast, cut into strips
- 1 egg, beaten
- 2 tablespoons almond flour
- 2 tablespoons desiccated coconut
- A dash of oregano
- A dash of paprika
- A dash of thyme
- Salt and pepper to taste

Directions:
1. Soak the chicken in egg.
2. In a mixing bowl, combine the rest of the ingredients until well-combined.
3. Dredge the chicken in the dry ingredients.
4. Place in the air fryer basket.
5. Cook for 20 minutes at 350°F.

298.Chicken Sausage, Cauliflower And Ham Gratin

Servings: 4
Cooking Time: 45 Minutes
Ingredients:
- 1/2 pound chicken sausages, smoked
- 1/2 pound ham, sliced
- 6 ounces cauliflower rice
- 2 garlic cloves, minced
- 8 ounces spinach
- 1/2 cup Ricotta cheese
- 1/2 cup Asiago cheese, grated
- 4 eggs
- 1/2 cup yogurt
- 1/2 cup milk
- Salt and ground black pepper, to taste
- 1 teaspoon smoked paprika

Directions:
1. Start by preheating your Air Fryer to 380 degrees F. Cook the sausages and ham for 10 minutes; set aside.
2. Meanwhile, in a preheated saucepan, cook the cauliflower and garlic for 4 minutes, stirring frequently; remove from the heat, add the spinach and cover with the lid.
3. Allow the spinach to wilt completely. Transfer the sautéed mixture to a baking pan. Add the reserved sausage and ham.
4. In a mixing dish, thoroughly combine the cheese, eggs, yogurt, milk, salt, pepper, and paprika. Pour the cheese mixture over the hash browns in the pan.
5. Place the baking pan in the cooking basket and cook approximately 30 minutes or until everything is thoroughly cooked. Bon appétit!

299.Chili, Lime & Corn Chicken Bbq

Servings:4
Cooking Time: 40 Minutes
Ingredients:
- ½ teaspoon cumin
- 1 tablespoon lime juice
- 1 teaspoon chili powder
- 2 chicken breasts
- 2 chicken thighs
- 2 cups barbecue sauce
- 2 teaspoon grated lime zest
- 4 ears of corn, cleaned
- Salt and pepper to taste

Directions:
1. Place all Ingredients in a Ziploc bag except for the corn. Allow to marinate in the fridge for at least 2 hours.
2. Preheat the air fryer to 390°F.
3. Place the grill pan accessory in the air fryer.
4. Grill the chicken and corn for 40 minutes.
5. Meanwhile, pour the marinade in a saucepan over medium heat until it thickens.
6. Before serving, brush the chicken and corn with the glaze.

300.Chicken Surprise

Servings: 2
Cooking Time: 30 Minutes
Ingredients:
- 2 chicken breasts, boneless and skinless
- 2 large eggs
- ½ cup skimmed milk
- 6 tbsp. soy sauce
- 1 cup flour
- 1 tsp. smoked paprika
- 1 tsp. salt
- ¼ tsp. black pepper
- ½ tsp. garlic powder
- 1 tbsp. olive oil
- 4 hamburger buns

Directions:
1. Slice the chicken breast into 2 – 3 pieces.
2. Place in a large bowl and drizzle with the soy sauce. Sprinkle on the smoked paprika, black pepper, salt, and garlic powder and mix well.
3. Allow to marinate for 30 – 40 minutes.
4. In the meantime, combine the eggs with the milk in a bowl. Put the flour in a separate bowl.
5. Dip the marinated chicken into the egg mixture before coating it with the flour. Cover each piece of chicken evenly.
6. Pre-heat the Air Fryer to 380°F.
7. Drizzle on the olive oil and put chicken pieces in the fryer.
8. Cook for 10 – 12 minutes. Flip the chicken once throughout the cooking process.
9. Toast the hamburger buns and put each slice of chicken between two buns to make a sandwich. Serve with ketchup or any other sauce of your choice.

301.Easy Chicken Fried Rice

Servings:3
Cooking Time: 20 Minutes
Ingredients:
- 1 cup frozen peas & carrots
- 1 packed cup cooked chicken, diced
- 1 tbsp vegetable oil
- 1/2 cup onion, diced
- 3 cups cold cooked white rice
- 6 tbsp soy sauce

Directions:
1. Lightly grease baking pan of air fryer with vegetable oil. Add frozen carrots and peas.
2. For 5 minutes, cook on 360°F.
3. Stir in chicken and cook for another 5 minutes.
4. Add remaining ingredients and toss well to mix.
5. Cook for another 10 minutes, while mixing halfway through.
6. Serve and enjoy.

302.Stuffed Chicken

Servings: 2
Cooking Time: 11 Minutes
Ingredients:
- 8 oz chicken fillet
- 3 oz Blue cheese
- ½ teaspoon salt
- ½ teaspoon thyme
- 1 teaspoon sesame oil

Directions:
1. Cut the fillet into halves and beat them gently with the help of the kitchen hammer. After this, make the horizontal cut in every fillet. Sprinkle the chicken with salt and thyme. Then fill it with Blue cheese and secure the cut with the help of the toothpick. Sprinkle the stuffed chicken fillets with sesame oil. Preheat the air fryer to 385F. Put the chicken fillets in the air fryer and cook them for 7 minutes. Then carefully flip the chicken fillets on another side and cook for 4 minutes more.

303.Chinese-style Sticky Turkey Thighs

Servings: 6
Cooking Time: 35 Minutes
Ingredients:
- 1 tablespoon sesame oil
- 2 pounds turkey thighs
- 1 teaspoon Chinese Five-spice powder
- 1 teaspoon pink Himalayan salt
- 1/4 teaspoon Sichuan pepper

- 6 tablespoons honey
- 1 tablespoon Chinese rice vinegar
- 2 tablespoons soy sauce
- 1 tablespoon sweet chili sauce
- 1 tablespoon mustard

Directions:
1. Preheat your Air Fryer to 360 degrees F.
2. Brush the sesame oil all over the turkey thighs. Season them with spices.
3. Cook for 23 minutes, turning over once or twice. Make sure to work in batches to ensure even cooking
4. In the meantime, combine the remaining ingredients in a wok (or similar type pan that is preheated over medium-high heat. Cook and stir until the sauce reduces by about a third.
5. Add the fried turkey thighs to the wok; gently stir to coat with the sauce.
6. Let the turkey rest for 10 minutes before slicing and serving. Enjoy!

304.Chicken Curry

Servings: 2
Cooking Time: 60 Minutes
Ingredients:
- 2 chicken thighs
- 1 small zucchini
- 2 cloves garlic
- 6 dried apricots
- 3 ½ oz. long turnip
- 6 basil leaves
- 1 tbsp. whole pistachios
- 1 tbsp. raisin soup
- 1 tbsp. olive oil
- 1 large pinch salt
- Pinch of pepper

- 1 tsp. curry powder

Directions:
1. Pre-heat Air Fryer at 320°F.
2. Cut the chicken into 2 thin slices and chop up the vegetables into bite-sized pieces.
3. In a dish, combine all of the ingredients, incorporating everything well.
4. Place in the fryer and cook for a minimum of 30 minutes.
5. Serve with rice if desired.

305.Chicken And Chickpeas Mix

Servings: 4
Cooking Time: 25 Minutes
Ingredients:
- 5 ounces bacon, cooked and crumbled
- 2 tablespoons olive oil
- 1 cup yellow onion, chopped
- 8 ounces canned chickpeas, drained
- 2 carrots, chopped
- 1 tablespoon parsley, chopped
- Salt and black pepper to taste
- 2 pounds chicken thighs, boneless
- 1 cup chicken stock
- 1 teaspoon balsamic vinegar

Directions:
1. Heat up a pan that fits your air fryer with the oil over medium heat.
2. Add the onions, carrots, salt and pepper; stir, and sauté for 3-4 minutes.
3. Add the chicken, stock, vinegar, and chickpeas; then toss.
4. Place the pan in the fryer and cook at 380 degrees F for 20 minutes.
5. Add the bacon and the parsley and toss again.
6. Divide everything between plates and serve.

BEEF,PORK & LAMB RECIPES

306.Pork Butt With Herb-garlic Sauce

Servings: 4
Cooking Time: 35 Minutes + Marinating Time
Ingredients:

- 1 pound pork butt, cut into pieces 2-inches long
- 1 teaspoon golden flaxseed meal
- 1 egg white, well whisked
- Salt and ground black pepper, to taste
- 1 tablespoon olive oil
- 1 tablespoon coconut aminos
- 1 teaspoon lemon juice, preferably freshly squeezed
- For the Coriander-Garlic Sauce:
- 3 garlic cloves, peeled
- 1/3 cup fresh parsley leaves
- 1/3 cup fresh coriander leaves
- 1/2 tablespoon salt
- 1 teaspoon lemon juice
- 1/3 cup extra-virgin olive oil

Directions:

1. Combine the pork strips with the flaxseed meal, egg white, salt, pepper, olive oil, coconut aminos, and lemon juice. Cover and refrigerate for 30 to 45 minutes.
2. After that, spritz the pork strips with a nonstick cooking spray.
3. Set your Air Fryer to cook at 380 degrees F. Press the power button and air-fry for 15 minutes; pause the machine, shake the basket and cook for 15 more minutes.
4. Meanwhile, puree the garlic in a food processor until finely minced. Now, puree the parsley, coriander, salt, and lemon juice. With the machine running, carefully pour in the olive oil.
5. Serve the pork with well-chilled sauce with and enjoy!

307.Pork Sausage Casserole

Servings:4
Cooking Time: 30 Minutes
Ingredients:

- 6 ounces flour, sifted
- 2 eggs
- 1 red onion, thinly sliced
- 1 garlic clove, minced
- Salt and ground black pepper, as required
- ¾ cup milk
- 2/3 cup cold water
- 8 small sausages
- 8 fresh rosemary sprigs

Directions:

1. In a bowl, mix together the flour, and eggs.
2. Add the onion, garlic, salt, and black pepper. Mix them well.

3. Gently, add in the milk, and water and mix until well combined.
4. In each sausage, pierce 1 rosemary sprig.
5. Set the temperature of air fryer to 320 degrees F. Grease a baking dish.
6. Arrange sausages into the prepared baking dish and top evenly with the flour mixture.
7. Air fry for about 30 minutes.
8. Remove from the air fryer and serve warm.

308.Beef And Plums Mix

Servings: 6
Cooking Time: 40 Minutes
Ingredients:

- 1½ pounds beef stew meat, cubed
- 3 tablespoons honey
- 2 tablespoons olive oil
- 9 ounces plums, pitted and halved
- 8 ounces beef stock
- 2 yellow onions, chopped
- 2 garlic cloves, minced
- Salt and black pepper to tastes
- 1 teaspoon turmeric powder
- 1 teaspoon ginger powder
- 1 teaspoon cinnamon powder

Directions:

1. In a pan that fits your air fryer, heat up the oil over medium heat.
2. Add the beef, stir, and brown for 2 minutes.
3. Add the honey, onions, garlic, salt, pepper, turmeric, ginger, and cinnamon; toss, and cook for 2-3 minutes more.
4. Add the plums and the stock; toss again.
5. Place the pan in the fryer and cook at 380 degrees for 30 minutes.
6. Divide everything into bowls and serve.

309.Mexican Chili Beef Sausage Meatballs

Servings: 4
Cooking Time: 25 Minutes
Ingredients:

- 1 cup green onion, finely minced
- 1/2 teaspoon parsley flakes
- 2 teaspoons onion flakes
- 1 pound chili sausage, crumbled
- 2 tablespoons flaxseed meal
- 3 cloves garlic, finely minced
- 1 teaspoon Mexican oregano
- 1 tablespoon poblano pepper, chopped
- Fine sea salt and ground black pepper, to taste
- ½ tablespoon fresh chopped sage

Directions:

1. Mix all ingredients in a bowl until the mixture has a uniform consistency.
2. Roll into bite-sized balls and transfer them to a baking dish.

3. Cook in the preheated Air Fryer at 345 degrees for 18 minutes. Serve on wooden sticks and enjoy!

310.Pork With Balsamic-raspberry Jam

Servings:4
Cooking Time: 30 Minutes
Ingredients:
- ¼ cup all-purpose flour
- ¼ cup milk
- 1 cup chopped pecans
- 1 cup panko breadcrumbs
- 2 large eggs, beaten
- 2 tablespoons raspberry jam
- 2 tablespoons sugar
- 2/3 cup balsamic vinegar
- 4 smoked pork chops
- Salt and pepper to taste

Directions:
1. Preheat the air fryer to 330°F.
2. Season pork chops with salt and pepper to taste.
3. In a small bowl, whisk together eggs and milk. Set aside.
4. Dip the pork chops in flour then in the egg mixture before dredging in the panko mixed with pecans.
5. Place in the air fryer and cook for 30 minutes.
6. Meanwhile, prepare the sauce by putting in the saucepan the remaining Ingredients. Season with salt and pepper.
7. Drizzle the pork chops with the sauce once cooked.

311.Simple Beef Burgers

Servings:6
Cooking Time:12 Minutes
Ingredients:
- 2 pounds ground beef
- 12 cheddar cheese slices
- 12 dinner rolls
- 6 tablespoons tomato ketchup
- Salt and black pepper, to taste

Directions:
1. Preheat the Air fryer to 390 °F and grease an Air fryer basket.
2. Mix the beef, salt and black pepper in a bowl.
3. Make small equal-sized patties from the beef mixture and arrange half of patties in the Air fryer basket.
4. Cook for about 12 minutes and top each patty with 1 cheese slice.
5. Arrange the patties between rolls and drizzle with ketchup.
6. Repeat with the remaining batch and dish out to serve hot.

312.Max's Meatloaf

Servings: 4
Cooking Time: 35 Minutes
Ingredients:
- 1 large onion, peeled and diced
- 2 kg. minced beef
- 1 tsp. Worcester sauce
- 3 tbsp. tomato ketchup
- 1 tbsp. basil
- 1 tbsp. oregano
- 1 tbsp. mixed herbs
- 1 tbsp. friendly bread crumbs
- Salt & pepper to taste

Directions:
1. In a large bowl, combine the mince with the herbs, Worcester sauce, onion and tomato ketchup, incorporating every component well.
2. Pour in the breadcrumbs and give it another stir.
3. Transfer the mixture to a small dish and cook for 25 minutes in the Air Fryer at 350°F.

313.Cheesy Meatball And Mushroom Casserole

Servings:4
Cooking Time:41 Minutes
Ingredients:
- 2 tablespoons Italian breadcrumbs
- 10 ounces lean ground pork
- 1 ½ cup mushrooms, sliced
- 3 carrots, peeled and shredded
- 1 teaspoon saffron
- 2 teaspoons fennel seeds
- 1/3 cup Monterey Jack cheese, preferably freshly grated
- 1/3 cup cream
- 2 medium-sized leeks, finely chopped
- 1/teaspoon dried dill weed
- 2 small-sized egg
- 1/2 teaspoon cumin
- ½ teaspoon fine sea salt
- Freshly ground black pepper, to taste

Directions:
1. Begin by preheating the air fryer to 400 degrees F.
2. In a bowl, mix the ingredients for the meatballs. Shape the mixture into mini meatballs.
3. In an air fryer baking dish, toss the carrots and mushrooms with the cream; cook for 23 minutes in the preheated air fryer.
4. Pause the machine and place the reserved meatballs in a single layer on top of the carrot/mushroom mixture.
5. Top with the grated Monterey Jack cheese; bake for 9 minutes longer. Serve warm.

314.Garlic Fillets

Servings: 4
Cooking Time: 15 Minutes
Ingredients:

- 1-pound beef filet mignon
- 1 teaspoon minced garlic
- 1 tablespoon peanut oil
- ½ teaspoon salt
- 1 teaspoon dried oregano

Directions:

1. Chop the beef into the medium size pieces and sprinkle with salt and dried oregano. Then add minced garlic and peanut oil and mix up the meat well. Place the bowl with meat in the fridge for 10 minutes to marinate. Meanwhile, preheat the air fryer to 400F. Put the marinated beef pieces in the air fryer and cook them for 10 minutes Then flip the beef on another side and cook for 5 minutes more.

315.Lamb Chops And Lemon Yogurt Sauce

Servings: 4
Cooking Time: 30 Minutes
Ingredients:

- 4 lamb chops
- A pinch of salt and black pepper
- 1 cup Greek yogurt
- 2 tablespoons coconut oil, melted
- 1 teaspoon lemon zest, grated
- ½ teaspoon turmeric powder

Directions:

1. In a bowl, mix the lamb chops with the rest of the ingredients and toss well. Put the chops in your air fryer's basket and cook at 380 degrees F for 15 minutes on each side. Divide between plates and serve.

316.Beef & Mushrooms

Servings: 1
Cooking Time: 3 Hours 15 Minutes
Ingredients:

- 6 oz. beef
- ¼ onion, diced
- ½ cup mushroom slices
- 2 tbsp. favorite marinade [preferably bulgogi]

Directions:

1. Slice or cube the beef and put it in a bowl.
2. Cover the meat with the marinade, place a layer of aluminum foil or saran wrap over the bowl, and place the bowl in the refrigerator for 3 hours.
3. Put the meat in a baking dish along with the onion and mushrooms
4. Air Fry at 350°F for 10 minutes. Serve hot.

317.Traditional Beefy Spaghetti

Servings:4
Cooking Time: 40 Minutes
Ingredients:

- 8- ounce spaghetti, cooked according to manufacturer's Directions:
- 1 egg
- 3 tablespoons grated Parmesan cheese
- 3 tablespoons butter, melted
- 1 cup small curd cottage cheese, divided
- 2 cups shredded mozzarella cheese, divided
- 1/2-pound ground beef
- 1/2 onion, chopped
- 1/2 (32 ounce) jar meatless spaghetti sauce
- 1/4 teaspoon seasoned salt

Directions:

1. Lightly grease baking pan of air fryer with cooking spray. Add ground beef and onion. For 10 minutes, cook on 360°F. Crumble and mix well halfway through cooking time. Discard excess fat.
2. Mix in seasoned salt and spaghetti sauce. Mix well and transfer to a bowl.
3. In a large bowl, whisk well butter, parmesan cheese, and eggs.
4. In same air fryer baking pan, spread evenly half of the pasta, add half the spaghettis sauce, and then half of the mozzarella and cottage cheese. Repeat layering.
5. Cover pan with foil.
6. Cook for another 20 minutes, remove foil and cook for another 10 minutes.
7. Serve and enjoy.

318.Smoked Sausage And Bacon Shashlik

Servings: 4
Cooking Time: 20 Minutes
Ingredients:

- 1 pound smoked Polish beef sausage, sliced
- 1 tablespoon mustard
- 1 tablespoon olive oil
- 2 tablespoons Worcestershire sauce
- 2 bell peppers, sliced
- Salt and ground black pepper, to taste

Directions:

1. Toss the sausage with the mustard, olive, and Worcestershire sauce. Thread sausage and peppers onto skewers.
2. Sprinkle with salt and black pepper.
3. Cook in the preheated Air Fryer at 360 degrees F for 11 minutes. Brush the skewers with the reserved marinade. Bon appétit!

319.Burger Patties

Servings: 6
Cooking Time: 15 Minutes
Ingredients:

- 1 lb. ground beef
- 6 cheddar cheese slices
- Pepper and salt to taste

Directions:
1. Pre-heat the Air Fryer to 350°F.
2. Sprinkle the salt and pepper on the ground beef.
3. Shape six equal portions of the ground beef into patties and put each one in the Air Fryer basket.
4. Air fry the patties for 10 minutes.
5. Top the patties with the cheese slices and air fry for one more minute.
6. Serve the patties on top of dinner rolls.

320.Sirloin With Yogurt 'n Curry-paprika

Servings:3
Cooking Time: 25 Minutes
Ingredients:
- ¼ cup mint, chopped
- ½ cup low-fat yogurt
- 1 ½ pounds boneless beef top loin steak
- 2 teaspoons curry powder
- 2 teaspoons paprika
- 3 tablespoons lemon juice
- 6 cloves of garlic, minced
- Salt and pepper to taste

Directions:
1. Place all Ingredients except for the green onions in a Ziploc bag and allow to marinate in the fridge for at least 2 hours.
2. Preheat the air fryer to 390°F.
3. Place the grill pan accessory in the air fryer.
4. Grill for 25 to 30 minutes.
5. Flip the steaks halfway through the cooking time for even grilling.

321.Pork Kebabs With Serrano Pepper

Servings: 3
Cooking Time: 22 Minutes
Ingredients:
- 2 tablespoons tomato puree
- 1/2 fresh serrano, minced
- 1/3 teaspoon paprika
- 1 pound pork, ground
- 1/2 cup green onions, finely chopped
- 3 cloves garlic, peeled and finely minced
- 1 teaspoon ground black pepper, or more to taste
- 1 teaspoon salt, or more to taste

Directions:
1. Thoroughly combine all ingredients in a mixing dish. Then, form your mixture into sausage shapes.
2. Cook for 18 minutes at 355 degrees F. Mound salad on a serving platter, top with air-fried kebabs and serve warm. Bon appétit!

322.Garlic Pork And Ginger Sauce

Servings: 4
Cooking Time: 35 Minutes

Ingredients:
- 1 pound pork tenderloin, cut into strips
- 1 garlic clove, minced
- A pinch of salt and black pepper
- 1 tablespoon ginger, grated
- 3 tablespoons coconut aminos
- 2 tablespoons coconut oil, melted

Directions:
1. Heat up a pan that fits the air fryer with the oil over medium-high heat, add the meat and brown for 3 minutes. Add the rest of the ingredients, cook for 2 minutes more, put the pan in the fryer and cook at 380 degrees F for 30 minutes Divide between plates and serve with a side salad.

323.Oregano-paprika On Breaded Pork

Servings:4
Cooking Time: 30 Minutes
Ingredients:
- ¼ cup water
- ¼ teaspoon dry mustard
- ½ teaspoon black pepper
- ½ teaspoon cayenne pepper
- ½ teaspoon garlic powder
- ½ teaspoon salt
- 1 cup panko breadcrumbs
- 1 egg, beaten
- 2 teaspoons oregano
- 4 lean pork chops
- 4 teaspoons paprika

Directions:
1. Preheat the air fryer to 390°F.
2. Pat dry the pork chops.
3. In a mixing bowl, combine the egg and water. Then set aside.
4. In another bowl, combine the rest of the Ingredients.
5. Dip the pork chops in the egg mixture and dredge in the flour mixture.
6. Place in the air fryer basket and cook for 25 to 30 minutes until golden.

324.Beef And Thyme Cabbage Mix

Servings: 4
Cooking Time: 25 Minutes
Ingredients:
- 2 pounds beef, cubed
- ½ pound bacon, chopped
- 2 shallots, chopped
- 1 napa cabbage, shredded
- 2 garlic cloves, minced
- A pinch of salt and black pepper
- 2 tablespoons olive oil
- 1 teaspoon thyme, dried
- 1 cup beef stock

Directions:
1. Heat up a pan that fits the air fryer with the oil over medium-high heat, add the beef and

brown for 3 minutes. Add the bacon, shallots and garlic and cook for 2 minutes more. Add the rest of the ingredients, toss, put the pan in the air fryer and cook at 390 degrees F for 20 minutes. Divide between plates and serve.

325.Pork And Garlic Sauce

Servings: 4
Cooking Time: 25 Minutes
Ingredients:
- 1 pound pork tenderloin, sliced
- A pinch of salt and black pepper
- 4 tablespoons butter, melted
- 2 teaspoons garlic, minced
- 1 teaspoon sweet paprika

Directions:
1. Heat up a pan that fits the air fryer with the butter over medium heat, add all the ingredients except the pork medallions, whisk well and simmer for 4-5 minutes. Add the pork, toss, put the pan in your air fryer and cook at 380 degrees F for 20 minutes. Divide between plates and serve with a side salad.

326.Spiced Hot Ribs

Servings: 4
Cooking Time: 35 Minutes
Ingredients:
- 1-pound pork baby back ribs
- ½ teaspoon fennel seeds
- ½ teaspoon ground cumin
- ½ teaspoon ground coriander
- ½ teaspoon smoked paprika
- ½ teaspoon garlic powder
- ½ teaspoon onion powder
- ¼ teaspoon ground nutmeg
- 1 teaspoon cayenne pepper
- 1 teaspoon dried oregano
- 1 tablespoon coconut oil, melted
- 4 tablespoons apple cider vinegar

Directions:
1. In the mixing bowl mix up fennel seeds, cumin, coriander, smoked paprika, garlic powder, onion powder, ground nutmeg, cayenne pepper, and dried oregano. Then rub the pork baby back ribs with spice mixture well and sprinkle with apple cider vinegar. Then brush the ribs with coconut oil and leave for 15 minutes to marinate. Then preheat the air fryer to 355F. Put the pork baby back ribs in the air fryer and cook them for 35 minutes. Flip the ribs on another side after 15 minutes of cooking.

327.Bbq Skirt Steak

Servings: 5
Cooking Time: 20 Minutes + Marinating Time

Ingredients:
- 2 pounds skirt steak
- 2 tablespoons tomato paste
- 1 tablespoon olive oil
- 1 tablespoon coconut aminos
- 1/4 cup rice vinegar
- 1 tablespoon fish sauce
- Sea salt, to taste
- 1/2 teaspoon dried dill
- 1/2 teaspoon dried rosemary
- 1/4 teaspoon black pepper, freshly cracked

Directions:
1. Place all ingredients in a large ceramic dish; let it marinate for 3 hours in your refrigerator.
2. Coat the sides and bottom of the Air Fryer with cooking spray.
3. Add your steak to the cooking basket; reserve the marinade. Cook the skirt steak in the preheated Air Fryer at 400 degrees F for 12 minutes, turning over a couple of times, basting with the reserved marinade.
4. Bon appétit!

328.Meatloaf With Sweet-sour Glaze

Servings:3
Cooking Time: 30 Minutes
Ingredients:
- ½ medium onion, chopped
- ½ Tbsp lightly dried (or fresh chopped) Parsley
- 1 Tbsp Worcestershire sauce
- 1 tsp (or 2 cloves) minced garlic
- 1 tsp dried basil
- 1/3 cup Kellogg's corn flakes crumbs
- 1-2 tsp freshly ground black pepper
- 1-2 tsp salt
- 1-pound lean ground beef (93% fat free), raw
- 3 tsp Splenda (or Truvia) brown sugar blend
- 5 Tbsp Heinz reduced-sugar ketchup
- 8-oz tomato sauce, divided

Directions:
1. Lightly grease baking pan of air fryer with cooking spray.
2. In a large bowl, mix well 6-oz tomato sauce, garlic, pepper, salt, corn flake crumbs, and onion. Stir in ground beef and mix well with hands.
3. Evenly spread ground beef mixture in pan, ensuring that it is lumped altogether.
4. In a medium bowl, whisk all remaining Ingredients together to make a glaze. Pour on top of ground beef.
5. Cover pan with foil.
6. For 15 minutes, cook on 360°F. Remove foil and continue cooking for another 10 minutes.

7. Let it stand for 5 minutes.
8. Serve and enjoy.

329.Five Spice Pork

Servings:4
Cooking Time:20 Minutes
Ingredients:
- 1-pound pork belly
- 2 tablespoons swerve
- 2 tablespoons dark soy sauce
- 1 tablespoon Shaoxing (cooking wine)
- 2 teaspoons garlic, minced
- 2 teaspoons ginger, minced
- 1 tablespoon hoisin sauce
- 1 teaspoon Chinese Five Spice

Directions:
1. Preheat the Air fryer to 390 °F and grease an Air fryer basket.
2. Mix all the ingredients in a bowl and place in the Ziplock bag.
3. Seal the bag, shake it well and refrigerate to marinate for about 1 hour.
4. Remove the pork from the bag and arrange it in the Air fryer basket.
5. Cook for about 15 minutes and dish out in a bowl to serve warm.

330.Sausage Meatballs With Parmesan And Marinara Sauce

Servings: 4
Cooking Time: 20 Minutes
Ingredients:
- 1 pound pork sausage meat
- 1 shallot, finely chopped
- 2 garlic cloves, finely minced
- 1/2 teaspoon fine sea salt
- 1/4 teaspoon ground black pepper, or more to taste
- 3/4 teaspoon paprika
- 1/2 cup parmesan cheese, preferably freshly grated
- 1/2 jar marinara sauce

Directions:
1. Mix all of the above ingredients, except the marinara sauce, in a large-sized dish, until everything is well incorporated.
2. Shape into meatballs. Air-fry them at 360 degrees F for 10 minutes; pause the Air Fryer, shake them up and cook for additional 6 minutes or until the balls are no longer pink in the middle.
3. Meanwhile, heat the marinara sauce over a medium flame. Serve the pork sausage meatballs with marinara sauce. Bon appétit!

331.Lemon Osso Bucco

Servings: 4
Cooking Time: 40 Minutes
Ingredients:
- 3 spring onions, chopped
- 1 garlic clove, diced
- 1 oz celery, chopped
- 1-pound veal shank, boneless, chopped
- ½ teaspoon salt
- ½ teaspoon ground black pepper
- 1 tablespoon ghee
- 1 tablespoon keto tomato sauce
- 2 tablespoons water
- ½ teaspoon dried thyme
- 1 teaspoon lemon juice
- 1 teaspoon sunflower oil

Directions:
1. Preheat the air fryer to 370F. In the mixing bowl mix up spring onions, garlic, celery, salt, ground black pepper, ghee, tomato sauce, water, dried thyme, lemon juice, and sunflower oil. Add the veal shank and mix up the ingredients carefully. Then cover the mixture with foil and transfer in the air fryer. Cook Osso Bucco for 40 minutes. Cool the cooked meal to the room temperature.

332.Spicy Pork Sausage With Eggs

Servings: 6
Cooking Time: 24 Minutes
Ingredients:
- 1 green bell pepper, seeded and thinly sliced
- 6 medium-sized eggs
- 1 Habanero pepper, seeded and minced
- 1/2 teaspoon sea salt
- 2 teaspoons fennel seeds
- 1 red bell pepper, seeded and thinly sliced
- 1 teaspoon tarragon
- 1/2 teaspoon freshly cracked black pepper
- 6 pork sausages

Directions:
1. Place the sausages and all peppers in the Air Fryer cooking basket. Cook at 335 degrees F for 9 minutes.
2. Divide the eggs among 6 ramekins; sprinkle each egg with the seasonings.
3. Cook for 11 more minutes at 395 degrees F. Serve warm with sausages. Bon appétit!

333.Meaty Pasta Bake From The Southwest

Servings:6
Cooking Time: 45 Minutes
Ingredients:
- 1 can (14-1/2 ounces each) diced tomatoes, undrained
- 1 cup shredded Monterey Jack cheese
- 1 cup uncooked elbow macaroni, cooked according to manufacturer's Directions:
- 1 jalapeno pepper, seeded and chopped
- 1 large onion, chopped

- 1 teaspoon chili powder
- 1 teaspoons salt
- 1/2 can (16 ounces) kidney beans, rinsed and drained
- 1/2 can (4 ounces) chopped green chilies, drained
- 1/2 can (6 ounces) tomato paste
- 1/2 teaspoon ground cumin
- 1/2 teaspoon pepper
- 1-pound ground beef
- 2 garlic cloves, minced

Directions:
1. Lightly grease baking pan of air fryer with cooking spray. Add ground beef, onion, and garlic. For 10 minutes, cook on 360°F. Halfway through cooking time, stir and crumble beef.
2. Mix in diced tomatoes, kidney beans, tomato paste, green chilies, salt, chili powder, cumin, and pepper. Mix well. Cook for another 10 minutes.
3. Stir in macaroni and mix well. Top with jalapenos and cheese.
4. Cover pan with foil.
5. Cook for 15 minutes at 390°F, remove foil and continue cooking for another 10 minutes until tops are lightly browned.
6. Serve and enjoy.

334.Super Simple Steaks

Servings:2
Cooking Time:14 Minutes
Ingredients:
- ½ pound quality cuts steak
- Salt and black pepper, to taste

Directions:
1. Preheat the Air fryer to 390 °F and grease an Air fryer basket.
2. Season the steaks evenly with salt and black pepper and transfer into the Air fryer basket.
3. Cook for about 14 minutes and dish out to serve.

335.Peach Puree On Ribeye

Servings:2
Cooking Time: 45 Minutes
Ingredients:
- ¼ cup balsamic vinegar
- 1 cup peach puree
- 1 tablespoon paprika
- 1 teaspoon thyme
- 1-pound T-bone steak
- 2 teaspoons lemon pepper seasoning
- Salt and pepper to taste

Directions:
1. Place all ingredients in a Ziploc bag and allow to marinate in the fridge for at least 2 hours.

2. Preheat the air fryer to 390°F.
3. Place the grill pan accessory in the air fryer.
4. Grill for 20 minutes and flip the meat halfway through the cooking time.

336.Tender And Creamy Beef With Sage

Servings: 2
Cooking Time: 13 Minutes
Ingredients:
- 1/3 cup sour cream
- ½ cup green onion, chopped
- 1 tablespoon mayonnaise
- 3 cloves garlic, smashed
- 1 pound beef flank steak, trimmed and cubed
- 2 tablespoons fresh sage, minced
- ½ teaspoon salt
- 1/3 teaspoon black pepper, or to taste

Directions:
1. Season your meat with salt and pepper; arrange beef cubes on the bottom of a baking dish that fits in your air fryer.
2. Stir in green onions and garlic; air-fry for about 7 minutes at 385 degrees F.
3. Once your beef starts to tender, add the cream, mayonnaise, and sage; air-fry an additional 8 minutes. Bon appétit!

337.Rosemary Lamb Steak

Servings: 2
Cooking Time: 12 Minutes
Ingredients:
- 12 oz lamb steak (6 oz each lamb steak)
- 1 teaspoon dried rosemary
- 1 teaspoon minced onion
- 1 tablespoon avocado oil
- ½ teaspoon salt

Directions:
1. Rub the lamb steaks with minced onion and salt. In the shallow bowl mix up dried rosemary and avocado oil. Sprinkle the meat with rosemary mixture. After this, preheat the air fryer to 400F. Put the lamb steaks in the air fryer in one layer and cook them for 6 minutes. Then flip the meat on another side and cook it for 6 minutes more.

338.Basil Beef And Avocado

Servings: 4
Cooking Time: 25 Minutes
Ingredients:
- 4 flank steaks
- 1 garlic clove, minced
- 1/3 cup beef stock
- 2 avocados, peeled, pitted and sliced
- 1 teaspoon chili flakes
- ½ cup basil, chopped
- 2 spring onions, chopped
- 2 teaspoons olive oil

- A pinch of salt and black pepper

Directions:
1. Heat up a pan that fits the air fryer with the oil over medium-high heat, add the steaks and cook for 2 minutes on each side. Add the rest of the ingredients except the avocados, put the pan in the air fryer and cook at 380 degrees F for 15 minutes. Add the avocado slices, cook for 5 minutes more, divide everything between plates and serve.

339.Christmas Filet Mignon Steak

Servings: 6
Cooking Time: 25 Minutes
Ingredients:
- 1/3 stick butter, at room temperature
- 1/2 cup heavy cream
- 1/2 medium-sized garlic bulb, peeled and pressed
- 6 filet mignon steaks
- 2 teaspoons mixed peppercorns, freshly cracked
- 1 ½ tablespoons apple cider
- A dash of hot sauce
- 1 ½ teaspoons sea salt flakes

Directions:
1. Season the mignon steaks with the cracked peppercorns and salt flakes. Roast the mignon steaks in the preheated Air Fryer for 24 minutes at 385 degrees F, turning once. Check for doneness and set aside, keeping it warm.
2. In a small nonstick saucepan that is placed over a moderate flame, mash the garlic to a smooth paste. Whisk in the rest of the above ingredients. Whisk constantly until it has a uniform consistency.
3. To finish, lay the filet mignon steaks on serving plates; spoon a little sauce onto each filet mignon. Bon appétit!

340.Veal Rolls

Servings:4
Cooking Time:15 Minutes
Ingredients:
- 4 (6-ounce) veal cutlets
- 2 tablespoons fresh sage leaves
- 4 cured ham slices
- 1 tablespoon unsalted butter, melted
- Salt and black pepper, to taste

Directions:
1. Preheat the Air fryer to 390 °F and grease an Air fryer basket.
2. Season the veal cutlets with salt and roll them up tightly.
3. Wrap 1 ham slice around each roll and coat with 1 tablespoon of the butter.
4. Top rolls with the sage leaves and transfer into the Air fryer basket.

5. Cook for about 10 minutes, flipping once in between and set the Air fryer to 300 °F.
6. Cook for about 5 more minutes and dish out to serve hot.

341.Tangy And Saucy Beef Fingers

Servings: 4
Cooking Time: 20 Minutes + Marinating Time
Ingredients:
- 1 ½ pounds sirloin steak
- 1/4 cup red wine
- 1/4 cup fresh lime juice
- 1 teaspoon garlic powder
- 1 teaspoon shallot powder
- 1 teaspoon celery seeds
- 1 teaspoon mustard seeds
- Coarse sea salt and ground black pepper, to taste
- 1 teaspoon red pepper flakes
- 2 eggs, lightly whisked
- 1 cup parmesan cheese
- 1 teaspoon paprika

Directions:
1. Place the steak, red wine, lime juice, garlic powder, shallot powder, celery seeds, mustard seeds, salt, black pepper, and red pepper in a large ceramic bowl; let it marinate for 3 hours.
2. Tenderize the cube steak by pounding with a mallet; cut into 1-inch strips.
3. In a shallow bowl, whisk the eggs. In another bowl, mix the parmesan cheese and paprika.
4. Dip the beef pieces into the whisked eggs and coat on all sides. Now, dredge the beef pieces in the parmesan mixture.
5. Cook at 400 degrees F for 14 minutes, flipping halfway through the cooking time.
6. Meanwhile, make the sauce by heating the reserved marinade in a saucepan over medium heat; let it simmer until thoroughly warmed. Serve the steak fingers with the sauce on the side. Enjoy!

342.German Schnitzel

Servings: 4
Cooking Time: 15 Minutes
Ingredients:
- 4 thin beef schnitzel
- 1 tbsp. sesame seeds
- 2 tbsp. paprika
- 3 tbsp. olive oil
- 4 tbsp. flour
- 2 eggs, beaten
- 1 cup friendly bread crumbs
- Pepper and salt to taste

Directions:
1. Pre-heat the Air Fryer at 350°F.

2. Sprinkle the pepper and salt on the schnitzel.
3. In a shallow dish, combine the paprika, flour, and salt
4. In a second shallow dish, mix the bread crumbs with the sesame seeds.
5. Place the beaten eggs in a bowl.
6. Coat the schnitzel in the flour mixture. Dip it into the egg before rolling it in the bread crumbs.
7. Put the coated schnitzel in the Air Fryer basket and allow to cook for 12 minutes before serving hot.

343.Sherry 'n Soy Garlicky Steak

Servings:3
Cooking Time: 50 Minutes
Ingredients:
- 1 tablespoon brown sugar
- ½ teaspoon dry mustard
- 1 clove of garlic, minced
- 1 ½ pounds beef top round steak
- 2 green onions, chopped
- 1/3 cup soy sauce
- 1/3 cup dry sherry

Directions:
1. Place all ingredients except for the green onions in a Ziploc bag and allow to marinate in the fridge for at least 2 hours.
2. Preheat the air fryer to 390°F.
3. Place the grill pan accessory in the air fryer. Add meat and cover top with foil.
4. Grill for 50 minutes.
5. Halfway through the cooking time, flip the meat for even grilling.
6. Meanwhile, pour the marinade into a saucepan and simmer for 10 minutes until the sauce thickens.
7. Baste the meat with the sauce and garnish with green onions before serving.

344.Chives On Bacon & Cheese Bake

Servings:6
Cooking Time: 50 Minutes
Ingredients:
- 4 slices bread, crusts removed
- 1 cup egg substitute (such as Egg Beaters®)
- 1 tablespoon chopped fresh chives
- 6 slices cooked bacon, crumbled
- 1 cup Cheddar cheese
- 1 1/2 cups skim milk

Directions:
1. Cook bacon in baking pan of air fryer for 10 minutes at 360°F. Once done, discard excess fat and then crumble bacon.
2. In a bowl, whisk well eggs. Stir in milk and chives.
3. In same air fryer baking pan, evenly spread bread slices. Pour egg mixture over it. Top

with bacon. Cover pan with foil and let it rest in the fridge for at least an hour.
4. Preheat air fryer to 330°F.
5. Cook while covered in foil for 20 minutes. Remove foil and sprinkle cheese. Continue cooking uncovered for another 15 minutes.
6. Serve and enjoy.

345.Seekh Kebab With Yogurt Sauce

Servings: 4
Cooking Time: 25 Minutes
Ingredients:
- 1 ½ pounds ground chuck
- 1 egg
- 1 medium-sized leek, chopped
- 2 garlic cloves, smashed
- 2 tablespoons fresh parsley, chopped
- 1 teaspoon fresh rosemary, chopped
- Sea salt, to taste
- 1/2 teaspoon ground black pepper
- 1/2 teaspoon chili powder
- 1 teaspoon garam masala
- 1 teaspoon ginger paste
- 1/2 teaspoon ground cumin
- Raita Sauce:
- 1 small-sized cucumber, grated and squeezed
- A pinch of salt
- 1 cup full-fat yogurt
- 1/4 cup fresh cilantro, coarsely chopped

Directions:
1. Combine all ingredients until everything is well incorporated. Press the meat mixture into a baking pan.
2. Cook in the preheated Air Fryer at 360 degrees F for 15 minutes. Taste for doneness with a meat thermometer.
3. Meanwhile, mix all ingredients for the sauce. Serve the warm meatloaf with the sauce on the side. Enjoy!

346.Garlicky Buttered Chops

Servings:4
Cooking Time: 30 Minutes
Ingredients:
- 1 tablespoons butter, melted
- 2 teaspoons chopped parsley
- 2 teaspoons grated garlic
- 4 pork chops
- Salt and pepper to taste

Directions:
1. Preheat the air fryer to 330°F.
2. Place the grill pan accessory in the air fryer.
3. Season the pork chops with the remaining Ingredients.
4. Place on the grill pan and cook for 30 minutes.
5. Flip the pork chops halfway through the cooking time.

347.Caraway, Sichuan 'n Cumin Lamb Kebabs

Servings:3
Cooking Time: 1 Hour
Ingredients:
- 1 ½ pounds lamb shoulder, bones removed and cut into pieces
- 1 tablespoon Sichuan peppercorns
- 1 teaspoon sugar
- 2 tablespoons cumin seeds, toasted
- 2 teaspoons caraway seeds, toasted
- 2 teaspoons crushed red pepper flakes
- Salt and pepper to taste

Directions:
1. Place all ingredients in bowl and allow the meat to marinate in the fridge for at least 2 hours.
2. Preheat the air fryer to 390°F.
3. Place the grill pan accessory in the air fryer.
4. Grill the meat for 15 minutes per batch.
5. Flip the meat every 8 minutes for even grilling.

348.Beef & Kale Omelet

Servings: 4
Cooking Time: 20 Minutes
Ingredients:
- Cooking spray
- ½ lb. leftover beef, coarsely chopped
- 2 garlic cloves, pressed
- 1 cup kale, torn into pieces and wilted
- 1 tomato, chopped
- ¼ tsp. sugar
- 4 eggs, beaten
- 4 tbsp. heavy cream
- ½ tsp. turmeric powder
- Salt and ground black pepper to taste
- 1/8 tsp. ground allspice

Directions:
1. Grease four ramekins with cooking spray.
2. Place equal amounts of each of the ingredients into each ramekin and mix well.
3. Air-fry at 360°F for 16 minutes, or longer if necessary. Serve immediately.

349.Garlic-rosemary Lamb Bbq

Servings:2
Cooking Time: 12 Minutes
Ingredients:
- 1-lb cubed lamb leg
- juice of 1 lemon
- fresh rosemary
- 3 smashed garlic cloves
- salt and pepper
- 1/2 cup olive oil

Directions:
1. In a shallow dish, mix well all Ingredients and marinate for 3 hours.
2. Thread lamb pieces in skewers. Place on skewer rack in air fryer.

3. For 12 minutes, cook on 390°F. Halfway through cooking time, turnover skewers. If needed, cook in batches.
4. Serve and enjoy.

350.Aromatic Pork Tenderloin With Herbs

Servings: 4
Cooking Time: 20 Minutes + Marinating Time
Ingredients:
- 1 pound pork tenderloin
- 4-5 garlic cloves, peeled and halved
- 1 teaspoon kosher salt
- 1/3 teaspoon ground black pepper
- 1 teaspoon dried basil
- 1/2 teaspoon dried oregano
- 1/2 teaspoon dried rosemary
- 1/2 teaspoon dried marjoram
- 2 tablespoons cooking wine

Directions:
1. Rub the pork with garlic halves; add the seasoning and drizzle with the cooking wine. Then, cut slits completely through pork tenderloin. Tuck the remaining garlic into the slits.
2. Wrap the pork tenderloin with foil; let it marinate overnight.
3. Roast at 360 degrees F for 15 to 17 minutes. Serve warm with roasted potatoes. Bon appétit!

351.Meat Balls With Mint Yogurt Dip From Morocco

Servings:2
Cooking Time: 25 Minutes
Ingredients:
- ¼ cup bread crumbs
- ¼ cup sour cream
- ½ cup Greek yogurt
- 1 clove of garlic, minced
- 1 egg, beaten
- 1 tablespoon mint, chopped
- 1 teaspoon cayenne pepper
- 1 teaspoon ground coriander
- 1 teaspoon ground cumin
- 1 teaspoon red chili paste
- 1-pound ground beef
- 2 cloves of garlic, minced
- 2 tablespoon flat leaf parsley, chopped
- 2 tablespoons buttermilk
- 2 tablespoons honey
- 2 tablespoons mint
- Salt and pepper to taste

Directions:
1. In a mixing bowl, combine the ground beef, cumin, coriander, cayenne pepper, red chili paste, minced garlic, parsley, chopped mint, egg, and bread crumbs. Season with salt and pepper to taste. Use your hands and form small balls. Set aside and allow to rest in the fridge for at least 30 minutes.
2. Preheat the air fryer to 330°F.

3. Place the meatballs in the air fryer basket and cook for 25 minutes. Give the air fryer basket a shake to cook evenly.
4. Meanwhile, mix the Greek yogurt, sour cream, buttermilk, mint, garlic, and honey in a bowl. Season with salt and pepper.
5. Serve the meatballs with the yogurt sauce.

352.Steak Rolls

Servings: 4
Cooking Time: 18 Minutes
Ingredients:
- 12 oz pork steaks (3 oz each steak)
- 1 green bell pepper
- 2 oz asparagus, trimmed
- 1 teaspoon ground black pepper
- ¼ teaspoon salt
- 1 teaspoon sunflower oil
- 1 teaspoon chili flakes
- 1 teaspoon avocado oil

Directions:
1. Beat every pork steak with the kitchen hammer gently. Then sprinkle the meat with chili flakes and avocado oil and place it in the air fryer in one layer. Cook the meat for 8 minutes at 375F. Then remove the meat from the air fryer and cool to the room temperature. Meanwhile, cut the bell pepper on the thin wedges. Mix up together pepper wedges and asparagus. Add ground black pepper, salt, and sunflower oil. Mix up the vegetables. After this, place the vegetables on the pork steaks and roll them. Secure the meat with toothpicks if needed. Then transfer the steak bundles in the air fryer in one layer and cook them for 10 minutes at 365F.

353.Ham And Veggie Air Fried Mix Recipe

Servings: 6
Cooking Time:30 Minutes
Ingredients:
- 1/4 cup butter
- 1/4 cup flour
- 6 oz. sweet peas
- 4 oz. mushrooms; halved
- 3 cups milk
- 1/2 tsp. thyme; dried
- 2 cups ham; chopped
- 1 cup baby carrots

Directions:
1. Heat up a large pan that fits your air fryer with the butter over medium heat, melt it, add flour and whisk well
2. Add milk and, well again and take off heat
3. Add thyme, ham, peas, mushrooms and baby carrots, toss, put in your air fryer and cook at 360 °F, for 20 minutes. Divide everything on plates and serve.

354.Garlic-rosemary Rubbed Beef Rib Roast

Servings:14
Cooking Time: 2 Hours
Ingredients:
- 1 cup dried porcini mushrooms
- 1 medium shallot, chopped
- 2 cloves of garlic, minced
- 2 cups water
- 3 tablespoons unsalted pepper
- 3 tablespoons vegetable oil
- 4 sprigs of thyme
- 6 ribs, beef rib roast
- Salt and pepper to taste

Directions:
1. Preheat the air fryer for 5 minutes.
2. Place all ingredients in a baking dish that will fit in the air fryer.
3. Place the dish in the air fryer and cook for 2 hours at 325°F.

355.Easy Beef Medallions With Parsley And Peppers

Servings: 4
Cooking Time: 30 Minutes
Ingredients:
- 2 tablespoons olive oil
- 2 small bunch parsley, roughly chopped
- 1 ½ pounds beef medallions
- 3 bell peppers, seeded and sliced
- 2 sprigs thyme
- 1 sprig rosemary
- Umami dust seasoning, to taste
- Salt and ground black pepper, to taste

Directions:
1. Firstly, arrange the vegetables on the bottom of the air fry Air Fryer basket; add seasonings and drizzle with olive oil. Roast for 8 minutes and pause the machine.
2. Now, place beef medallions on top of the vegetables.
3. Roast for 18 minutes longer at 375 degrees, stirring once halfway through. To serve, sprinkle with umami dust seasoning and enjoy!

356.Beef And Zucchini Sauté

Servings: 4
Cooking Time: 25 Minutes
Ingredients:
- 1 pound beef meat, cut into thin strips
- 1 zucchini, roughly cubed
- 2 tablespoons coconut aminos
- 2 garlic cloves, minced
- ¼ cup cilantro, chopped
- 2 tablespoons avocado oil

Directions:
1. Heat up a pan that fits your air fryer with the oil over medium heat, add the meat and brown for 5 minutes. Add the rest of the ingredients, toss, put the pan in the fryer

and cook at 380 degrees F for 20 minutes. Divide everything into bowls and serve.

357.Spicy Pork With Herbs And Candy Onions

Servings: 4
Cooking Time: 1 Hour
Ingredients:
- 1 rosemary sprig, chopped
- 1 thyme sprig, chopped
- 1 teaspoon dried sage, crushed
- Sea salt and ground black pepper, to taste
- 1 teaspoon cayenne pepper
- 2 teaspoons sesame oil
- 2 pounds pork leg roast, scored
- 1/2 pound candy onions, peeled
- 2 chili peppers, minced
- 4 cloves garlic, finely chopped

Directions:
1. Start by preheating your Air Fryer to 400 degrees F.
2. Then, mix the seasonings with the sesame oil.
3. Rub the seasoning mixture all over the pork leg. Cook in the preheated Air Fryer for 40 minutes.
4. Add the candy onions, peppers and garlic and cook an additional 12 minutes. Slice the pork leg. Afterwards, spoon the pan juices over the meat and serve with the candy onions. Bon appétit!

358.Char-grilled Skirt Steak With Fresh Herbs

Servings:3
Cooking Time: 30 Minutes
Ingredients:
- 1 ½ pounds skirt steak, trimmed
- 1 tablespoon lemon zest
- 1 tablespoon olive oil
- 2 cups fresh herbs like tarragon, sage, and mint, chopped
- 4 cloves of garlic, minced
- Salt and pepper to taste

Directions:
1. Preheat the air fryer to 390°F.
2. Place the grill pan accessory in the air fryer.
3. Season the steak with salt, pepper, lemon zest, herbs, and garlic.
4. Brush with oil.
5. Grill for 15 minutes and if needed cook in batches.

359.Bacon Wrapped Filet Mignon

Servings:2
Cooking Time:15 Minutes
Ingredients:
- 2 bacon slices
- 2 (6-ounces) filet mignon steaks
- Salt and black pepper, to taste
- 1 teaspoon avocado oil

Directions:

1. Preheat the Air fryer to 375 °F and grease an Air fryer basket.
2. Wrap each mignon steak with 1 bacon slice and secure with a toothpick.
3. Season the steak generously with salt and black pepper and coat with avocado oil.
4. Arrange the steaks in the Air fryer basket and cook for about 15 minutes, flipping once in between.
5. Dish out the steaks and cut into desired size slices to serve.

360.Adobo Pork Chops

Servings: 5
Cooking Time: 20 Minutes
Ingredients:
- 5 pork chops
- 1 tablespoon lemon juice
- 1 tablespoon sesame oil
- ½ teaspoon garlic powder
- 1 teaspoon adobo seasonings
- 1/3 cup coconut flour
- 3 eggs, beaten

Directions:
1. Sprinkle the pork chops with lemon juice, garlic powder, and adobo seasonings. Then dip the meat in the beaten eggs and coat in the coconut flour. Repeat the same steps with remaining beaten eggs and coconut flour. After this, sprinkle the pork chops with sesame oil and put in the air fryer in one layer. Cook 3 pork chops per one time. Cook the pork chops for 10 minutes at 350F. Then flip them on another side and cook for 10 minutes more.

361.Meatballs With Herbs And Mozzarella

Servings: 4
Cooking Time: 20 Minutes
Ingredients:
- 1/2 pound ground pork
- 1/2 pound ground beef
- 1 shallot, chopped
- 2 garlic cloves, minced
- 1 tablespoon coriander, chopped
- 1 teaspoon fresh mint, minced
- Sea salt and ground black pepper, to taste
- 1/2 teaspoon mustard seeds
- 1 teaspoon fennel seeds
- 1 teaspoon ground cumin
- 1 cup mozzarella, sliced

Directions:
1. In a mixing bowl, combine all ingredients, except the mozzarella.
2. Shape the mixture into balls and transfer them to a lightly greased cooking basket.
3. Cook the meatballs in the preheated Air Fryer at 380 degrees for 10 minutes. Check the meatballs halfway through the cooking time.

4. Top with sliced mozzarella and bake for 3 minutes more. To serve, arrange on a nice serving platter. Bon appétit!

362.Beef Schnitzel

Servings: 1
Cooking Time: 30 Minutes
Ingredients:
- 1 egg
- 1 thin beef schnitzel
- 3 tbsp. friendly bread crumbs
- 2 tbsp. olive oil
- 1 parsley, roughly chopped
- ½ lemon, cut in wedges

Directions:
1. Pre-heat your Air Fryer to the 360°F.
2. In a bowl combine the bread crumbs and olive oil to form a loose, crumbly mixture.
3. Beat the egg with a whisk.
4. Coat the schnitzel first in the egg and then in the bread crumbs, ensuring to cover it fully.
5. Place the schnitzel in the Air Fryer and cook for 12 – 14 minutes. Garnish the schnitzel with the lemon wedges and parsley before serving.

363.Mustard Chives And Basil Lamb

Servings: 4
Cooking Time: 30 Minutes
Ingredients:
- 8 lamb cutlets
- A pinch of salt and black pepper
- A drizzle of olive oil
- 2 garlic cloves, minced
- ¼ cup mustard
- 1 tablespoon chives, chopped
- 1 tablespoon basil, chopped
- 1 tablespoon oregano, chopped
- 1 tablespoon mint chopped

Directions:
1. In a bowl, mix the lamb with the rest of the ingredients and rub well. Put the cutlets in your air fryer's basket and cook at 380 degrees F for 15 minutes on each side. Divide between plates and serve with a side salad.

364.Spicy And Saucy Pork Sirloin

Servings: 3
Cooking Time: 55 Minutes
Ingredients:
- 2 teaspoons peanut oil
- 1 ½ pounds pork sirloin
- Coarse sea salt and ground black pepper, to taste
- 1 tablespoon smoked paprika
- 1/4 cup prepared salsa sauce

Directions:
1. Start by preheating your Air Fryer to 360 degrees F.
2. Drizzle the oil all over the pork sirloin. Sprinkle with salt, black pepper, and paprika.
3. Cook for 50 minutes in the preheated Air Fryer.
4. Remove the roast from the Air Fryer and shred with two forks. Mix in the salsa sauce. Enjoy!

365.Pork Roulade

Servings: 2
Cooking Time: 17 Minutes
Ingredients:
- 2 pork chops
- 1 teaspoon German mustard
- 1 teaspoon scallions, diced
- 1 pickled cucumber, diced
- 1 teaspoon almond butter
- ½ teaspoon ground black pepper
- 1 teaspoon olive oil

Directions:
1. Beat the pork chops gently with the help of the kitchen hammer and place them o the chopping board overlap. Then rub the meat with ground black pepper and German mustard. Top it with scallions, diced pickled cucumber, and almond butter. Roll the meat into the roulade and secure it with the kitchen thread. Then sprinkle the roulade with olive oil. Preheat the air fryer to 390F. Put the roulade in the air fryer and cook it for 17 minutes. Slice the cooked roulade.

366.Beef Fajita Keto Burrito

Servings: 4
Cooking Time: 20 Minutes
Ingredients:
- 1 pound rump steak
- 1 teaspoon garlic powder
- 1/2 teaspoon onion powder
- 1/2 teaspoon cayenne pepper
- 1 teaspoon piri piri powder
- 1 teaspoon Mexican oregano
- Salt and ground black pepper, to taste
- 1 cup Mexican cheese blend
- 1 head romaine lettuce, separated into leaves

Directions:
1. Toss the rump steak with the garlic powder, onion powder, cayenne pepper, piri piri powder, Mexican oregano, salt, and black pepper.
2. Cook in the preheated Air Fryer at 390 degrees F for 10 minutes. Slice against the grain into thin strips. Add the cheese blend and cook for 2 minutes more.
3. Spoon the beef mixture onto romaine lettuce leaves; roll up burrito-style and serve.

FISH & SEAFOOD RECIPES

367.Fish And Cauliflower Cakes

Servings: 4
Cooking Time: 2 Hours 20 Minutes
Ingredients:
- 1/2 pound cauliflower florets
- 1/2 teaspoon English mustard
- 2 tablespoons butter, room temperature
- 1/2 tablespoon cilantro, minced
- 2 tablespoons sour cream
- 2 ½ cups cooked white fish
- Salt and freshly cracked black pepper, to savor

Directions:
1. Boil the cauliflower until tender. Then, purée the cauliflower in your blender. Transfer to a mixing dish.
2. Now, stir in the fish, cilantro, salt, and black pepper.
3. Add the sour cream, English mustard, and butter; mix until everything's well incorporated. Using your hands, shape into patties.
4. Place in the refrigerator for about 2 hours. Cook for 13 minutes at 395 degrees F. Serve with some extra English mustard.

368.Squid Mix

Servings: 4
Cooking Time: 17 Minutes
Ingredients:
- 17 ounces squids, cleaned and cut into medium pieces
- ½ cup veggie stock
- 1½ tablespoons red chili powder
- Salt and black pepper to taste
- ¼ teaspoon turmeric powder
- 4 garlic cloves, minced
- ½ teaspoon cumin seeds
- 3 tablespoons olive oil
- ¼ teaspoon mustard seeds
- 1-inch ginger, minced

Directions:
1. Place all ingredients in a pan that fits your air fryer and mix well.
2. Insert the pan into the fryer and cook at 380 degrees F for 17 minutes.
3. Divide between plates and serve.

369.Simple Sesame Squid On The Grill

Servings:3
Cooking Time: 10 Minutes
Ingredients:
- 1 ½ pounds squid, cleaned
- 2 tablespoon toasted sesame oil
- Salt and pepper to taste

Directions:
1. Preheat the air fryer at 390°F.
2. Place the grill pan accessory in the air fryer.
3. Season the squid with sesame oil, salt and pepper.
4. Grill the squid for 10 minutes.

370.Crispy Mustardy Fish Fingers

Servings: 4
Cooking Time: 20 Minutes
Ingredients:
- 1 ½ pounds tilapia pieces (fingers)
- 1/2 cup all-purpose flour
- 2 eggs
- 1 tablespoon yellow mustard
- 1 cup cornmeal
- 1 teaspoon garlic powder
- 1 teaspoon onion powder
- Sea salt and ground black pepper, to taste
- 1/2 teaspoon celery powder
- 2 tablespoons peanut oil

Directions:
1. Pat dry the fish fingers with a kitchen towel.
2. To make a breading station, place the all-purpose flour in a shallow dish. In a separate dish, whisk the eggs with mustard.
3. In a third bowl, mix the remaining ingredients.
4. Dredge the fish fingers in the flour, shaking the excess into the bowl; dip in the egg mixture and turn to coat evenly; then, dredge in the cornmeal mixture, turning a couple of times to coat evenly.
5. Cook in the preheated Air Fryer at 390 degrees F for 5 minutes; turn them over and cook another 5 minutes. Enjoy!

371.Prawn Burgers

Servings:2
Cooking Time:6 Minutes
Ingredients:
- ½ cup prawns, peeled, deveined and finely chopped
- ½ cup breadcrumbs
- 2-3 tablespoons onion, finely chopped
- 3 cups fresh baby greens
- ½ teaspoon ginger, minced
- ½ teaspoon garlic, minced
- ½ teaspoon red chili powder
- ½ teaspoon ground cumin
- ¼ teaspoon ground turmeric
- Salt and ground black pepper, as required

Directions:
1. Preheat the Air fryer to 390 °F and grease an Air fryer basket.
2. Mix the prawns, breadcrumbs, onion, ginger, garlic, and spices in a bowl.

3. Make small-sized patties from the mixture and transfer to the Air fryer basket.
4. Cook for about 6 minutes and dish out in a platter.
5. Serve immediately warm alongside the baby greens.

372.Fried Haddock Fillets

Servings: 2
Cooking Time: 20 Minutes
Ingredients:
- 2 haddock fillets
- 1/2 cup parmesan cheese, freshly grated
- 1 teaspoon dried parsley flakes
- 1 egg, beaten
- 1/2 teaspoon coarse sea salt
- 1/4 teaspoon ground black pepper
- 1/4 teaspoon cayenne pepper
- 2 tablespoons olive oil

Directions:
1. Start by preheating your Air Fryer to 360 degrees F. Pat dry the haddock fillets and set aside.
2. In a shallow bowl, thoroughly combine the parmesan and parsley flakes. Mix until everything is well incorporated.
3. In a separate shallow bowl, whisk the egg with salt, black pepper, and cayenne pepper.
4. Dip the haddock fillets into the egg. Then, dip the fillets into the parmesan mixture until well coated on all sides.
5. Drizzle the olive oil all over the fish fillets. Lower the coated fillets into the lightly greased Air Fryer basket. Cook for 11 to 13 minutes. Bon appétit!

373.Air Fried Catfish

Servings: 4
Cooking Time: 20 Minutes
Ingredients:
- 4 catfish fillets
- 1 tbsp olive oil
- 1/4 cup fish seasoning
- 1 tbsp fresh parsley, chopped

Directions:
1. Preheat the air fryer to 400 F.
2. Spray air fryer basket with cooking spray.
3. Seasoned fish with seasoning and place into the air fryer basket.
4. Drizzle fish fillets with oil and cook for 10 minutes.
5. Turn fish to another side and cook for 10 minutes more.
6. Garnish with parsley and serve.

374.Buttered Baked Cod With Wine

Servings:2
Cooking Time: 12 Minutes
Ingredients:
- 1 tablespoon butter
- 1 tablespoon butter
- 2 tablespoons dry white wine
- 1/2 pound thick-cut cod loin
- 1-1/2 teaspoons chopped fresh parsley
- 1-1/2 teaspoons chopped green onion
- 1/2 lemon, cut into wedges
- 1/4 sleeve buttery round crackers (such as Ritz®), crushed
- 1/4 lemon, juiced

Directions:
1. In a small bowl, melt butter in microwave. Whisk in crackers.
2. Lightly grease baking pan of air fryer with remaining butter. And melt for 2 minutes at 390°F.
3. In a small bowl whisk well lemon juice, white wine, parsley, and green onion.
4. Coat cod filets in melted butter. Pour dressing. Top with butter-cracker mixture.
5. Cook for 10 minutes at 390°F.
6. Serve and enjoy with a slice of lemon.

375.Mediterranean Grilled Scallops

Servings: 2
Cooking Time: 2 Hour 12 Minutes
Ingredients:
- 1 1/2 tablespoons coconut aminos
- 1 tablespoon Mediterranean seasoning mix
- 1/3 cup shallots, chopped
- 1/2 tablespoon balsamic vinegar
- 1 1/2 tablespoons olive oil
- 1 clove garlic, chopped
- 1/2 teaspoon ginger, grated
- 1 pound scallops, cleaned
- Belgian endive, for garnish

Directions:
1. In a small-sized sauté pan that is placed over a moderate flame, simmer all ingredients, minus scallops and Belgian endive. Allow this mixture to cool down completely.
2. After that, add the scallops and let them marinate for at least 2 hours in the refrigerator.
3. Arrange the scallops in a single layer in the Air Fryer grill pan. Spritz with a cooking oil. Air-fry at 345 degrees for 10 minutes, turning halfway through.
4. Serve immediately with Belgian endive. Bon appétit!

376.Cajun Spiced Lemon-shrimp Kebabs

Servings:2
Cooking Time: 10 Minutes
Ingredients:
- 1 tsp cayenne
- 1 tsp garlic powder
- 1 tsp kosher salt

- 1 tsp onion powder
- 1 tsp oregano
- 1 tsp paprika
- 12 pcs XL shrimp
- 2 lemons, sliced thinly crosswise
- 2 tbsp olive oil

Directions:
1. In a bowl, mix all Ingredients except for sliced lemons. Marinate for 10 minutes.
2. Thread 3 shrimps per steel skewer.
3. Place in skewer rack.
4. Cook for 5 minutes at 390°F.
5. Serve and enjoy with freshly squeezed lemon.

377.Halibut Cakes With Horseradish Mayo

Servings: 4
Cooking Time: 20 Minutes
Ingredients:
- Halibut Cakes:
- 1 pound halibut
- 2 tablespoons olive oil
- 1/2 teaspoon cayenne pepper
- 1/4 teaspoon black pepper
- Salt, to taste
- 2 tablespoons cilantro, chopped
- 1 shallot, chopped
- 2 garlic cloves, minced
- 1/2 cup Romano cheese, grated
- 1/2 cup breadcrumbs
- 1 egg, whisked
- 1 tablespoon Worcestershire sauce
- Mayo Sauce:
- 1 teaspoon horseradish, grated
- 1/2 cup mayonnaise

Directions:
1. Start by preheating your Air Fryer to 380 degrees F. Spritz the Air Fryer basket with cooking oil.
2. Mix all ingredients for the halibut cakes in a bowl; knead with your hands until everything is well incorporated.
3. Shape the mixture into equally sized patties. Transfer your patties to the Air Fryer basket. Cook the fish patties for 10 minutes, turning them over halfway through.
4. Mix the horseradish and mayonnaise. Serve the halibut cakes with the horseradish mayo. Bon appétit!

378.Salmon And Creamy Chives Sauce

Servings: 4
Cooking Time: 20 Minutes
Ingredients:
- 4 salmon fillets, boneless
- A pinch of salt and black pepper
- ½ cup heavy cream
- 1 tablespoon chives, chopped
- 1 teaspoon lemon juice

- 1 teaspoon dill, chopped
- 2 garlic cloves, minced
- ¼ cup ghee, melted

Directions:
1. In a bowl, mix all the ingredients except the salmon and whisk well. Arrange the salmon in a pan that fits the air fryer, drizzle the sauce all over, introduce the pan in the machine and cook at 360 degrees F for 20 minutes. Divide everything between plates and serve.

379.Breaded Hake

Servings:2
Cooking Time:12 Minutes
Ingredients:
- 1 egg
- 4 ounces breadcrumbs
- 4 (6-ounces) hake fillets
- 1 lemon, cut into wedges
- 2 tablespoons vegetable oil

Directions:
1. Preheat the Air fryer to 350 °F and grease an Air fryer basket.
2. Whisk the egg in a shallow bowl and mix breadcrumbs and oil in another bowl.
3. Dip hake fillets into the whisked egg and then, dredge in the breadcrumb mixture.
4. Arrange the hake fillets into the Air fryer basket in a single layer and cook for about 12 minutes.
5. Dish out the hake fillets onto serving plates and serve, garnished with lemon wedges.

380.Shrimp Scampi

Servings: 4
Cooking Time: 10 Minutes
Ingredients:
- 1 lb shrimp, peeled and deveined
- 10 garlic cloves, peeled
- 2 tbsp olive oil
- 1 fresh lemon, cut into wedges
- 1/4 cup parmesan cheese, grated
- 2 tbsp butter, melted

Directions:
1. Preheat the air fryer to 370 F.
2. Mix together shrimp, lemon wedges, olive oil, and garlic cloves in a bowl.
3. Pour shrimp mixture into the air fryer pan and place into the air fryer and cook for 10 minutes.
4. Drizzle with melted butter and sprinkle with parmesan cheese.
5. Serve and enjoy.

381.Best Cod Ever

Servings:2
Cooking Time:7 Minutes
Ingredients:

- 2 (4-ounce) skinless codfish fillets, cut into rectangular pieces
- ½ cup flour
- 3 eggs
- 1 green chili, chopped finely
- 3 scallions, chopped finely
- 2 garlic cloves, minced
- 1 teaspoon light soy sauce
- Salt and black pepper, to taste

Directions:
1. Preheat the Air fryer to 375 °F and grease an Air fryer basket.
2. Place the flour in a shallow dish and mix remaining ingredients in another shallow dish except cod.
3. Coat each fillet with the flour and then dip into the egg mixture.
4. Place the cod in the Air fryer basket and cook for about 7 minutes.
5. Dish out in a platter and serve warm.

382.Tuna And Potato Cakes

Servings:4
Cooking Time:12 Minutes
Ingredients:
- 1 onion, chopped
- 1 green chili, seeded and finely chopped
- 2 (6-ounces) cans tuna, drained
- 1 medium boiled potato, mashed
- 1 cup breadcrumbs
- ½ tablespoon olive oil
- 1 tablespoon fresh ginger, grated
- Salt, as required

Directions:
1. Preheat the Air fryer to 390 °F and grease an Air fryer basket.
2. Heat olive oil in a frying pan and add onions, ginger, and green chili.
3. Sauté for about 30 seconds and add the tuna.
4. Stir fry for about 3 minutes and dish out the tuna mixture onto a large bowl.
5. Add mashed potato, celery, and salt and mix well.
6. Make 4 equal-sized patties from the mixture.
7. Place the breadcrumbs in a shallow bowl and whisk the egg in another bowl.
8. Dredge each patty with breadcrumbs, then dip into egg and coat again with the breadcrumbs.
9. Arrange tuna cakes into the Air fryer basket and cook for about 3 minutes.
10. Flip the side and cook for about 5 minutes.
11. 1Dish out the tuna cakes onto serving plates and serve warm.

383.Paprika Prawns

Servings: 5
Cooking Time: 5 Minutes

Ingredients:
- 3-pound prawns, peeled
- 1 tablespoon ground turmeric
- 1 teaspoon smoked paprika
- 1 tablespoon coconut milk
- 1 teaspoon avocado oil
- ½ teaspoon salt

Directions:
1. Put the prawns in the bowl and sprinkle them with ground turmeric, smoked paprika, and salt. Then add coconut milk and leave them for 10 minutes to marinate. Meanwhile, preheat the air fryer to 400F. Put the marinated prawns in the air fryer basket and sprinkle with avocado oil. Cook the prawns for 3 minutes. Then shake them well and cook for 2 minutes more.

384.Cod And Cauliflower Patties

Servings: 4
Cooking Time: 12 Minutes
Ingredients:
- ½ cup cauliflower, shredded
- 4 oz cod fillet, chopped
- 1 egg, beaten
- 1 teaspoon chives, chopped
- ¼ teaspoon chili flakes
- 1 teaspoon salt
- ½ teaspoon ground cumin
- 2 tablespoons coconut flour
- 1 spring onion, chopped
- 1 tablespoon sesame oil

Directions:
1. Grind the chopped cod fillet and put it in the mixing bowl. Add shredded cauliflower, egg, chives, chili flakes, salt, ground cumin, and chopped onion. Stir the mixture until homogenous and add coconut flour. Stir it again. After this, make the medium size patties. Preheat the air fryer to 385F. Place the patties in the air fryer basket and sprinkle with sesame oil. Cook the fish patties for 8 minutes. Then flip them on another side and cook for 4 minutes more or until the patties are light brown.

385.Ghee Shrimp And Green Beans

Servings: 4
Cooking Time: 15 Minutes
Ingredients:
- 1 pound shrimp, peeled and deveined
- A pinch of salt and black pepper
- ½ pound green beans, trimmed and halved
- Juice of 1 lime
- 2 tablespoons cilantro, chopped
- ¼ cup ghee, melted

Directions:
1. In a pan that fits your air fryer, mix all the ingredients, toss, introduce in the fryer and

cook at 360 degrees F for 15 minutes shaking the fryer halfway. Divide into bowls and serve.

386. Fijan Coconut Fish

Servings: 2
Cooking Time: 20 Minutes + Marinating Time
Ingredients:
- 1 cup coconut milk
- 2 tablespoons lime juice
- 2 tablespoons Shoyu sauce
- Salt and white pepper, to taste
- 1 teaspoon turmeric powder
- 1/2 teaspoon ginger powder
- 1/2 Thai Bird's Eye chili, seeded and finely chopped
- 1 pound tilapia
- 2 tablespoons olive oil

Directions:
1. In a mixing bowl, thoroughly combine the coconut milk with the lime juice, Shoyu sauce, salt, pepper, turmeric, ginger, and chili pepper. Add tilapia and let it marinate for 1 hour.
2. Brush the Air Fryer basket with olive oil. Discard the marinade and place the tilapia fillets in the Air Fryer basket.
3. Cook the tilapia in the preheated Air Fryer at 400 degrees F for 6 minutes; turn them over and cook for 6 minutes more. Work in batches.
4. Serve with some extra lime wedges if desired. Enjoy!

387. Pesto Sauce Over Fish Filet

Servings:3
Cooking Time: 20 Minutes
Ingredients:
- 1 bunch fresh basil
- 1 cup olive oil
- 1 tablespoon parmesan cheese, grated
- 2 cloves of garlic,
- 2 tablespoons pine nuts
- 3 white fish fillets
- Salt and pepper to taste

Directions:
1. In a food processor, combine all ingredients except for the fish fillets.
2. Pulse until smooth.
3. Place the fish in a baking dish and pour over the pesto sauce.
4. Place in the air fryer and cook for 20 minutes at 400°F.

388. Creamy Cod Strips

Servings: 4
Cooking Time: 6 Minutes
Ingredients:
- 10 oz cod fillet

- 1 tablespoon coconut flour
- 1 tablespoon coconut flakes
- 1 egg, beaten
- 1 teaspoon ground turmeric
- ½ teaspoon salt
- 1 tablespoon heavy cream
- 1 teaspoon olive oil

Directions:
1. Cut the cod fillets on the fries strips. After this, in the mixing bowl mix up coconut flour, coconut flakes, ground turmeric, and salt. In the other bowl mix up egg and heavy cream. After this, dip the fish fries in the egg mixture. Then coat them in the coconut flour mixture. Repeat the steps again. Preheat the air fryer to 400F. Put the fish fries in the air fryer basket in one layer and sprinkle them with olive oil. Cook the meal for 3 minutes. Then flip the fish fries on another side and cook for 3 minutes more.

389. Whitefish Cakes

Servings: 4
Cooking Time: 1 Hr. 20 Minutes
Ingredients:
- 1 ½ cups whitefish fillets, minced
- 1 ½ cups green beans, finely chopped
- ½ cup scallions, chopped
- 1 chili pepper, deveined and minced
- 1 tbsp. red curry paste
- 1 tsp. sugar
- 1 tbsp. fish sauce
- 2 tbsp. apple cider vinegar
- 1 tsp. water
- Sea salt flakes, to taste
- ½ tsp. cracked black peppercorns
- 1 ½ teaspoons butter, at room temperature
- 1 lemon

Directions:
1. Place all of the ingredients a bowl, following the order in which they are listed.
2. Combine well with a spatula or your hands.
3. Mold the mixture into several small cakes and refrigerate for 1 hour.
4. Put a piece of aluminum foil in the cooking basket and lay the cakes on top.
5. Cook at 390°F for 10 minutes. Turn each fish cake over before air-frying for another 5 minutes.
6. Serve the fish cakes with a side of cucumber relish.

390. Trout And Tomato Zucchinis Mix

Servings: 4
Cooking Time: 15 Minutes
Ingredients:
- 3 zucchinis, cut in medium chunks
- 4 trout fillets, boneless
- 2 tablespoons olive oil

- ¼ cup keto tomato sauce
- Salt and black pepper to the taste
- 1 garlic clove, minced
- 1 tablespoon lemon juice
- ½ cup cilantro, chopped

Directions:
1. In a pan that fits your air fryer, mix the fish with the other ingredients, toss, introduce in the fryer and cook at 380 degrees F for 15 minutes. Divide everything between plates and serve right away.

391.Parmesan Walnut Salmon

Servings: 4
Cooking Time: 12 Minutes
Ingredients:
- 4 salmon fillets
- 1/4 cup parmesan cheese, grated
- 1/2 cup walnuts
- 1 tsp olive oil
- 1 tbsp lemon rind

Directions:
1. Preheat the air fryer to 370 F.
2. Spray an air fryer baking dish with cooking spray.
3. Place salmon on a baking dish.
4. Add walnuts into the food processor and process until finely ground.
5. Mix ground walnuts with parmesan cheese, oil, and lemon rind. Stir well.
6. Spoon walnut mixture over the salmon and press gently.
7. Place in the air fryer and cook for 12 minutes.
8. Serve and enjoy.

392.Haddock With Cheese Sauce

Servings:4
Cooking Time:8 Minutes
Ingredients:
- 4 (6-ounce) haddock fillets
- 6 tablespoons fresh basil, chopped
- 4 tablespoons pine nuts
- 2 tablespoons Parmesan cheese, grated
- 2 tablespoons olive oil
- Salt and black pepper, to taste

Directions:
1. Preheat the Air fryer to 360 °F and grease an Air fryer basket.
2. Season the haddock fillets with salt and black pepper and coat evenly with olive oil.
3. Transfer the haddock fillets in the Air fryer basket and cook for about 8 minutes.
4. Meanwhile, put rest of the ingredients in a food processor and pulse until smooth to make cheese sauce.
5. Dish out the haddock fillets in the bowl and top with cheese sauce to serve.

393.Ale-battered Fish With Potato Mash

Servings:4
Cooking Time: 20 Minutes
Ingredients:
- 2 eggs
- 1 cup ale beer
- 1 ½ cups flour
- Salt and black pepper to taste
- 4 white fish fillets
- 2 cups mashed potatoes

Directions:
1. Preheat your Air Fryer to 390 F. Spray the air fryer basket with cooking spray.
2. Beat the eggs in a bowl with ale beer, salt, and black pepper. Pat dry the fish fillets with paper towels and dredge them in the flour; shake off the excess. Dip in the egg mixture and then in the flour again. Spray with cooking spray and add to the cooking basket. Cook for 15 minutes, flipping halfway through. Serve with potato mash and lemon wedges.

394.Citrusy Branzini On The Grill

Servings:2
Cooking Time: 15 Minutes
Ingredients:
- 2 branzini fillets
- Salt and pepper to taste
- 3 lemons, juice freshly squeezed
- 2 oranges, juice freshly squeezed

Directions:
1. Place all ingredients in a Ziploc bag. Allow to marinate in the fridge for 2 hours.
2. Preheat the air fryer at 390°F.
3. Place the grill pan accessory in the air fryer.
4. Place the fish on the grill pan and cook for 15 minutes until the fish is flaky.

395.Sesame Prawns With Firecracker Sauce

Servings:4
Cooking Time: 20 Minutes
Ingredients:
- Salt and black pepper to taste
- 1 egg
- ½ cup flour
- ¼ cup sesame seeds
- ¾ cup seasoned breadcrumbs
- Firecracker sauce
- ⅓ cup sour cream
- 2 tbsp buffalo sauce
- ¼ cup spicy ketchup
- 1 green onion, chopped

Directions:
1. Preheat your Air Fryer to 390 F. Spray the air fryer basket with cooking spray.

2. Beat the eggs in a bowl with salt. In a separate bowl, mix seasoned breadcrumbs with sesame seeds. In a third bowl, pour the flour mixed with black pepper.
3. Dip prawns in the flour and then in the eggs, and finally in the breadcrumb mixture. Spray with cooking spray and add to the cooking basket. Cook for 10 minutes, flipping halfway through.
4. Meanwhile, mix well all the sauce ingredients, except for the green onion in a bowl. Serve the prawns with firecracker sauce.

396.Crusty Pesto Salmon

Servings: 2
Cooking Time: 15 Minutes
Ingredients:
- ¼ cup s, roughly chopped
- ¼ cup pesto
- 2 x 4-oz. salmon fillets
- 2 tbsp. unsalted butter, melted

Directions:
1. Mix the s and pesto together.
2. Place the salmon fillets in a round baking dish, roughly six inches in diameter.
3. Brush the fillets with butter, followed by the pesto mixture, ensuring to coat both the top and bottom. Put the baking dish inside the fryer.
4. Cook for twelve minutes at 390°F.
5. The salmon is ready when it flakes easily when prodded with a fork. Serve warm.

397.Cajun Fish Cakes With Cheese

Servings: 4
Cooking Time: 30 Minutes
Ingredients:
- 2 catfish fillets
- 1 cup all-purpose flour
- 3 ounces butter
- 1 teaspoon baking powder
- 1 teaspoon baking soda
- 1/2 cup buttermilk
- 1 teaspoon Cajun seasoning
- 1 cup Swiss cheese, shredded

Directions:
1. Bring a pot of salted water to a boil. Boil the fish fillets for 5 minutes or until it is opaque. Flake the fish into small pieces.
2. Mix the remaining ingredients in a bowl; add the fish and mix until well combined. Shape the fish mixture into 12 patties.
3. Cook in the preheated Air Fryer at 380 degrees F for 15 minutes. Work in batches. Enjoy!

398.Pistachio Crusted Salmon

Servings:1

Cooking Time: 15 Minutes
Ingredients:
- 1 tsp mustard
- 3 tbsp pistachios
- A pinch of sea salt
- A pinch of garlic powder
- A pinch of black pepper
- 1 tsp lemon juice
- 1 tsp grated Parmesan cheese
- 1 tsp olive oil

Directions:
1. Preheat the air fryer to 350 F, and whisk mustard and lemon juice together. Season the salmon with salt, pepper, and garlic powder. Brush the olive oil on all sides. Brush the mustard mixture onto salmon.
2. Chop the pistachios finely and combine them with the Parmesan cheese; sprinkle on top of the salmon. Place the salmon in the air fryer basket with the skin side down. Cook for 12 minutes, or to your liking.

399.Shrimp, Mushroom 'n Rice Casserole

Servings:2
Cooking Time: 35 Minutes
Ingredients:
- 1 tablespoon butter
- 1/2 (10.75 ounce) can condensed cream of shrimp soup
- 1/2 teaspoon vegetable oil
- 1/2-pound small shrimp, peeled and deveined
- 1/2 (4 ounce) can sliced mushrooms, drained
- 1/2 (8 ounce) container sour cream
- 1/3 cup shredded Cheddar cheese
- 3/4 cup uncooked instant rice
- 3/4 cup water

Directions:
1. Lightly grease baking pan of air fryer with cooking spray. Add rice, water, mushrooms, and butter. Cover with foil. For 20 minutes, cook on 360°F.
2. Open foil cover, stir in shrimps, return foil and let it rest for 5 minutes.
3. Remove foil completely and stir in sour cream. Mix well and evenly spread rice.
4. Top with cheese.
5. Cook for 7 minutes at 390°F until tops are lightly browned.
6. Serve and enjoy.

400.Korean-style Salmon Patties

Servings: 4
Cooking Time: 15 Minutes
Ingredients:
- 1 pound salmon
- 1 egg
- 1 garlic clove, minced

- 2 green onions, minced
- 1/2 cup rolled oats
- Sauce:
- 1 teaspoon rice wine
- 1 ½ tablespoons soy sauce
- 1 teaspoon honey
- A pinch of salt
- 1 teaspoon gochugaru (Korean red chili pepper flakes

Directions:
1. Start by preheating your Air Fryer to 380 degrees F. Spritz the Air Fryer basket with cooking oil.
2. Mix the salmon, egg, garlic, green onions, and rolled oats in a bowl; knead with your hands until everything is well incorporated.
3. Shape the mixture into equally sized patties. Transfer your patties to the Air Fryer basket.
4. Cook the fish patties for 10 minutes, turning them over halfway through.
5. Meanwhile, make the sauce by whisking all ingredients. Serve the warm fish patties with the sauce on the side.

401.Rockfish With Greek Avocado Cream

Servings: 4
Cooking Time: 15 Minutes + Marinating Time
Ingredients:
- For the Fish Fillets:
- 1 1/2 tablespoons balsamic vinegar
- 1/2 cup vegetable broth
- 1/3 teaspoon shallot powder
- 1 tablespoon soy sauce
- 4 Rockfish fillets
- 1 teaspoon ground black pepper
- 1 ½ tablespoons olive oil
- Fine sea salt, to taste
- 1/3 teaspoon garlic powder
- For the Avocado Cream:
- 2 tablespoons Greek-style yogurt
- 1 clove garlic, peeled and minced
- 1 teaspoon ground black pepper
- 1/2 tablespoon olive oil
- 1/3 cup vegetable broth
- 1 avocado
- 1/2 teaspoon lime juice
- 1/3 teaspoon fine sea salt

Directions:
1. In a bowl, wash and pat the fillets dry using some paper towels. Add all the seasonings. In another bowl, stir in the remaining ingredients for the fish fillets.
2. Add the seasoned fish fillets; cover and let the fillets marinate in your refrigerator at least 3 hours.
3. Then, set your Air Fryer to cook at 325 degrees F. Cook marinated rockfish fillets in the air fryer grill basket for 9 minutes.

4. In the meantime, prepare the avocado sauce by mixing all the ingredients with an immersion blender or regular blender. Serve the rockfish fillets topped with the avocado sauce. Enjoy!

402.Summer Fish Packets

Servings: 2
Cooking Time: 20 Minutes
Ingredients:
- 2 snapper fillets
- 1 shallot, peeled and sliced
- 2 garlic cloves, halved
- 1 bell pepper, sliced
- 1 small-sized serrano pepper, sliced
- 1 tomato, sliced
- 1 tablespoon olive oil
- 1/4 teaspoon freshly ground black pepper
- 1/2 teaspoon paprika
- Sea salt, to taste
- 2 bay leaves

Directions:
1. Place two parchment sheets on a working surface. Place the fish in the center of one side of the parchment paper.
2. Top with the shallot, garlic, peppers, and tomato. Drizzle olive oil over the fish and vegetables. Season with black pepper, paprika, and salt. Add the bay leaves.
3. Fold over the other half of the parchment. Now, fold the paper around the edges tightly and create a half moon shape, sealing the fish inside.
4. Cook in the preheated Air Fryer at 390 degrees F for 15 minutes. Serve warm.

403.Chinese Garlic Shrimp

Servings:5
Cooking Time: 15 Minutes
Ingredients:
- Juice of 1 lemon
- 1 tsp sugar
- 3 tbsp peanut oil
- 2 tbsp cornstarch
- 2 scallions, chopped
- ¼ tsp Chinese powder
- Chopped chili to taste
- Salt and black pepper to taste
- 4 garlic cloves

Directions:
1. Preheat air fryer to 370 F. In a Ziploc bag, mix lemon juice, sugar, pepper, half of oil, cornstarch, powder, Chinese powder and salt. Add in the shrimp and massage to coat evenly. Let sit for 10 minutes.
2. Add the remaining peanut oil, garlic, scallions, and chili to a pan, and fry for 5 minutes over medium heat. Place the marinated shrimp in your air fryer's basket

and cover with the sauce. Cook for 10 minutes, until nice and crispy. Serve.

404. Lemon Garlic Shrimp

Servings: 2
Cooking Time: 15 Minutes
Ingredients:
- 1 medium lemon
- ½ lb. medium shrimp, shelled and deveined
- ½ tsp. Old Bay seasoning
- 2 tbsp. unsalted butter, melted
- ½ tsp. minced garlic

Directions:
1. Grate the rind of the lemon into a bowl. Cut the lemon in half and juice it over the same bowl. Toss in the shrimp, Old Bay, and butter, mixing everything to make sure the shrimp is completely covered.
2. Transfer to a round baking dish roughly six inches wide, then place this dish in your fryer.
3. Cook at 400°F for six minutes. The shrimp is cooked when it turns a bright pink color.
4. Serve hot, drizzling any leftover sauce over the shrimp.

405. Celery Leaves 'n Garlic-oil Grilled Turbot

Servings: 2
Cooking Time: 20 Minutes
Ingredients:
- ½ cup chopped celery leaves
- 1 clove of garlic, minced
- 2 tablespoons olive oil
- 2 whole turbot, scaled and head removed
- Salt and pepper to taste

Directions:
1. Preheat the air fryer to 390°F.
2. Place the grill pan accessory in the air fryer.
3. Season the turbot with salt, pepper, garlic, and celery leaves.
4. Brush with oil.
5. Place on the grill pan and cook for 20 minutes until the fish becomes flaky.

406. Easy Bacon Shrimp

Servings: 4
Cooking Time: 7 Minutes
Ingredients:
- 16 shrimp, deveined
- 1/4 tsp pepper
- 16 bacon slices

Directions:
1. Preheat the air fryer to 390 F.
2. Spray air fryer basket with cooking spray.
3. Wrap shrimp with bacon slice and place into the air fryer basket and cook for 5 minutes.

4. Turn shrimp to another side and cook for 2 minutes more. Season shrimp with pepper.
5. Serve and enjoy.

407. Basil Paprika Calamari

Servings: 2
Cooking Time: 4 Minutes
Ingredients:
- 8 oz calamari, peeled, trimmed
- 1 teaspoon ghee, melted
- 1 teaspoon fresh basil, chopped
- ½ teaspoon smoked paprika
- ½ teaspoon white pepper
- 1 tablespoon apple cider vinegar

Directions:
1. In the shallow bowl mix up melted ghee, basil, smoked paprika, white pepper, and apple cider vinegar. After this, sprinkle the calamari with ghee mixture and leave for 15 minutes to marinate. After this, roughly slice the calamari. Preheat the air fryer to 400F. Put the sliced calamari in the air fryer and cook for 2 minutes. Shake the seafood well and cook for 2 minutes more.

408. Tempting Seafood Platter With Shell Pasta

Servings: 4
Cooking Time: 18 Minutes
Ingredients:
- 14-ounce shell pasta
- 4 (4-ounce) salmon steaks
- ½ pound cherry tomatoes, halved
- 8 large prawns, peeled and deveined
- 2 tablespoons fresh thyme, chopped
- 4 tablespoons pesto, divided
- 2 tablespoons olive oil
- 2 tablespoons fresh lemon juice

Directions:
1. Preheat the Air fryer to 390 °F and grease a baking dish.
2. Cook pasta in a large pan of salted water for about 10 minutes.
3. Meanwhile, spread pesto in the bottom of a baking dish.
4. Arrange salmon steaks and cherry tomatoes over pesto and drizzle evenly with olive oil.
5. Top with prawns and sprinkle with lemon juice and thyme.
6. Transfer the baking dish in the Air fryer and cook for about 8 minutes.
7. Serve the seafood mixture with pasta and enjoy.

409. Halibut With Thai Lemongrass Marinade

Servings: 2
Cooking Time: 45 Minutes
Ingredients:

- 2 tablespoons tamari sauce
- 2 tablespoons fresh lime juice
- 2 tablespoons olive oil
- 1 teaspoon Thai curry paste
- 1/2 inch lemongrass, finely chopped
- 1 teaspoon basil
- 2 cloves garlic, minced
- 2 tablespoons shallot, minced
- Sea salt and ground black pepper, to taste
- 2 halibut steaks

Directions:
1. Place all ingredients in a ceramic dish; let it marinate for 30 minutes.
2. Place the halibut steaks in the lightly greased cooking basket.
3. Bake in the preheated Air Fryer at 400 degrees F for 9 to 10 minutes, basting with the reserved marinade and flipping them halfway through the cooking time. Bon appétit!

410.Japanese Citrus Soy Squid

Servings:4
Cooking Time: 10 Minutes
Ingredients:
- ½ cup mirin
- 1 cup soy sauce
- 1/3 cup yuzu or orange juice, freshly squeezed
- 2 cups water
- 2 pounds squid body, cut into rings

Directions:
1. Place all ingredients in a Ziploc bag and allow the squid rings to marinate in the fridge for at least 2 hours.
2. Preheat the air fryer at 390°F.
3. Place the grill pan accessory in the air fryer.
4. Grill the squid rings for 10 minutes.
5. Meanwhile, pour the marinade over a sauce pan and allow to simmer for 10 minutes or until the sauce has reduced.
6. Baste the squid rings with the sauce before serving.

411.Butterflied Sriracha Prawns Grilled

Servings:2
Cooking Time: 15 Minutes
Ingredients:
- 1-pound large prawns, shells removed and cut lengthwise or butterflied
- 1 tablespoon sriracha
- 2 tablespoons melted butter
- 2 tablespoons minced garlic
- 1teaspoon fish sauce
- 1 tablespoon lime juice
- Salt and pepper to taste

Directions:
1. Preheat the air fryer at 390°F.
2. Place the grill pan accessory in the air fryer.

3. Season the prawns with the rest of the ingredients.
4. Place on the grill pan and cook for 15 minutes. Make sure to flip the prawns halfway through the cooking time.

412.Sesame Seeds Coated Haddock

Servings:4
Cooking Time:14 Minutes
Ingredients:
- 4 tablespoons plain flour
- 2 eggs
- ½ cup sesame seeds, toasted
- ½ cup breadcrumbs
- 4 (6-ounces) frozen haddock fillets
- 1/8 teaspoon dried rosemary, crushed
- Salt and ground black pepper, as required
- 3 tablespoons olive oil

Directions:
1. Preheat the Air fryer to 390 °F and grease an Air fryer basket.
2. Place the flour in a shallow bowl and whisk the eggs in a second bowl.
3. Mix sesame seeds, breadcrumbs, rosemary, salt, black pepper and olive oil in a third bowl until a crumbly mixture is formed.
4. Coat each fillet with flour, dip into whisked eggs and finally, dredge into the breadcrumb mixture
5. Arrange haddock fillets into the Air fryer basket in a single layer and cook for about 14 minutes, flipping once in between.
6. Dish out the haddock fillets onto serving plates and serve hot.

413.Spicy Prawns

Servings: 2
Cooking Time: 8 Minutes
Ingredients:
- 6 prawns
- 1/4 tsp pepper
- 1/2 tsp chili powder
- 1 tsp chili flakes
- 1/4 tsp salt

Directions:
1. Preheat the air fryer to 350 F.
2. In a bowl, mix together spices add prawns.
3. Spray air fryer basket with cooking spray.
4. Transfer prawns into the air fryer basket and cook for 8 minutes.
5. Serve and enjoy.

414.Salmon With Shrimp & Pasta

Servings:4
Cooking Time: 18 Minutes
Ingredients:
- 14 ounces pasta (of your choice)
- 4 tablespoons pesto, divided
- 4 (4-ounces) salmon steaks

- 2 tablespoons olive oil
- ½ pound cherry tomatoes, chopped
- 8 large prawns, peeled and deveined
- 2 tablespoons fresh lemon juice
- 2 tablespoons fresh thyme, chopped

Directions:
1. In a large pan of salted boiling water, add the pasta and cook for about 8-10 minutes or until desired doneness.
2. Meanwhile, in the bottom of a baking dish, spread 1 tablespoon of pesto.
3. Place salmon steaks and tomatoes over pesto in a single layer and drizzle evenly with the oil.
4. Now, add the prawns on top in a single layer.
5. Drizzle with lemon juice and sprinkle with thyme.
6. Set the temperature of air fryer to 390 degrees F.
7. Arrange the baking dish in air fryer and air fry for about 8 minutes.
8. Once done, remove the salmon mixture from air fryer.
9. Drain the pasta and transfer into a large bowl.
10. Add the remaining pesto and toss to coat well.
11. Add the pasta evenly onto each serving plate and top with salmon mixture.
12. Serve immediately.

415.Balsamic Cod

Servings: 4
Cooking Time: 15 Minutes
Ingredients:
- 4 cod fillets, boneless
- Salt and black pepper to the taste
- 1 cup parmesan
- 4 tablespoons balsamic vinegar
- A drizzle of olive oil
- 3 spring onions, chopped

Directions:
1. Season fish with salt, pepper, grease with the oil, and coat it in parmesan. Put the fillets in your air fryer's basket and cook at 370 degrees F for 14 minutes. Meanwhile, in a bowl, mix the spring onions with salt, pepper and the vinegar and whisk. Divide the cod between plates, drizzle the spring onions mix all over and serve with a side salad.

416.Catfish With Spring Onions And Avocado

Servings: 4
Cooking Time: 15 Minutes
Ingredients:
- 2 teaspoons oregano, dried

- 2 teaspoons cumin, ground
- 2 teaspoons sweet paprika
- A pinch of salt and black pepper
- 4 catfish fillets
- 1 avocado, peeled and cubed
- ½ cup spring onions, chopped
- 2 tablespoons cilantro, chopped
- 2 teaspoons olive oil
- 2 tablespoons lemon juice

Directions:
1. In a bowl, mix all the ingredients except the fish and toss. Arrange this in a baking pan that fits the air fryer, top with the fish, introduce the pan in the machine and cook at 360 degrees F for 15 minutes, flipping the fish halfway. Divide between plates and serve.

417.Egg Frittata With Smoked Trout

Servings:6
Cooking Time: 15 Minutes
Ingredients:
- 1 onion, chopped
- 2 fillets smoked trout, shredded
- 2 tablespoons coconut oil
- 2 tablespoons olive oil
- 6 eggs, beaten
- Salt and pepper to taste

Directions:
1. Preheat the air fryer for 5 minutes.
2. Place all ingredients in a mixing bowl until well-combined.
3. Pour into a baking dish that will fit in the air fryer.
4. Cook for 15 minutes at 400°F.

418.Cod Cakes(2)

Servings:6
Cooking Time:14 Minutes
Ingredients:
- 1 pound cod fillet
- 1 egg
- 1/3 cup coconut, grated and divided
- 1 scallion, finely chopped
- 2 tablespoons fresh parsley, chopped
- 1 teaspoon fresh lime zest, finely grated
- 1 teaspoon red chili paste
- Salt, as required
- 1 tablespoon fresh lime juice

Directions:
1. Preheat the Air fryer to 375 °F and grease an Air fryer basket.
2. Put the cod fillet, lime zest, egg, chili paste, salt and lime juice in a food processor and pulse until smooth.
3. Transfer the cod mixture into a bowl and add scallion, parsley and 2 tablespoons of coconut.

4. Mix until well combined and make 12 equal-sized round cakes from the mixture.
5. Place the remaining coconut in a shallow bowl and coat the cod cakes with coconut.
6. Arrange cod cakes into the Air fryer basket in 2 batches and cook for about 7 minutes.
7. Dish out in 2 serving plates and serve warm.

419.Cod With Avocado Mayo Sauce

Servings: 2
Cooking Time: 20 Minutes
Ingredients:
- 2 cod fish fillets
- 1 egg
- Sea salt, to taste
- 2 teaspoons olive oil
- 1/2 avocado, peeled, pitted, and mashed
- 1 tablespoon mayonnaise
- 3 tablespoons sour cream
- 1/2 teaspoon yellow mustard
- 1 teaspoon lemon juice
- 1 garlic clove, minced
- 1/4 teaspoon black pepper
- 1/4 teaspoon salt
- 1/4 teaspoon hot pepper sauce

Directions:
1. Start by preheating your Air Fryer to 360 degrees F. Spritz the Air Fryer basket with cooking oil.
2. Pat dry the fish fillets with a kitchen towel. Beat the egg in a shallow bowl. Add in the salt and olive oil.
3. Dip the fish into the egg mixture, making sure to coat thoroughly. Cook in the preheated Air Fryer approximately 12 minutes.
4. Meanwhile, make the avocado sauce by mixing the remaining ingredients in a bowl. Place in your refrigerator until ready to serve.
5. Serve the fish fillets with chilled avocado sauce on the side. Bon appétit!

420.Grilled Squid With Aromatic Sesame Oil

Servings:3
Cooking Time: 10 Minutes
Ingredients:
- 1 ½ pounds squid, cleaned
- 2 tablespoon toasted sesame oil
- Salt and pepper to taste

Directions:
1. Preheat the air fryer to 390°F.
2. Place the grill pan accessory in the air fryer.
3. Season the squid with sesame oil, salt and pepper.
4. Grill the squid for 10 minutes.

421.Spicy Salmon

Servings:2
Cooking Time: 11 Minutes
Ingredients:
- 1 teaspoon smoked paprika
- 1 teaspoon cayenne pepper
- 1 teaspoon onion powder
- 1 teaspoon garlic powder
- Salt and ground black pepper, as required
- 2 (6-ounces) (1½-inch thick) salmon fillets
- 2 teaspoons olive oil

Directions:
1. Add the spices in a bowl and mix well.
2. Drizzle the salmon fillets with oil and then, rub with the spice mixture.
3. Set the temperature of air fryer to 390 degrees F. Grease an air fryer basket.
4. Arrange salmon fillets into the prepared air fryer basket in a single layer.
5. Air fry for about 9-11 minutes.
6. Remove from air fryer and place the salmon fillets onto the serving plates.
7. Serve hot.

422.Soy-orange Flavored Squid

Servings:4
Cooking Time: 10 Minutes
Ingredients:
- ½ cup mirin
- 1 cup soy sauce
- 1/3 cup yuzu or orange juice, freshly squeezed
- 2 cups water
- 2 pounds squid body, cut into rings

Directions:
1. Place all ingredients in a Ziploc bag and allow the squid rings to marinate in the fridge for at least 2 hours.
2. Preheat the air fryer to 390°F.
3. Place the grill pan accessory in the air fryer.
4. Grill the squid rings for 10 minutes.
5. Meanwhile, pour the marinade over a sauce pan and allow to simmer for 10 minutes or until the sauce has reduced.
6. Baste the squid rings with the sauce before serving.

423.Lemon Butter Scallops

Servings: 1
Cooking Time: 30 Minutes
Ingredients:
- 1 lemon
- 1 lb. scallops
- ½ cup butter
- ¼ cup parsley, chopped

Directions:
1. Juice the lemon into a Ziploc bag.

2. Wash your scallops, dry them, and season to taste. Put them in the bag with the lemon juice. Refrigerate for an hour.
3. Remove the bag from the refrigerator and leave for about twenty minutes until it returns to room temperature. Transfer the scallops into a foil pan that is small enough to be placed inside the fryer.
4. Pre-heat the fryer at 400°F and put the rack inside.
5. Place the foil pan on the rack and cook for five minutes.
6. In the meantime, melt the butter in a saucepan over a medium heat. Zest the lemon over the saucepan, then add in the chopped parsley. Mix well.
7. Take care when removing the pan from the fryer. Transfer the contents to a plate and drizzle with the lemon-butter mixture. Serve hot.

424.Nutritious Salmon

Servings: 2
Cooking Time: 10 Minutes
Ingredients:
- 2 salmon fillets
- 1 tbsp olive oil
- 1/4 tsp ground cardamom
- 1/2 tsp paprika
- Salt

Directions:
1. Preheat the air fryer to 350 F.
2. Coat salmon fillets with olive oil and season with paprika, cardamom, and salt and place into the air fryer basket.
3. Cook salmon for 10-12 minutes. Turn halfway through.
4. Serve and enjoy.

425.Spicy Tuna Casserole

Servings: 4
Cooking Time: 20 Minutes
Ingredients:
- 5 eggs, beaten
- 1/2 chili pepper, deveined and finely minced
- 1 ½ tablespoons sour cream
- 1/3 teaspoon dried oregano
- 1/2 tablespoon sesame oil
- 1/3 cup yellow onions, chopped
- 2 cups canned tuna
- 1/2 bell pepper, deveined and chopped
- 1/3 teaspoon dried basil
- Fine sea salt and ground black pepper, to taste

Directions:

1. Warm sesame oil in a nonstick skillet that is preheated over a moderate flame. Then, sweat the onions and peppers for 4 minutes, or until they are just fragrant.
2. Add chopped canned tuna and stir until heated through.
3. Meanwhile, lightly grease a baking dish with a pan spray. Throw in sautéed tuna/pepper mix. Add the remaining ingredients in the order listed above.
4. Bake for 12 minutes at 325 degrees F. Eat warm garnished with Tabasco sauce if desired.

426.Fish Finger Sandwich

Servings:4
Cooking Time: 20 Minutes
Ingredients:
- 2 tbsp flour
- 10 capers
- 4 bread rolls
- 2 oz breadcrumbs
- 4 tbsp pesto sauce
- 4 lettuce leaves
- Salt and pepper, to taste

Directions:
1. Preheat air fryer to 370 F. Season the fillets with salt and pepper, and coat them with the flour; dip in the breadcrumbs. Arrange the fillets onto a baking mat and cook in the fryer for 10 to 15 minutes. Cut the bread rolls in half. Place a lettuce leaf on top of the bottom halves; put the fillets over. Spread a tbsp of pesto sauce on top of each fillet, and top with the remaining halves.

427.Coconut Calamari

Servings: 2
Cooking Time: 6 Minutes
Ingredients:
- 6 oz calamari, trimmed
- 2 tablespoons coconut flakes
- 1 egg, beaten
- 1 teaspoon Italian seasonings
- Cooking spray

Directions:
1. Slice the calamari into the rings and sprinkle them with Italian seasonings. Then transfer the calamari rings in the bowl with a beaten egg and stir them gently. After this, sprinkle the calamari rings with coconut flakes and shake well. Preheat the air fryer to 400F. Put the calamari rings in the air fryer basket and spray them with cooking spray. Cook the meal for 3 minutes. Then gently stir the calamari and cook them for 3 minutes more.

428.Cauliflower Bombs With Sweet & Sour Sauce

Servings: 4
Cooking Time: 25 Minutes
Ingredients:
- Cauliflower Bombs:
- 1/2 pound cauliflower
- 2 ounces Ricotta cheese
- 1/3 cup Swiss cheese
- 1 egg
- 1 tablespoon Italian seasoning mix
- Sweet & Sour Sauce:
- 1 red bell pepper, jarred
- 1 clove garlic, minced
- 1 teaspoon sherry vinegar
- 1 tablespoon tomato puree
- 2 tablespoons olive oil
- Salt and black pepper, to taste

Directions:
1. Blanch the cauliflower in salted boiling water about 3 to 4 minutes until al dente. Drain well and pulse in a food processor.
2. Add the remaining ingredients for the cauliflower bombs; mix to combine well.
3. Bake in the preheated Air Fryer at 375 degrees F for 16 minutes, shaking halfway through the cooking time.
4. In the meantime, pulse all ingredients for the sauce in your food processor until combined. Season to taste. Serve the cauliflower bombs with the Sweet & Sour Sauce on the side. Bon appétit!

429.Crunchy Asparagus With Mediterranean Aioli

Servings: 4
Cooking Time: 50 Minutes
Ingredients:
- Crunchy Asparagus:
- 2 eggs
- 3/4 cup breadcrumbs
- 2 tablespoons Parmesan cheese
- Sea salt and ground white pepper, to taste
- 1/2 pound asparagus, cleaned and trimmed
- Cooking spray
- Mediterranean Aioli:
- 4 garlic cloves, minced
- 4 tablespoons olive oil mayonnaise
- 1 tablespoons lemon juice, freshly squeezed

Directions:
1. Start by preheating your Air Fryer to 400 degrees F.
2. In a shallow bowl, thoroughly combine the eggs, breadcrumbs, Parmesan cheese, salt, and white pepper.

3. Dip the asparagus spears in the egg mixture; roll to coat well. Cook in the preheated Air Fryer for 5 to 6 minutes; work in two batches.
4. Place the garlic on a piece of aluminum foil and spritz with cooking spray. Wrap the garlic in the foil.
5. Cook in the preheated Air Fryer at 400 degrees for 12 minutes. Check the garlic, open the top of the foil and continue to cook for 10 minutes more.
6. Let it cool for 10 to 15 minutes; remove the cloves by squeezing them out of the skins; mash the garlic and add the mayo and fresh lemon juice; whisk until everything is well combined.
7. Serve the asparagus with the chilled aioli on the side. Bon appétit!

430.Lava Rice Bites

Servings:4
Cooking Time:20 Minutes
Ingredients:
- 3 cups cooked risotto
- 1/3 cup Parmesan cheese, grated
- 1 egg, beaten
- 3-ounce mozzarella cheese, cubed
- ¾ cup bread crumbs
- 1 tablespoon olive oil

Directions:
1. Preheat the Air fryer to 390 °F and grease an Air fryer basket.
2. Mix risotto, olive oil, Parmesan cheese and egg in a bowl until well combined.
3. Make small equal-sized balls from mixture and put a mozzarella cube in the center of each ball.
4. Smooth the risotto mixture with your finger to cover the cheese.
5. Place the bread crumbs in a shallow dish and coat the balls evenly in bread crumbs.
6. Transfer the balls into the Air fryer basket and cook for about 10 minutes.
7. Dish out and serve warm.

431.Sugar Snap Bacon

Servings: 4
Cooking Time: 10 Minutes
Ingredients:
- 3 cups sugar snap peas
- ½ tbsp lemon juice
- 2 tbsp bacon fat
- 2 tsp garlic
- ½ tsp red pepper flakes

Directions:
1. In a skillet, cook the bacon fat until it begins to smoke.
2. Add the garlic and cook for 2 minutes.

3. Add the sugar peas and lemon juice.
4. Cook for 2-3 minutes.
5. Remove and sprinkle with red pepper flakes and lemon zest.
6. Serve!

432.Cocktail Flanks

Servings: 4
Cooking Time: 45 Minutes
Ingredients:
- 1x 12-oz. package cocktail franks
- 1x 8-oz. can crescent rolls

Directions:
1. 1 Drain the cocktail franks and dry with paper towels.
2. 2 Unroll the crescent rolls and slice the dough into rectangular strips, roughly 1" by 1.5".
3. 3 Wrap the franks in the strips with the ends poking out. Leave in the freezer for 5 minutes.
4. 4 Pre-heat the Air Fryer to 330°F.
5. 5 Take the franks out of the freezer and put them in the cooking basket. Cook for 6 – 8 minutes.
6. 6 Reduce the heat to 390°F and cook for another 3 minutes or until a golden-brown color is achieved.

433.Chicken, Mushroom & Spinach Pizza

Servings: 4
Cooking Time: 25 Minutes
Ingredients:
- 10 ½ oz. minced chicken
- 1 tsp. garlic powder
- 1 tsp. black pepper
- 2 tbsp. tomato basil sauce
- 5 button mushrooms, sliced thinly
- Handful of spinach

Directions:
1. 1 Pre-heat your Air Fryer at 450°F.
2. 2 Add parchment paper onto your baking tray.
3. 3 In a large bowl add the chicken with the black pepper and garlic powder.
4. 4 Add one spoonful of the chicken mix onto your baking tray.
5. 5 Flatten them into 7-inch rounds.
6. 6 Bake in the Air Fryer for about 10 minutes.
7. 7 Take out off the Air Fryer and add the tomato basil sauce onto each round.
8. 8 Add the mushroom on top. Bake again for 5 minutes.
9. 9 Serve immediately.

434.Cheese Dill Mushrooms

Servings: 6
Cooking Time: 5 Minutes
Ingredients:
- 9 oz mushrooms, cut stems

- 1 tsp dried parsley
- 1 tsp dried dill
- 6 oz cheddar cheese, shredded
- 1 tbsp butter
- 1/2 tsp salt

Directions:
1. Chop mushrooms stem finely and place into the bowl.
2. Add parsley, dill, cheese, butter, and salt into the bowl and mix until well combined.
3. Preheat the air fryer to 400 F.
4. Stuff bowl mixture into the mushroom caps and place into the air fryer basket.
5. Cook mushrooms for 5 minutes.
6. Serve and enjoy.

435.Beef Jerky

Servings: 4
Cooking Time: 250 Minutes
Ingredients:
- ¼ tsp. garlic powder
- ¼ tsp. onion powder
- ¼ cup soy sauce
- 2 tsp. Worcestershire sauce
- 1 lb. flat iron steak, thinly sliced

Directions:
1. In a bowl, combine the garlic powder, onion powder, soy sauce, and Worcestershire sauce. Marinade the beef slices with the mixture in an airtight bag, shaking it well to ensure the beef is well-coated. Leave to marinate for at least two hours
2. Place the meat in the basket of your air fryer, making sure it is evenly spaced. Cook the beef slices in more than one batch if necessary.
3. Cook for four hours at 160°F.
4. Allow to cool before serving. You can keep the jerky in an airtight container for up to a week, if you can resist it that long.

436.Creamy Sausage Bites

Servings:6
Cooking Time: 9 Minutes
Ingredients:
- 1 cup ground pork sausages
- ¼ cup almond flour
- ¼ teaspoon baking powder
- ¼ teaspoon salt
- 1 teaspoon flax meal
- 1 egg, beaten
- ½ teaspoon dried dill
- 2 tablespoons heavy cream
- 1 teaspoon sunflower oil

Directions:
1. In the bowl mix up ground pork sausages, almond flour, baking powder, salt, flax meal, egg, dried dill, and heavy cream. Make the small balls from the mixture. Preheat the air

fryer to 400F. Place the sausage balls in the air fryer in one layer and cook them for 9 minutes. Flip the balls on another side after 5 minutes of cooking.

437.Flax Cheese Chips

Servings: 2
Cooking Time: 20 Minutes
Ingredients:
- 1 ½ cup cheddar cheese
- 4 tbsp ground flaxseed meal
- Seasonings of your choice

Directions:
1. Preheat your fryer to 425°F/220°C.
2. Spoon 2 tablespoons of cheddar cheese into a mound, onto a non-stick pad.
3. Spread out a pinch of flax seed on each chip.
4. Season and bake for 10-15 minutes.

438.Crispy Eggplant Slices

Servings:4
Cooking Time: 16 Minutes
Ingredients:
- 1 medium eggplant, peeled and cut into ½-inch round slices
- Salt, as required
- ½ cup all-purpose flour
- 2 eggs, beaten
- 1 cup Italian-style breadcrumbs
- ¼ cup olive oil

Directions:
1. In a colander, add the eggplant slices and sprinkle with salt.
2. Set aside for about 45 minutes and pat dry the eggplant slices.
3. Add the flour in a shallow dish.
4. Crack the eggs in a second dish and beat well.
5. In a third dish, mix together the oil, and breadcrumbs.
6. Coat each eggplant slice with flour, then dip into beaten eggs and finally, evenly coat with the breadcrumbs mixture.
7. Set the temperature of Air Fryer to 390 degrees F.
8. Arrange the eggplant slices in an Air Fryer basket in a single layer in 2 batches.
9. Air Fry for about 8 minutes.
10. Serve.

439.Honey Carrots

Servings: 4
Cooking Time: 20 Minutes
Ingredients:
- 1 tbsp. honey
- 3 cups baby carrots or carrots, cut into bite-size pieces
- 1 tbsp. olive oil
- Sea salt to taste
- Ground black pepper to taste

Directions:
1. In a bowl, combine the carrots, honey, and olive oil, coating the carrots completely. Sprinkle on some salt and ground black pepper.
2. Transfer the carrots to the Air Fryer and cook at 390°F for 12 minutes. Serve immediately.

440.Mushroom Bites

Servings: 6
Cooking Time: 12 Minutes
Ingredients:
- Salt and black pepper to the taste
- 1 and ¼ cups coconut flour
- 2 garlic clove, minced
- 2 tablespoons basil, minced
- ½ pound mushrooms, minced
- 1 egg, whisked

Directions:
1. In a bowl, mix all the ingredients except the cooking spray, stir well and shape medium balls out of this mix. Arrange the balls in your air fryer's basket, grease them with cooking spray and bake at 350 degrees F for 6 minutes on each side. Serve as an appetizer.

441.Rutabaga Fries

Servings: 8
Cooking Time: 18 Minutes
Ingredients:
- 1 lb rutabaga, cut into fries shape
- 2 tsp olive oil
- 1 tsp garlic powder
- 1/2 tsp chili pepper
- 1/2 tsp salt

Directions:
1. Add all ingredients into the large mixing bowl and toss to coat.
2. Preheat the air fryer to 365 F.
3. Transfer rutabaga fries into the air fryer basket and cook for 18 minutes. Shake 2-3 times.
4. Serve and enjoy.

442.Artichokes And Cream Cheese Dip

Servings: 6
Cooking Time: 25 Minutes
Ingredients:
- 2 teaspoons olive oil
- 2 spring onions, minced
- 1 pound artichoke hearts, steamed and chopped
- 2 garlic cloves, minced
- 6 ounces cream cheese, soft
- ½ cup almond milk
- 1 cup mozzarella, shredded

- A pinch of salt and black pepper

Directions:
1. Grease a baking pan that fits the air fryer with the oil and mix all the ingredients except the mozzarella inside. Sprinkle the cheese all over, introduce the pan in the air fryer and cook at 370 degrees F for 25 minutes. Divide into bowls and serve as a party dip.

443.Dad's Boozy Wings

Servings: 4
Cooking Time: 1 Hour 15 Minutes
Ingredients:
- 2 teaspoons coriander seeds
- 1 ½ tablespoons soy sauce
- 1/3 cup vermouth
- 3/4 pound chicken wings
- 1 ½ tablespoons each fish sauce
- 2 tablespoons melted butter
- 1 teaspoon seasoned salt
- Freshly ground black pepper, to taste

Directions:
1. Rub the chicken wings with the black pepper and seasoned salt; now, add the other ingredients.
2. Next, soak the chicken wings in this mixture for 55 minutes in the refrigerator.
3. Air-fry the chicken wings at 365 degrees F for 16 minutes or until warmed through. Bon appétit!

444.Oriental Spinach Samosa

Servings: 2
Cooking Time: 45 Minutes
Ingredients:
- ¾ cup boiled and blended spinach puree
- ¼ cup green peas
- ½ tsp. sesame seeds
- Ajwain, salt, chaat masala, chili powder to taste
- 2 tsp. olive oil
- 1 tsp. chopped fresh coriander leaves
- 1 tsp. garam masala
- ¼ cup boiled and cut potatoes
- ½ 1 cup flour
- ½ tsp. cooking soda

Directions:
1. In a bowl, combine the Ajwain, flour, cooking soda and salt to form a dough-like consistency. Pour in one teaspoon of the oil and the spinach puree. Continue to mix the dough, ensuring it is smooth.
2. Refrigerate for 20 minutes. Add another teaspoon of oil to a saucepan and sauté the potatoes and peas for 5 minutes.
3. Stir in the sesame seeds, coriander, and any other spices you desire.

4. Use your hands to shape equal sized amounts of the dough into small balls. Mold these balls into cone-shapes.
5. Fill each cone with the potatoes and peas mixture and seal.
6. Pre-heat your Air Fryer to 390°F.
7. Put the samosas in the basket and cook for 10 minutes.
8. Serve the samosas with the sauce of your choice.

445.Crunchy Roasted Pepitas

Servings: 4
Cooking Time: 20 Minutes
Ingredients:
- 2 cups fresh pumpkin seeds with shells
- 1 tablespoon olive oil
- 1 teaspoon sea salt
- 1 teaspoon ground coriander
- 1 teaspoon cayenne pepper

Directions:
1. Toss the pumpkin seeds with the olive oil.
2. Spread in an even layer in the Air Fryer basket; roast the seeds at 350 degrees F for 15 minutes, shaking the basket every 5 minutes.
3. Immediately toss the seeds with the salt, coriander, salt, and cayenne pepper. Enjoy!

446.Mexican-style Corn On The Cob With Bacon

Servings: 4
Cooking Time: 20 Minutes
Ingredients:
- 2 slices bacon
- 4 ears fresh corn, shucked and cut into halves
- 1 avocado, pitted, peeled and mashed
- 1 teaspoon ancho chili powder
- 2 garlic cloves
- 2 tablespoons cilantro, chopped
- 1 teaspoon lime juice
- Salt and black pepper, to taste

Directions:
1. Start by preheating your Air Fryer to 400 degrees F. Cook the bacon for 6 to 7 minutes; chop into small chunks and reserve.
2. Spritz the corn with cooking spray. Cook at 395 degrees F for 8 minutes, turning them over halfway through the cooking time.
3. Mix the reserved bacon with the remaining ingredients. Spoon the bacon mixture over the corn on the cob and serve immediately. Bon appétit!

447.Barbecue Little Smokies

Servings: 6
Cooking Time: 20 Minutes
Ingredients:

- 1 pound beef cocktail wieners
- 10 ounces barbecue sauce

Directions:
1. Start by preheating your Air Fryer to 380 degrees F.
2. Prick holes into your sausages using a fork and transfer them to the baking pan.
3. Cook for 13 minutes. Spoon the barbecue sauce into the pan and cook an additional 2 minutes.
4. Serve with toothpicks. Bon appétit!

448.Summer Meatball Skewers

Servings: 6
Cooking Time: 20 Minutes
Ingredients:
- 1/2 pound ground pork
- 1/2 pound ground beef
- 1 teaspoon dried onion flakes
- 1 teaspoon fresh garlic, minced
- 1 teaspoon dried parsley flakes
- Salt and black pepper, to taste
- 1 red pepper, 1-inch pieces
- 1 cup pearl onions
- 1/2 cup barbecue sauce

Directions:
1. Mix the ground meat with the onion flakes, garlic, parsley flakes, salt, and black pepper. Shape the mixture into 1-inch balls.
2. Thread the meatballs, pearl onions, and peppers alternately onto skewers.
3. Microwave the barbecue sauce for 10 seconds.
4. Cook in the preheated Air Fryer at 380 degrees for 5 minutes. Turn the skewers over halfway through the cooking time. Brush with the sauce and cook for a further 5 minutes. Work in batches.
5. Serve with the remaining barbecue sauce and enjoy!

449.Broccoli Cheese Nuggets

Servings: 4
Cooking Time: 15 Minutes
Ingredients:
- 1/4 cup almond flour
- 2 cups broccoli florets, cooked until soft
- 1 cup cheddar cheese, shredded
- 2 egg whites
- 1/8 tsp salt

Directions:
1. Preheat the air fryer to 325 F.
2. Spray air fryer basket with cooking spray.
3. Add cooked broccoli into the bowl and using masher mash broccoli into the small pieces.
4. Add remaining ingredients to the bowl and mix well to combine.

5. Make small nuggets from broccoli mixture and place into the air fryer basket.
6. Cook broccoli nuggets for 15 minutes. Turn halfway through.
7. Serve and enjoy.

450.Spicy Dip

Servings: 6
Cooking Time: 5 Minutes
Ingredients:
- 12 oz hot peppers, chopped
- 1 1/2 cups apple cider vinegar
- Pepper
- Salt

Directions:
1. Add all ingredients into the air fryer baking dish and stir well.
2. Place dish in the air fryer and cook at 380 F for 5 minutes.
3. Transfer pepper mixture into the blender and blend until smooth.
4. Serve and enjoy.

451.Roasted Almonds

Servings: 8
Cooking Time: 8 Minutes
Ingredients:
- 2 cups almonds
- 1/4 tsp pepper
- 1 tsp paprika
- 1 tbsp garlic powder
- 1 tbsp soy sauce

Directions:
1. Add pepper, paprika, garlic powder, and soy sauce in a bowl and stir well.
2. Add almonds and stir to coat.
3. Spray air fryer basket with cooking spray.
4. Add almonds in air fryer basket and cook for 6-8 minutes at 320 F. Shake basket after every 2 minutes.
5. Serve and enjoy.

452.Cheesy Spinach Triangles

Servings: 6
Cooking Time: 20 Minutes
Ingredients:
- 3 cups mozzarella, shredded
- 4 tablespoons coconut flour
- ½ cup almond flour
- 2 eggs, whisked
- A pinch of salt and black pepper
- 6 ounces spinach, chopped
- ¼ cup parmesan, grated
- 4 ounces cream cheese, soft
- 2 tablespoons ghee, melted

Directions:
1. In a bowl, mix the mozzarella with coconut and almond flour, eggs, salt and pepper, stir well until you obtain a dough and roll it well

114

on a parchment paper. Cut into triangles and leave them aside for now. In a bowl, mix the spinach with parmesan, cream cheese, salt and pepper and stir really well. Divide this into the center of each dough triangle, roll and seal the edges. Brush the rolls with the ghee, place them in your air fryer's basket and cook at 360 degrees F for 20 minutes. Serve as an appetizer.

453.Coconut Cheese Sticks

Servings:4
Cooking Time: 4 Minutes
Ingredients:
- 1 egg, beaten
- 4 tablespoons coconut flakes
- 1 teaspoon ground paprika
- 6 oz Provolone cheese
- Cooking spray

Directions:
1. Cut the cheese into sticks. Then dip every cheese stick in the beaten egg. After this, mix up coconut flakes and ground paprika. Coat the cheese sticks in the coconut mixture. Preheat the air fryer to 400F. Put the cheese sticks in the air fryer and spray them with cooking spray. Cook the meal for 2 minutes from each side. Cool them well before serving.

454.Parmesan Zucchini Bites

Servings: 6
Cooking Time: 10 Minutes
Ingredients:
- 1 egg, lightly beaten
- 4 zucchinis, grated and squeeze out all liquid
- 1 cup shredded coconut
- 1 tsp Italian seasoning
- 1/2 cup parmesan cheese, grated

Directions:
1. Add all ingredients into the bowl and mix until well combined.
2. Spray air fryer basket with cooking spray.
3. Make small balls from zucchini mixture and place into the air fryer basket and cook at 400 F for 10 minutes.
4. Serve and enjoy.

455.Mozzarella Sticks

Servings: 4
Cooking Time: 60 Minutes
Ingredients:
- 6 x 1-oz. mozzarella string cheese sticks
- 1 tsp. dried parsley
- ½ oz. pork rinds, finely ground
- ½ cup parmesan cheese, grated
- 2 eggs

Directions:

1. Halve the mozzarella sticks and freeze for forty-five minutes. Optionally you can leave them longer and place in a Ziploc bag to prevent them from becoming freezer burned.
2. In a small bowl, combine the dried parsley, pork rinds, and parmesan cheese.
3. In a separate bowl, beat the eggs with a fork.
4. Take a frozen mozzarella stick and dip it into the eggs, then into the pork rind mixture, making sure to coat it all over. Proceed with the rest of the cheese sticks, placing each coated stick in the basket of your air fryer.
5. Cook at 400°F for ten minutes, until they are golden brown.
6. Serve hot, with some homemade marinara sauce if desired.

456.Coconut Salmon Bites

Servings: 12
Cooking Time: 10 Minutes
Ingredients:
- 2 avocados, peeled, pitted and mashed
- 4 ounces smoked salmon, skinless, boneless and chopped
- 2 tablespoons coconut cream
- 1 teaspoon avocado oil
- 1 teaspoon dill, chopped
- A pinch of salt and black pepper

Directions:
1. In a bowl, mix all the ingredients, stir well and shape medium balls out of this mix. Place them in your air fryer's basket and cook at 350 degrees F for 10 minutes. Serve as an appetizer.

457.Zucchini Chips

Servings: 2
Cooking Time: 30 Minutes
Ingredients:
- 3 medium zucchini, sliced
- 1 tsp. parsley, chopped
- 3 tbsp. parmesan cheese, grated
- Pepper to taste
- Salt to taste

Directions:
1. Pre-heat the Air Fryer to 425°F.
2. Put the sliced zucchini on a sheet of baking paper and spritz with cooking spray.
3. Combine the cheese, pepper, parsley, and salt. Use this mixture to sprinkle over the zucchini.
4. Transfer to the Air Fryer and cook for 25 minutes, ensuring the zucchini slices have crisped up nicely before serving.

458.Lemon Tofu

Servings: 4

Cooking Time: 15 Minutes
Ingredients:
- 1 lb tofu, drained and pressed
- 1 tbsp arrowroot powder
- 1 tbsp tamari
- For sauce:
- 2 tsp arrowroot powder
- 2 tbsp erythritol
- 1/2 cup water
- 1/3 cup lemon juice
- 1 tsp lemon zest

Directions:
1. Cut tofu into cubes. Add tofu and tamari into the zip-lock bag and shake well.
2. Add 1 tbsp arrowroot into the bag and shake well to coat the tofu. Set aside for 15 minutes.
3. Meanwhile, in a bowl, mix together all sauce ingredients and set aside.
4. Spray air fryer basket with cooking spray.
5. Add tofu into the air fryer basket and cook at 390 F for 10 minutes. Shake halfway through.
6. Add cooked tofu and sauce mixture into the pan and cook over medium-high heat for 3-5 minutes.
7. Serve and enjoy.

459.Bacon-wrapped Shrimp

Servings:6
Cooking Time:7 Minutes
Ingredients:
- 1 pound bacon, sliced thinly
- 1 pound shrimp, peeled and deveined
- Salt, to taste

Directions:
1. Preheat the Air fryer to 390 °F and grease an Air fryer basket.
2. Wrap 1 shrimp with a bacon slices, covering completely.
3. Repeat with the remaining shrimp and bacon slices.
4. Arrange the bacon wrapped shrimps in a baking dish and freeze for about 15 minutes.
5. Place the shrimps in an Air fryer basket and cook for about 7 minutes.
6. Dish out and serve warm.

460.Cod Nuggets

Servings:4
Cooking Time:10 Minutes
Ingredients:
- 1 cup all-purpose flour
- 2 eggs
- ¾ cup breadcrumbs
- 1 pound cod, cut into 1x2½-inch strips
- A pinch of salt
- 2 tablespoons olive oil

Directions:
1. Preheat the Air fryer to 390 °F and grease an Air fryer basket.
2. Place flour in a shallow dish and whisk the eggs in a second dish.
3. Place breadcrumbs, salt, and olive oil in a third shallow dish.
4. Coat the cod strips evenly in flour and dip in the eggs.
5. Roll into the breadcrumbs evenly and arrange the nuggets in an Air fryer basket.
6. Cook for about 10 minutes and dish out to serve warm.

461.Hot Cheesy Dip

Servings: 6
Cooking Time: 12 Minutes
Ingredients:
- 12 ounces coconut cream
- 2 teaspoons keto hot sauce
- 8 ounces cheddar cheese, grated

Directions:
1. In ramekin, mix the cream with hot sauce and cheese and whisk. Put the ramekin in the fryer and cook at 390 degrees F for 12 minutes. Whisk, divide into bowls and serve as a dip.

462.Sweet Potato Wedges

Servings: 2
Cooking Time: 25 Minutes
Ingredients:
- 2 large sweet potatoes, cut into wedges
- 1 tbsp. olive oil
- 1 tsp. chili powder
- 1 tsp. mustard powder
- 1 tsp. cumin
- 1 tbsp. Mexican seasoning
- Pepper to taste
- Salt to taste

Directions:
1. Pre-heat the Air Fryer at 350°F.
2. Place all of the ingredients into a bowl and combine well to coat the sweet potatoes entirely.
3. Place the wedges in the Air Fryer basket and air fry for 20 minutes, shaking the basket at 5-minute intervals.

463.Air Fryer Plantains

Servings:4
Cooking Time:10 Minutes
Ingredients:
- 2 ripe plantains
- 2 teaspoons avocado oil
- 1/8 teaspoon salt

Directions:
1. Preheat the Air fryer to 400 °F and grease an Air fryer basket.

2. Mix the plantains with avocado oil and salt in a bowl.
3. Arrange the coated plantains in the Air fryer basket and cook for about 10 minutes.
4. Dish out in a bowl and serve immediately.

464.Artichoke Dip

Servings: 6
Cooking Time: 24 Minutes
Ingredients:
- 15 oz artichoke hearts, drained
- 1 tsp Worcestershire sauce
- 3 cups arugula, chopped
- 1 cup cheddar cheese, shredded
- 1 tbsp onion, minced
- 1/2 cup mayonnaise

Directions:
1. Preheat the air fryer to 325 F.
2. Add all ingredients into the blender and blend until smooth.
3. Pour artichoke mixture into air fryer baking dish and place into the air fryer basket.
4. Cook dip for 24 minutes.
5. Serve with vegetables and enjoy.

465.Bruschetta With Fresh Tomato And Basil

Servings: 3
Cooking Time: 15 Minutes
Ingredients:
- 1/2 Italian bread, sliced
- 2 garlic cloves, peeled
- 2 tablespoons extra-virgin olive oil
- 2 ripe tomatoes, chopped
- 1 teaspoon dried oregano
- Salt, to taste
- 8 fresh basil leaves, roughly chopped

Directions:
1. Place the bread slices on the lightly greased Air Fryer grill pan. Bake at 370 degrees F for 3 minutes.
2. Cut a clove of garlic in half and rub over one side of the toast; brush with olive oil. Add the chopped tomatoes. Sprinkle with oregano and salt.
3. Increase the temperature to 380 degrees F. Cook in the preheated Air Fryer for 3 minutes more.
4. Garnish with fresh basil and serve. Bon appétit!

466.Paprika Chips

Servings: 4
Cooking Time: 5 Minutes
Ingredients:
- 8 ounces cheddar cheese, shredded
- 1 teaspoon sweet paprika

Directions:

1. Divide the cheese in small heaps in a pan that fits the air fryer, sprinkle the paprika on top, introduce the pan in the machine and cook at 400 degrees F for 5 minutes. Cool the chips down and serve them.

467.Thai Chili Chicken Wings

Servings: 6
Cooking Time: 16 Minutes
Ingredients:
- 1/2 lb chicken wings
- 1 tsp paprika
- 1/3 cup Thai chili sauce
- 2 tsp garlic powder
- 2 tsp ginger powder
- 2 1/2 tbsp dry sherry
- Pepper
- Salt

Directions:
1. Toss chicken wings with dry sherry, paprika, garlic powder, ginger, powder, pepper, and salt.
2. Add chicken wings into the air fryer basket and cook at 365 F for 16 minutes.
3. Serve with Thai chili sauce and enjoy.

468.Paprika Bacon Shrimp

Servings: 10
Cooking Time: 45 Minutes
Ingredients:
- 1 ¼ pounds shrimp, peeled and deveined
- 1 teaspoon paprika
- 1/2 teaspoon ground black pepper
- 1/2 teaspoon red pepper flakes, crushed
- 1 tablespoon salt
- 1 teaspoon chili powder
- 1 tablespoon shallot powder
- 1/4 teaspoon cumin powder
- 1 ¼ pounds thin bacon slices

Directions:
1. Toss the shrimps with all the seasoning until they are coated well.
2. Next, wrap a slice of bacon around the shrimps, securing with a toothpick; repeat with the remaining ingredients; chill for 30 minutes.
3. Air-fry them at 360 degrees F for 7 to 8 minutes, working in batches. Serve with cocktail sticks if desired. Enjoy!

469.Parmigiana Tomato Chips

Servings: 4
Cooking Time: 15 Minutes
Ingredients:
- 4 Roma tomatoes, sliced
- 2 tablespoons olive oil
- Sea salt and white pepper, to taste
- 1 teaspoon Italian seasoning mix
- 1/2 cup Parmesan cheese, grated

Directions:
1. Start by preheating your Air Fryer to 350 degrees F. Generously grease the Air Fryer basket with nonstick cooking oil.
2. Toss the sliced tomatoes with the remaining ingredients. Transfer them to the cooking basket without overlapping.
3. Cook in the preheated Air Fryer for 5 minutes. Shake the cooking basket and cook an additional 5 minutes. Work in batches.
4. Serve with Mediterranean aioli for dipping, if desired. Bon appétit!

470.Stuffed Mushrooms

Servings: 4
Cooking Time: 25 Minutes
Ingredients:
- 6 small mushrooms
- 1 tbsp. onion, peeled and diced
- 1 tbsp. friendly bread crumbs
- 1 tbsp. olive oil
- 1 tsp. garlic, pureed
- 1 tsp. parsley
- Salt and pepper to taste

Directions:
1. 1 Combine the bread crumbs, oil, onion, parsley, salt, pepper and garlic in a bowl.
2. 2 Scoop the stalks out of the mushrooms and spoon equal portions of the crumb mixture in the caps. Transfer to the Air Fryer and cook for 10 minutes at 350°F.
3. 3 Serve with mayo dip if desired.

471.Cheesy Eggplant Crisps

Servings: 4
Cooking Time: 45 Minutes
Ingredients:
- 1 eggplant, peeled and thinly sliced
- Salt
- 1/2 cup almond meal
- 1/4 cup canola oil
- 1/2 cup water
- 1 teaspoon garlic powder
- 1/2 teaspoon dried dill weed
- 1/2 teaspoon ground black pepper, to taste

Directions:
1. Salt the eggplant slices and let them stay for about 30 minutes. Squeeze the eggplant slices and rinse them under cold running water.
2. Toss the eggplant slices with the other ingredients. Cook at 390 degrees F for 13 minutes, working in batches.
3. Serve with a sauce for dipping. Bon appétit!

472.Polenta Sticks

Servings:4
Cooking Time: 6 Minutes
Ingredients:
- 2½ cups cooked polenta
- Salt, as required
- ¼ cup Parmesan cheese, shredded

Directions:
1. Add the polenta evenly into a greased baking dish and with the back of a spoon, smooth the top surface.
2. Cover the baking dish and refrigerate for about 1 hour or until set.
3. Remove from the refrigerator and cut down the polenta into the desired size slices.
4. Set the temperature of Air Fryer to 350 degrees F. Grease a baking dish.
5. Arrange the polenta sticks into the prepared baking dish in a single layer and sprinkle with salt.
6. Place the baking dish into an Air Fryer basket.
7. Air Fry for about 5-6 minutes.
8. Top with the cheese and serve.

473.Basil Pork Bites

Servings: 6
Cooking Time: 25 Minutes
Ingredients:
- 2 pounds pork belly, cut into strips
- 2 tablespoons olive oil
- 2 teaspoons fennel seeds
- A pinch of salt and black pepper
- A pinch of basil, dried

Directions:
1. In a bowl, mix all the ingredients, toss and put the pork strips in your air fryer's basket and cook at 425 degrees F for 25 minutes. Divide into bowls and serve as a snack.

474.Chinese-style Glazed Baby Carrots

Servings: 6
Cooking Time: 20 Minutes
Ingredients:
- 1 pound baby carrots
- 2 tablespoons sesame oil
- 1/2 teaspoon Szechuan pepper
- 1 teaspoon Wuxiang powder (Five-spice powder)
- 3-4 drops liquid Stevia
- 1 large garlic clove, crushed
- 1 (1-inch) piece fresh ginger root, peeled and grated
- 2 tablespoons tamari sauce

Directions:
1. Start by preheating your Air Fryer to 380 degrees F.
2. Toss all ingredients together and place them in the Air Fryer basket.
3. Cook for 15 minutes, shaking the basket halfway through the cooking time. Enjoy!

475.Brussels Sprout Crisps

Servings: 4
Cooking Time: 20 Minutes
Ingredients:
- 1 pound Brussels sprouts, ends and yellow leaves removed and halved lengthwise
- Salt and black pepper, to taste
- 1 tablespoon toasted sesame oil
- 1 teaspoon fennel seeds
- Chopped fresh parsley, for garnish

Directions:
1. Place the Brussels sprouts, salt, pepper, sesame oil, and fennel seeds in a resealable plastic bag. Seal the bag and shake to coat.
2. Air-fry at 380 degrees F for 15 minutes or until tender. Make sure to flip them over halfway through the cooking time.
3. Serve sprinkled with fresh parsley. Bon appétit!

476.Crispy Kale Chips

Servings:4
Cooking Time:3 Minutes
Ingredients:
- 1 head fresh kale, stems and ribs removed and cut into 1½ inch pieces
- 1 tablespoon olive oil
- 1 teaspoon soy sauce

Directions:
1. Preheat the Air fryer to 380 °F and grease an Air fryer basket.
2. Mix together all the ingredients in a bowl until well combined.
3. Arrange the kale in the Air fryer basket and cook for about 3 minutes, flipping in between.
4. Dish out and serve warm.

477.Crunchy Spicy Chickpeas

Servings:4
Cooking Time:20 Minutes
Ingredients:
- 1 (15-ounce) can chickpeas, rinsed and drained
- 1 tablespoon olive oil
- ½ teaspoon ground cumin
- ½ teaspoon cayenne pepper
- ½ teaspoon smoked paprika
- Salt, taste

Directions:
1. Preheat the Air fryer to 390 °F and grease an Air fryer basket.
2. Mix together all the ingredients in a bowl and toss to coat well.
3. Place half of the chickpeas in the Air fryer basket and cook for about 10 minutes.
4. Repeat with the remaining chickpeas and dish out to serve warm.

478.Fennel And Parmesan Dip

Servings: 8
Cooking Time: 25 Minutes
Ingredients:
- 3 tablespoons olive oil
- 3 fennel bulbs, trimmed and cut into wedges
- A pinch of salt and black pepper
- 4 garlic cloves, minced
- ¼ cup parmesan, grated

Directions:
1. Put the fennel in the air fryer's basket and bake at 380 degrees F for 20 minutes. In a blender, combine the roasted fennel with the rest of the ingredients and pulse well. Put the spread in a ramekin, introduce it in the fryer and cook at 380 degrees F for 5 minutes more. Divide into bowls and serve as a dip.

479.Mix Nuts

Servings: 8
Cooking Time: 15 Minutes
Ingredients:
- 2 cup mixed nuts
- 1 tsp. chipotle chili powder
- 1 tsp. ground cumin
- 1 tbsp. butter, melted
- 1 tsp. pepper
- 1 tsp. salt

Directions:
1. In a bowl, combine all of the ingredients, coating the nuts well.
2. Set your Air Fryer to 350°F and allow to heat for 5 minutes.
3. Place the mixed nuts in the fryer basket and roast for 4 minutes, shaking the basket halfway through the cooking time.

480.Cheese Dip

Servings: 10
Cooking Time: 10 Minutes
Ingredients:
- 1 pound mozzarella, shredded
- 1 tablespoon thyme, chopped
- 6 garlic cloves, minced
- 3 tablespoons olive oil
- 1 teaspoon rosemary, chopped
- A pinch of salt and black pepper

Directions:
1. In a pan that fits your air fryer, mix all the ingredients, whisk really well, introduce in the air fryer and cook at 370 degrees F for 10 minutes. Divide into bowls and serve right away.

481.Mascarpone Duck Wraps

Servings:6
Cooking Time: 6 Minutes

Ingredients:

- 1-pound duck fillet, boiled
- 1 tablespoon mascarpone
- 1 teaspoon chili flakes
- 1 teaspoon onion powder
- 6 wonton wraps
- 1 egg yolk, whisked
- Cooking spray

Directions:

1. Shred the boiled duck fillet and mix it up with mascarpone, chili flakes, and onion powder. After this, fill the wonton wraps with the duck mixture and roll them in the shape of pies. Brush the duck pies with the egg yolk. Preheat the air fryer to 385F. Put the duck pies in the air fryer and spray them with the cooking spray. Cook the snack for 3 minutes from each side.

482.Avocado Fries

Servings: 4
Cooking Time: 20 Minutes
Ingredients:

- ½ cup panko
- ½ tsp. salt
- 1 whole avocado
- 1 oz. aquafaba

Directions:

1. In a shallow bowl, stir together the panko and salt.
2. In a separate shallow bowl, add the aquafaba.
3. Dip the avocado slices into the aquafaba, before coating each one in the panko.
4. Place the slices in your Air Fryer basket, taking care not to overlap any. Air fry for 10 minutes at 390°F.

483.Coconut Chicken Wings

Servings:4
Cooking Time: 10 Minutes
Ingredients:

- 4 chicken wings
- 1 teaspoon keto tomato sauce
- 2 tablespoons coconut cream
- 1 teaspoon nut oil
- ¼ teaspoon salt

Directions:

1. Sprinkle the chicken wings with tomato sauce, nut oil, coconut cream, and salt. Massage the chicken wings with the help of the fingertips and put in the air fryer. Cook the chicken at 400f for 6 minutes. Then flip the wings on another side and cook for 4 minutes more.

484.Shrimp Dip

Servings: 4
Cooking Time: 20 Minutes

Ingredients:

- 1 pound shrimp, peeled, deveined and minced
- 2 tablespoons ghee, melted
- ¼ pound mushrooms, minced
- ½ cup mozzarella, shredded
- 4 garlic cloves, minced
- 1 tablespoon parsley, chopped
- Salt and black pepper to the taste

Directions:

1. In a bowl, mix all the ingredients, stir well, divide into small ramekins and place them in your air fryer's basket. Cook at 360 degrees F for 20 minutes and serve as a party dip.

485.Old-fashioned Onion Rings

Servings:4
Cooking Time:10 Minutes
Ingredients:

- 1 large onion, cut into rings
- 1¼ cups all-purpose flour
- 1 cup milk
- 1 egg
- ¾ cup dry bread crumbs
- Salt, to taste

Directions:

1. Preheat the Air fryer to 360 °F and grease the Air fryer basket.
2. Mix together flour and salt in a dish.
3. Whisk egg with milk in a second dish until well mixed.
4. Place the breadcrumbs in a third dish.
5. Coat the onion rings with the flour mixture and dip into the egg mixture.
6. Lastly dredge in the breadcrumbs and transfer the onion rings in the Air fryer basket.
7. Cook for about 10 minutes and dish out to serve warm.

486.Cumin Pork Sticks

Servings:4
Cooking Time: 12 Minutes
Ingredients:

- 2 eggs, beaten
- 4 tablespoons flax meal
- ½ teaspoon chili powder
- ¼ teaspoon ground cumin
- 8 oz pork loin
- 1 teaspoon sunflower oil

Directions:

1. Cut the pork loin into the sticks and sprinkle with chili powder and cumin powder. Then dip the pork sticks in the eggs and coat in the flax meal. Place the meat in the air fryer and sprinkle with sunflower oil. Cook the snack at 400F for 6 minutes. Then

flip the pork sticks on another side and cook for 6 minutes more.

487.Chili Pepper Kale Chips

Servings: 14
Cooking Time: 8 Minutes
Ingredients:
- 1 lb kale, wash, dry and cut into pieces
- 2 tsp olive oil
- 1 tsp chili pepper
- 1 tsp salt

Directions:
1. Preheat the air fryer to 370 F.
2. Add kale pieces into the air fryer basket. Drizzle kale with oil.
3. Sprinkle chili pepper and salt over the kale and toss well.
4. Cook kale for 5 minutes. Shake well and cook for 3 minutes more.
5. Serve and enjoy.

488.Saucy Chicken Wings With Sage

Servings: 4
Cooking Time: 1 Hour 10 Minutes

Ingredients:
- 1/3 cup almond flour
- 1/3 cup buttermilk
- 1 ½ pound chicken wings
- 1 tablespoon tamari sauce
- 1/3 teaspoon fresh sage
- 1 teaspoon mustard seeds
- 1/2 teaspoon garlic paste
- 1/2 teaspoon freshly ground mixed peppercorns
- 1/2 teaspoon seasoned salt
- 2 teaspoons fresh basil

Directions:
1. Place the seasonings along with the garlic paste, chicken wings, buttermilk, and tamari sauce in a large-sized mixing dish. Let it soak about 55 minutes; drain the wings.
2. Dredge the wings in the almond flour and transfer them to the Air Fryer cooking basket.
3. Air-fry for 16 minutes at 355 degrees F. Serve on a nice serving platter with a dressing on the side. Bon appétit!

DESSERTS RECIPES

489.Apple Cake

Servings:6
Cooking Time:45 Minutes
Ingredients:
- 1 cup all-purpose flour
- ½ teaspoon baking soda
- 1 egg
- 2 cups apples, peeled, cored and chopped
- 1/3 cup brown sugar
- 1 teaspoon ground nutmeg
- 1 teaspoon ground cinnamon
- Salt, to taste
- 5 tablespoons plus 1 teaspoon vegetable oil
- ¾ teaspoon vanilla extract

Directions:
1. Preheat the Air fryer to 355 °F and grease a baking pan lightly.
2. Mix flour, sugar, spices, baking soda and salt in a bowl until well combined.
3. Whisk egg with oil and vanilla extract in another bowl.
4. Stir in the flour mixture slowly and fold in the apples.
5. Pour this mixture into the baking pan and cover with the foil paper.
6. Transfer the baking pan into the Air fryer and cook for about 40 minutes.
7. Remove the foil and cook for 5 more minutes.
8. Allow to cool completely and cut into slices to serve.

490.White Chocolate Rum Molten Cake

Servings: 4
Cooking Time: 20 Minutes
Ingredients:
- 2 ½ ounces butter, at room temperature
- 3 ounces white chocolate
- 2 eggs, beaten
- 1/2 cup powdered sugar
- 1/3 cup self-rising flour
- 1 teaspoon rum extract
- 1 teaspoon vanilla extract

Directions:
1. Begin by preheating your Air Fryer to 370 degrees F. Spritz the sides and bottom of four ramekins with cooking spray.
2. Melt the butter and white chocolate in a microwave-safe bowl. Mix the eggs and sugar until frothy.
3. Pour the butter/chocolate mixture into the egg mixture. Stir in the flour, rum extract, and vanilla extract. Mix until everything is well incorporated.
4. Scrape the batter into the prepared ramekins. Bake in the preheated Air Fryer for 9 to 11 minutes.
5. Let stand for 2 to 3 minutes. Invert on a plate while warm and serve. Bon appétit!

491.Banana-choco Brownies

Servings:12
Cooking Time: 30 Minutes
Ingredients:
- 2 cups almond flour
- 2 teaspoons baking powder
- ½ teaspoon baking powder
- ½ teaspoon baking soda
- ½ teaspoon salt
- 1 over-ripe banana
- 3 large eggs
- ½ teaspoon stevia powder
- ¼ cup coconut oil
- 1 tablespoon vinegar
- 1/3 cup almond flour
- 1/3 cup cocoa powder

Directions:
1. Preheat the air fryer for 5 minutes.
2. Combine all ingredients in a food processor and pulse until well-combined.
3. Pour into a baking dish that will fit in the air fryer.
4. Place in the air fryer basket and cook for 30 minutes at 350°F or if a toothpick inserted in the middle comes out clean.

492.Cream Doughnuts

Servings:8
Cooking Time:16 Minutes
Ingredients:
- 4 tablespoons butter, softened and divided
- 2 egg yolks
- 2¼ cups plain flour
- 1½ teaspoons baking powder
- ½ cup sugar
- 1 teaspoon salt
- ½ cup sour cream
- ½ cup heavy cream

Directions:
1. Preheat the Air fryer to 355 °F and grease an Air fryer basket lightly.
2. Sift together flour, baking powder and salt in a large bowl.
3. Add sugar and cold butter and mix until a coarse crumb is formed.
4. Stir in the egg yolks, ½ of the sour cream and 1/3 of the flour mixture and mix until a dough is formed.
5. Add remaining sour cream and 1/3 of the flour mixture and mix until well combined.

6. Stir in the remaining flour mixture and combine well.
7. Roll the dough into ½ inch thickness onto a floured surface and cut into donuts with a donut cutter.
8. Coat butter on both sides of the donuts and arrange in the Air fryer basket.
9. Cook for about 8 minutes until golden and top with heavy cream to serve.

493.Cheesy Orange Fritters

Servings:8
Cooking Time:15 Minutes
Ingredients:
- 1 ½ tablespoons orange juice
- 3/4 pound cream cheese, at room temperature
- 1 teaspoon freshly grated orange rind
- 3/4 cup whole milk
- 1 teaspoon vanilla extract
- 1 ¼ cups all-purpose flour
- 1/3 cup white sugar
- 1/3 teaspoon ground cinnamon
- 1/2 teaspoon ground anise star

Directions:
1. Thoroughly combine all ingredients in a mixing dish.
2. Next step, drop a teaspoonful of the mixture into the air fryer cooking basket; air-fry for 4 minutes at 340 degrees F.
3. Dust with icing sugar, if desired. Bon appétit!

494.English-style Scones With Raisins

Servings: 6
Cooking Time: 20 Minutes
Ingredients:
- 1 ½ cups all-purpose flour
- 1/4 cup brown sugar
- 1 teaspoon baking powder
- 1/4 teaspoon sea salt
- 1/4 teaspoon ground cloves
- 1/2 teaspoon ground cardamom
- 1 teaspoon ground cinnamon
- 1/2 cup raisins
- 6 tablespoons butter, cooled and sliced
- 1/2 cup double cream
- 2 eggs, lightly whisked
- 1/2 teaspoon vanilla essence

Directions:
1. In a mixing bowl, thoroughly combine the flour, sugar, baking powder, salt, cloves, cardamom cinnamon, and raisins. Mix until everything is combined well.
2. Add the butter and mix again.
3. In another mixing bowl, combine the double cream with the eggs and vanilla; beat until creamy and smooth.
4. Stir the wet ingredients into the dry mixture. Roll your dough out into a circle and cut into wedges.
5. Bake in the preheated Air Fryer at 360 degrees for 11 minutes, rotating the pan halfway through the cooking time. Bon appétit!

495.Easy Chocolate Brownies

Servings: 8
Cooking Time: 30 Minutes
Ingredients:
- 1 stick butter, melted
- 1/2 cup caster sugar
- 1/2 cup white sugar
- 1 egg
- 1 teaspoon vanilla essence
- 1/2 cup all-purpose flour
- 1 teaspoon baking powder
- 1/2 cup cocoa powder
- A pinch of salt
- A pinch of ground cardamom

Directions:
1. Start by preheating your Air Fryer to 350 degrees F. Now, spritz the sides and bottom of a baking pan with cooking spray.
2. In a mixing dish, beat the melted butter with sugar until fluffy. Next, fold in the egg and beat again.
3. After that, add the vanilla, flour, baking powder, cocoa, salt, and ground cardamom. Mix until everything is well combined.
4. Bake in the preheated Air Fryer for 20 to 22 minutes. Enjoy!

496.Ricotta Lemon Cake

Servings: 8
Cooking Time: 40 Minutes
Ingredients:
- 1 lb ricotta
- 4 eggs
- 1 lemon juice
- 1 lemon zest
- ¼ cup erythritol

Directions:
1. Preheat the air fryer to 325 F.
2. Spray air fryer baking dish with cooking spray.
3. In a bowl, beat ricotta cheese until smooth.
4. Whisk in the eggs one by one.
5. Whisk in lemon juice and zest.
6. Pour batter into the prepared baking dish and place into the air fryer.
7. Cook for 40 minutes.
8. Allow to cool completely then slice and serve.

497.Butter Marshmallow Fluff Turnover

Servings: 4

Cooking Time: 35 Minutes
Ingredients:
- 4 sheets filo pastry, defrosted
- 4 tbsp. chunky peanut butter
- 4 tsp. marshmallow fluff
- 2 oz. butter, melted
- Pinch of sea salt

Directions:
1. Pre-heat the Air Fryer to 360°F.
2. Roll out the pastry sheets. Coat one with a light brushing of butter.
3. Lay a second pastry sheet on top of the first one. Brush once again with butter. Repeat until all 4 sheets have been used.
4. Slice the filo layers into four strips, measuring roughly 3 inches x 12 inches.
5. Spread one tablespoon of peanut butter and one teaspoon of marshmallow fluff on the underside of each pastry strip.
6. Take the tip of each sheet and fold it backwards over the filling, forming a triangle. Repeat this action in a zigzag manner until the filling is completely enclosed.
7. Seal the ends of each turnover with a light brushing of butter.
8. Put the turnovers in the fryer basket and cook for 3 – 5 minutes, until they turn golden brown and puffy.
9. Sprinkle a little sea salt over each turnover before serving.

498. Tea Cookies

Servings:15
Cooking Time:25 Minutes
Ingredients:
- ½ cup salted butter, softened
- 2 cups almond meal
- 1 organic egg
- 1 teaspoon ground cinnamon
- 2 teaspoons sugar
- 1 teaspoon organic vanilla extract

Directions:
1. Preheat the Air fryer to 370 °F and grease an Air fryer basket.
2. Mix all the ingredients in a bowl until well combined.
3. Make equal sized balls from the mixture and transfer in the Air fryer basket.
4. Cook for about 5 minutes and press down each ball with fork.
5. Cook for about 20 minutes and allow the cookies cool to serve with tea.

499. Bakery-style Hazelnut Cookies

Servings: 6
Cooking Time: 20 Minutes
Ingredients:
- 1 ½ cups all-purpose flour

- 1 teaspoon baking soda
- 1 teaspoon fine sea salt
- 1 stick butter
- 1 cup brown sugar
- 2 teaspoons vanilla
- 2 eggs, at room temperature
- 1 cup hazelnuts, coarsely chopped

Directions:
1. Begin by preheating your Air Fryer to 350 degrees F.
2. Mix the flour with the baking soda, and sea salt.
3. In the bowl of an electric mixer, beat the butter, brown sugar, and vanilla until creamy. Fold in the eggs, one at a time, and mix until well combined.
4. Slowly and gradually, stir in the flour mixture. Finally, fold in the coarsely chopped hazelnuts.
5. Divide the dough into small balls using a large cookie scoop; drop onto the prepared cookie sheets. Bake for 10 minutes or until golden brown, rotating the pan once or twice through the cooking time.
6. Work in batches and cool for a couple of minutes before removing to wire racks. Enjoy!

500. Lusciously Easy Brownies

Servings:8
Cooking Time: 20 Minutes
Ingredients:
- 1 egg
- 2 tablespoons and 2 teaspoons unsweetened cocoa powder
- 1/2 cup white sugar
- 1/2 teaspoon vanilla extract
- 1/4 cup butter
- 1/4 cup all-purpose flour
- 1/8 teaspoon salt
- 1/8 teaspoon baking powder
- Frosting Ingredients
- 1 tablespoon and 1-1/2 teaspoons butter, softened
- 1 tablespoon and 1-1/2 teaspoons unsweetened cocoa powder
- 1-1/2 teaspoons honey
- 1/2 teaspoon vanilla extract
- 1/2 cup confectioners' sugar

Directions:
1. Lightly grease baking pan of air fryer with cooking spray. Melt ¼ cup butter for 3 minutes. Stir in vanilla, eggs, and sugar. Mix well.
2. Stir in baking powder, salt, flour, and cocoa mix well. Evenly spread.
3. For 20 minutes, cook on 300°F.

4. In a small bowl, make the frosting by mixing well all Ingredients. Frost brownies while still warm.
5. Serve and enjoy.

501.Chocolate Lover's Muffins

Servings:8
Cooking Time:10 Minutes
Ingredients:
- 1½ cups all-purpose flour
- 2 teaspoons baking powder
- 1 egg
- 1 cup yogurt
- ½ cup mini chocolate chips
- ¼ cup sugar
- Salt, to taste
- 1/3 cup vegetable oil
- 2 teaspoons vanilla extract

Directions:
1. Preheat the Air fryer to 355 °F and grease 8 muffin cups lightly.
2. Mix flour, baking powder, sugar and salt in a bowl.
3. Whisk egg, oil, yogurt and vanilla extract in another bowl.
4. Combine the flour and egg mixtures and mix until a smooth mixture is formed.
5. Fold in the chocolate chips and divide this mixture into the prepared muffin cups.
6. Transfer into the Air fryer basket and cook for about 10 minutes.
7. Refrigerate for 2 hours and serve chilled.

502.Easy Spanish Churros

Servings: 4
Cooking Time: 20 Minutes
Ingredients:
- 3/4 cup water
- 1 tablespoon swerve
- 1/4 teaspoon sea salt
- 1/4 teaspoon grated nutmeg
- 1/4 teaspoon ground cloves
- 6 tablespoons butter
- 3/4 cup almond flour
- 2 eggs

Directions:
1. To make the dough, boil the water in a pan over medium-high heat; now, add the swerve, salt, nutmeg, and cloves; cook until dissolved.
2. Add the butter and turn the heat to low. Gradually stir in the almond flour, whisking continuously, until the mixture forms a ball.
3. Remove from the heat; fold in the eggs one at a time, stirring to combine well.
4. Pour the mixture into a piping bag with a large star tip. Squeeze 4-inch strips of dough into the greased Air Fryer pan.

5. Cook at 410 degrees F for 6 minutes, working in batches. Bon appétit!

503.Chocolate Fudgy Brownies

Servings: 8
Cooking Time: 30 Minutes
Ingredients:
- 1 stick butter, melted
- 1 cup swerve
- 2 eggs
- 1 teaspoon vanilla essence
- 2 tablespoons flaxseed meal
- 1 cup coconut flour
- 1 teaspoon baking powder
- 1/2 cup cocoa powder, unsweetened
- A pinch of salt
- A pinch of ground cardamom

Directions:
1. Start by preheating your Air Fryer to 350 degrees F. Now, spritz the sides and bottom of a baking pan with cooking spray.
2. In a mixing dish, beat the melted butter with swerve until fluffy. Next, fold in the eggs and beat again.
3. After that, add the vanilla, flour, baking powder, cocoa, salt, and ground cardamom. Mix until everything is well combined.
4. Bake in the preheated Air Fryer for 20 to 22 minutes. Enjoy!

504.Simple Coffee Cake

Servings:2
Cooking Time: 30 Minutes
Ingredients:
- ½ tsp instant coffee
- 1 tbsp black coffee, brewed
- 1 egg
- ¼ cup sugar
- ¼ cup flour
- 1 tsp cocoa powder
- A pinch of salt
- Powdered sugar, for icing

Directions:
1. Preheat the air fryer to 330 F.
2. Grease a small ring cake pan. Beat the sugar and egg together in a bowl. Beat in cocoa, instant and black coffee; stir in salt and flour. Transfer the batter to the prepared pan. Cook for 15 minutes.

505.Strawberry Muffins

Servings: 12
Cooking Time: 15 Minutes
Ingredients:
- 3 eggs
- 1 tsp ground cinnamon
- 2 tsp baking powder
- 2 1/2 cups almond flour
- 2/3 cup fresh strawberries, diced

- 1/3 cup heavy cream
- 1 tsp vanilla
- 1/2 cup Swerve
- 5 tbsp butter

Directions:
1. Preheat the air fryer 325 F.
2. Add butter and sweetener in a bowl and beat using a hand mixer until smooth.
3. Add eggs, cream, and vanilla and beat until frothy.
4. In another bowl, sift together almond flour, cinnamon, baking powder, and salt.
5. Add almond flour mixture to wet ingredients and mix until well combined.
6. Add strawberries and fold well.
7. Pour batter into the silicone muffin molds and place into the air fryer basket in batches.
8. Cook muffins for 15 minutes.
9. Serve and enjoy.

506.Apple Tart

Servings:2
Cooking Time:25 Minutes
Ingredients:
- 2½-ounce butter, chopped and divided
- 3 ½-ounce flour
- 1 egg yolk
- 1 large apple, peeled, cored and cut into 12 wedges
- 1-ounce sugar

Directions:
1. Preheat the Air fryer to 390 °F and grease a baking pan lightly.
2. Mix half of the butter and flour in a bowl until a soft dough is formed.
3. Roll the dough into 6-inch round on a floured surface.
4. Place the remaining butter and sugar in a baking pan and arrange the apple wedges in a circular pattern.
5. Top with rolled dough and press gently along the edges of the pan.
6. Transfer the baking pan in the Air fryer basket and cook for about 25 minutes.
7. Dish out and serve hot.

507.Almond Pumpkin Cookies

Servings: 8
Cooking Time: 8 Minutes
Ingredients:
- ¼ cup almond flour
- ½ cup pumpkin puree
- 3 tbsp swerve
- ½ tsp baking soda
- 1 tbsp coconut flakes
- ½ tsp cinnamon
- Pinch of salt

Directions:

1. Preheat the air fryer to 360 F.
2. Add all ingredients into the bowl and mix until well combined.
3. Spray air fryer basket with cooking spray.
4. Make cookies from bowl mixture and place into the air fryer and cook for 8 minutes.
5. Serve and enjoy.

508.Air Fried Apricots In Whiskey Sauce

Servings:4
Cooking Time:45 Minutes
Ingredients:
- 1 pound apricot, pitted and halved
- 1/4 cup whiskey
- 1 teaspoon pure vanilla extract
- 1/2 stick butter, room temperature
- 2-4 whole cloves
- 1 cup cool whip, for serving
- 1/2 cup maple syrup

Directions:
1. In a small-sized saucepan that is placed over a moderate flame, heat the maple syrup, vanilla, and butter; simmer until the butter has melted.
2. Add the whiskey and stir to combine. Arrange the apricots wedges on the bottom of a lightly greased baking dish.
3. Pour the sauce over the apricots; scatter whole cloves over the top. Then, transfer the baking dish to the preheated air fryer.
4. Air-fryer at 380 degrees F for 35 minutes. Top with cool whip and serve. Bon appétit!

509.Raspberry Pudding Surprise

Servings: 1
Cooking Time: 40 Minutes
Ingredients:
- 3 tbsp chia seeds
- ½ cup unsweetened milk
- 1 scoop chocolate protein powder
- ¼ cup raspberries, fresh or frozen
- 1 tsp honey

Directions:
1. Combine the milk, protein powder and chia seeds together.
2. Let rest for 5 minutes before stirring.
3. Refrigerate for 30 minutes.
4. Top with raspberries.
5. Serve!

510.Anise And Orange Cake

Servings: 6
Cooking Time: 30 Minutes
Ingredients:
- 1/3 cup hazelnuts, roughly chopped
- 3 tablespoons sugar free orange marmalade
- 1 stick butter
- 2 eggs plus 1 egg yolk, beaten
- 5 tablespoons liquid monk fruit

- 6 ounces unbleached almond flour
- 1 teaspoon baking soda
- 1/2 teaspoon baking powder
- 1/2 ground anise seed
- 1/2 teaspoon ground cinnamon
- 1/2 teaspoon ground allspice
- Pan oil

Directions:
1. Lightly grease a cake pan using a pan oil.
2. Now, whip the liquid monk fruit and butter in a mixing bowl; whip until pale and smooth. Fold in the eggs, hazelnuts and marmalade; beat again until everything's well mixed.
3. Throw in the almond flour, baking soda, baking powder, allspice, anise star, and ground cinnamon. Bake in the preheated Air Fryer at 310 degrees F for about 20 minutes.
4. After that, use a tester to check for doneness. To finish, add the frosting. Bon appétit!

511.Semolina Cake

Servings:8
Cooking Time:15 Minutes
Ingredients:
- 2½ cups semolina
- 1 cup milk
- 1 cup Greek yogurt
- 2 teaspoons baking powder
- ½ cup walnuts, chopped
- ½ cup vegetable oil
- 1 cup sugar
- Pinch of salt

Directions:
1. Preheat the Air fryer to 360 °F and grease a baking pan lightly.
2. Mix semolina, oil, milk, yogurt and sugar in a bowl until well combined.
3. Cover the bowl and keep aside for about 15 minutes.
4. Stir in the baking soda, baking powder and salt and fold in the walnuts.
5. Transfer the mixture into the baking pan and place in the Air fryer.
6. Cook for about 15 minutes and dish out to serve.

512.Peanuts Almond Biscuits

Servings: 6
Cooking Time: 35 Minutes
Ingredients:
- 4 oz peanuts, chopped
- 2 tablespoons peanut butter
- ½ teaspoon apple cider vinegar
- 1 egg, beaten
- 6 oz almond flour
- ¼ cup of coconut milk

- 2 teaspoons Erythritol
- 1 teaspoon vanilla extract
- Cooking spray

Directions:
1. In the bowl mix up peanut butter, apple cider vinegar, egg, almond flour, coconut milk, Erythritol, and vanilla extract. When the mixture is homogenous, add peanuts and knead the smooth dough. Then spray the cooking mold with cooking spray and place the dough inside. Preheat the air fryer to 350F. Put the mold with biscuits in the air fryer and cook it for 25 minutes. Then slice the cooked biscuits into pieces and return back in the air fryer. Cook them for 10 minutes more. Cool the cooked biscuits completely.

513.Luscious Cheesecake

Servings:8
Cooking Time:25 Minutes
Ingredients:
- 17.6-ounce ricotta cheese
- 3 eggs
- 3 tablespoons corn starch
- ¾ cup sugar
- 1 tablespoon fresh lemon juice
- 2 teaspoons vanilla extract
- 1 teaspoon fresh lemon zest, grated finely

Directions:
1. Preheat the Air fryer to 320 °F and grease a baking dish lightly.
2. Mix all the ingredients in a bowl and transfer the mixture into the baking dish.
3. Place the baking dish in the Air fryer basket and cook for 25 about minutes.
4. Dish out and serve immediately.

514.Almond Cookies

Servings: 8
Cooking Time: 15 Minutes
Ingredients:
- 1 and ½ cups almonds, crushed
- 2 tablespoons erythritol
- ½ teaspoon baking powder
- ¼ teaspoon almond extract
- 2 eggs, whisked

Directions:
1. In a bowl, mix all the ingredients and whisk well. Scoop 8 servings of this mix on a baking sheet that fits the air fryer which you've lined with parchment paper. Put the baking sheet in your air fryer and cook at 350 degrees F for 15 minutes. Serve cold.

515.Bread Pudding

Servings:2
Cooking Time:12 Minutes
Ingredients:

- 1 cup milk
- 1 egg
- 2 tablespoons raisins, soaked in hot water for about 15 minutes
- 2 bread slices, cut into small cubes
- 1 tablespoon chocolate chips
- 1 tablespoon brown sugar
- ½ teaspoon ground cinnamon
- ¼ teaspoon vanilla extract
- 1 tablespoon sugar

Directions:
1. Preheat the Air fryer to 375 °F and grease a baking dish lightly.
2. Mix milk, egg, brown sugar, cinnamon and vanilla extract until well combined.
3. Stir in the raisins and mix well.
4. Arrange the bread cubes evenly in the baking dish and top with the milk mixture.
5. Refrigerate for about 20 minutes and sprinkle with chocolate chips and sugar.
6. Transfer the baking pan into the Air fryer and cook for about 12 minutes.
7. Dish out and serve immediately.

516.Classic Buttermilk Biscuits

Servings:4
Cooking Time:8 Minutes
Ingredients:
- ½ cup cake flour
- 1¼ cups all-purpose flour
- ¾ teaspoon baking powder
- ¼ cup + 2 tablespoons butter, cut into cubes
- ¾ cup buttermilk
- 1 teaspoon granulated sugar
- Salt, to taste

Directions:
1. Preheat the Air fryer to 400 °F and grease a pie pan lightly.
2. Sift together flours, baking soda, baking powder, sugar and salt in a large bowl.
3. Add cold butter and mix until a coarse crumb is formed.
4. Stir in the buttermilk slowly and mix until a dough is formed.
5. Press the dough into ½ inch thickness onto a floured surface and cut out circles with a 1¾-inch round cookie cutter.
6. Arrange the biscuits in a pie pan in a single layer and brush butter on them.
7. Transfer into the Air fryer and cook for about 8 minutes until golden brown.

517.All-star Banana Fritters

Servings:5
Cooking Time: 15 Minutes
Ingredients:
- 5 bananas, sliced
- 1 tsp salt
- 3 tbsp sesame seeds
- 1 cup water
- 2 eggs, beaten
- 1 tsp baking powder
- ½ tbsp sugar

Directions:
1. Preheat the air fryer to 340 F.
2. In a bowl, mix salt, sesame seeds, flour, baking powder, eggs, sugar, and water.
3. Coat sliced bananas with the flour mixture; place the prepared slices in the air fryer basket; cook for 8 minutes.

518.Easy 'n Delicious Brownies

Servings:8
Cooking Time: 20 Minutes
Ingredients:
- 1/4 cup butter
- 1/2 cup white sugar
- 1 egg
- 1/2 teaspoon vanilla extract
- 2 tablespoons and 2 teaspoons unsweetened cocoa powder
- 1/4 cup all-purpose flour
- 1/8 teaspoon salt
- 1/8 teaspoon baking powder
- 1 tablespoon and 1-1/2 teaspoons butter, softened
- 1 tablespoon and 1-1/2 teaspoons unsweetened cocoa powder
- 1-1/2 teaspoons honey
- 1/2 teaspoon vanilla extract
- 1/2 cup confectioners' sugar

Directions:
1. Lightly grease baking pan of air fryer with cooking spray. Melt ¼ cup butter for 3 minutes. Stir in vanilla, eggs, and sugar. Mix well.
2. Stir in baking powder, salt, flour, and cocoa mix well. Evenly spread.
3. For 20 minutes, cook on 300°F.
4. In a small bowl, make the frosting by mixing well all Ingredients. Frost brownies while still warm.
5. Serve and enjoy.

519.Toasted Coconut Flakes

Servings: 1
Cooking Time: 5 Minutes
Ingredients:
- 1 cup unsweetened coconut flakes
- 2 tsp. coconut oil, melted
- ¼ cup granular erythritol
- Salt

Directions:
1. In a large bowl, combine the coconut flakes, oil, granular erythritol, and a pinch of salt, ensuring that the flakes are coated completely.

2. Place the coconut flakes in your fryer and cook at 300°F for three minutes, giving the basket a good shake a few times throughout the cooking time. Fry until golden and serve.

520.Rustic Baked Apples

Servings: 4
Cooking Time: 25 Minutes
Ingredients:
- 4 Gala apples
- 1/4 cup rolled oats
- 1/4 cup sugar
- 2 tablespoons honey
- 1/3 cup walnuts, chopped
- 1 teaspoon cinnamon powder
- 1/2 teaspoon ground cardamom
- 1/2 teaspoon ground cloves
- 2/3 cup water

Directions:
1. Use a paring knife to remove the stem and seeds from the apples, making deep holes.
2. In a mixing bowl, combine together the rolled oats, sugar, honey, walnuts, cinnamon, cardamom, and cloves.
3. Pour the water into an Air Fryer safe dish. Place the apples in the dish.
4. Bake at 340 degrees F for 17 minutes. Serve at room temperature. Bon appétit!

521.Pumpkin Cinnamon Pudding

Servings: 4
Cooking Time: 25 Minutes
Ingredients:
- 3 cups pumpkin puree
- 3 tbsp. honey
- 1 tbsp. ginger
- 1 tbsp. cinnamon
- 1 tsp. clove
- 1 tsp. nutmeg
- 1 cup full-fat cream
- 2 eggs
- 1 cup sugar

Directions:
1. Pre-heat your Air Fryer to 390°F.
2. In a bowl, stir all of the ingredients together to combine.
3. Grease the inside of a small baking dish.
4. Pour the mixture into the dish and transfer to the fryer. Cook for 15 minutes. Serve with whipped cream if desired.

522.Pear & Apple Crisp With Walnuts

Servings: 6
Cooking Time: 25 Minutes
Ingredients:
- ½ lb. apples, cored and chopped
- ½ lb. pears, cored and chopped
- 1 cup flour
- 1 cup sugar

- 1 tbsp. butter
- 1 tsp. ground cinnamon
- ¼ tsp. ground cloves
- 1 tsp. vanilla extract
- ¼ cup chopped walnuts
- Whipped cream, to serve

Directions:
1. Lightly grease a baking dish and place the apples and pears inside.
2. Combine the rest of the ingredients, minus the walnuts and the whipped cream, until a coarse, crumbly texture is achieved.
3. Pour the mixture over the fruits and spread it evenly. Top with the chopped walnuts.
4. Air bake at 340°F for 20 minutes or until the top turns golden brown.
5. When cooked through, serve at room temperature with whipped cream.

523.Cocoa Bombs

Servings: 12
Cooking Time: 8 Minutes
Ingredients:
- 2 cups macadamia nuts, chopped
- 4 tablespoons coconut oil, melted
- 1 teaspoon vanilla extract
- ¼ cup cocoa powder
- 1/3 cup swerve

Directions:
1. In a bowl, mix all the ingredients and whisk well. Shape medium balls out of this mix, place them in your air fryer and cook at 300 degrees F for 8 minutes. Serve cold.

524.Fruity Tacos

Servings:2
Cooking Time: 5 Minutes
Ingredients:
- 2 soft shell tortillas
- 4 tablespoons strawberry jelly
- ¼ cup blueberries
- ¼ cup raspberries
- 2 tablespoons powdered sugar

Directions:
1. Set the temperature of air fryer to 300 degrees F. Lightly, grease an air fryer basket.
2. Arrange the tortillas onto a smooth surface.
3. Spread two tablespoons of strawberry jelly over each tortilla and top each with berries.
4. Sprinkle each with the powdered sugar.
5. Arrange tortillas into the prepared air fryer basket.
6. Air fry for about 5 minutes or until crispy.
7. Remove from the air fryer and transfer the tortillas onto a platter.
8. Serve warm.

525.Hearty Apricot Crumbles

Servings:4

Cooking Time: 30 Minutes

Ingredients:
- 1 cup fresh blackberries
- ½ cup sugar
- 2 tbsp lemon Juice
- 1 cup flour
- Salt as needed
- 5 tbsp butter

Directions:
1. Add the apricot cubes to a bowl and mix with lemon juice, 2 tbsp sugar, and blackberries. Scoop the mixture into a greased dish and spread it evenly. In another bowl, mix flour and remaining sugar.
2. Add 1 tbsp of cold water and butter and keep mixing until you have a crumbly mixture. Preheat the air fryer to 390 F and place the fruit mixture in the cooking basket. Top with crumb mixture and cook for 20 minutes.

526.Authentic Indian Gulgulas

Servings: 3
Cooking Time: 20 Minutes

Ingredients:
- 1 banana, mashed
- 1/4 cup sugar
- 1 egg
- 1/2 teaspoon vanilla essence
- 1/4 teaspoon ground cardamom
- 1/4 teaspoon cinnamon
- 1/2 milk
- 3/4 cup all-purpose flour
- 1 teaspoon baking powder

Directions:
1. In a mixing bowl, whisk the mashed banana with the sugar and egg; add the vanilla, cardamom, and cinnamon and mix to combine well.
2. Gradually pour in the milk and mix again. Stir in the flour and baking powder. Mix until everything is well incorporated.
3. Drop a spoonful of batter onto the greased Air Fryer pan. Cook in the preheated Air Fryer at 360 degrees F for 5 minutes, flipping them halfway through the cooking time.
4. Repeat with the remaining batter and serve warm. Enjoy!

527.Raspberry Muffins

Servings: 10
Cooking Time: 35 Minutes

Ingredients:
- 1 egg
- 1 cup frozen raspberries, coated with some flour
- 1 ½ cups flour

- ½ cup sugar
- ⅓ cup vegetable oil
- 2 tsp. baking powder
- Yogurt, as needed
- 1 tsp. lemon zest
- 2 tbsp. lemon juice
- Pinch of sea salt

Directions:
1. Pre-heat the Air Fryer to 350°F
2. Place all of the dry ingredients in a bowl and combine well.
3. Beat the egg and pour it into a cup. Mix it with the oil and lemon juice. Add in the yogurt, to taste.
4. Mix together the dry and wet ingredients.
5. Add in the lemon zest and raspberries.
6. Coat the insides of 10 muffin tins with a little butter.
7. Spoon an equal amount of the mixture into each muffin tin.
8. Transfer to the fryer, and cook for 10 minutes, in batches if necessary.

528.Pecan-cranberry Cake

Servings:6
Cooking Time: 25 Minutes

Ingredients:
- 1 1/2 cups Almond Flour
- 1 tsp baking powder
- 1/2 cup fresh cranberries
- 1/2 tsp vanilla extract
- 1/4 cup cashew milk (or use any dairy or non-dairy milk you prefer)
- 1/4 cup chopped pecans
- 1/4 cup Monk fruit (or use your preferred sweetener)
- 1/4 tsp cinnamon
- 1/8 tsp salt
- 2 large eggs

Directions:
1. In blender, add all wet Ingredients and mix well. Add all dry Ingredients except for cranberries and pecans. Blend well until smooth.
2. Lightly grease baking pan of air fryer with cooking spray. Pour in batter. Drizzle cranberries on top and then followed by pecans.
3. For 20 minutes, cook on 330°F.
4. Let stand for 5 minutes.
5. Serve and enjoy.

529.Pumpkin Muffins

Servings: 10
Cooking Time: 20 Minutes

Ingredients:
- 4 large eggs
- 1/2 cup pumpkin puree
- 1 tbsp pumpkin pie spice

- 1 tbsp baking powder, gluten-free
- 2/3 cup erythritol
- 1 tsp vanilla
- 1/3 cup coconut oil, melted
- 1/2 cup almond flour
- 1/2 cup coconut flour
- 1/2 tsp sea salt

Directions:
1. Preheat the air fryer to 325 F.
2. In a large bowl, stir together coconut flour, pumpkin pie spice, baking powder, erythritol, almond flour, and sea salt.
3. Stir in eggs, vanilla, coconut oil, and pumpkin puree until well combined.
4. Pour batter into the silicone muffin molds and place into the air fryer basket in batches.
5. Cook muffins for 20 minutes.
6. Serve and enjoy.

530.Mom's Orange Rolls

Servings: 6
Cooking Time: 1 Hour 20 Minutes
Ingredients:
- 1/2 cup milk
- 1/4 cup granulated sugar
- 1 tablespoon yeast
- 1/2 stick butter, at room temperature
- 1 egg, at room temperature
- 1/4 teaspoon salt
- 2 cups all-purpose flour
- 2 tablespoons fresh orange juice
- Filling:
- 2 tablespoons butter
- 4 tablespoons white sugar
- 1 teaspoon ground star anise
- 1/4 teaspoon ground cinnamon
- 1 teaspoon vanilla paste
- 1/2 cup confectioners' sugar

Directions:
1. Heat the milk in a microwave safe bowl and transfer the warm milk to the bowl of a stand electric mixer. Add the granulated sugar and yeast, and mix to combine well. Cover and let it sit until the yeast is foamy.
2. Then, beat the butter on low speed. Fold in the egg and mix again. Add salt and flour. Add the orange juice and mix on medium speed until a soft dough forms.
3. Knead the dough on a lightly floured surface. Cover it loosely and let it sit in a warm place about 1 hour or until doubled in size. Then, spritz the bottom and sides of a baking pan with cooking oil (butter flavored.
4. Roll your dough out into a rectangle.
5. Spread 2 tablespoons of butter all over the dough. In a mixing dish, combine the white sugar, ground star anise, cinnamon, and vanilla; sprinkle evenly over the dough.

6. Then, roll up your dough to form a log. Cut into 6 equal rolls and place them in the parchment-lined Air Fryer basket.
7. Bake at 350 degrees for 12 minutes, turning them halfway through the cooking time. Dust with confectioners' sugar and enjoy!

531.Speedy Chocolate Cookie

Servings:4
Cooking Time: 15 Minutes
Ingredients:
- 1 cup flour
- ¼ tsp baking powder
- 1/8 tsp salt
- ¼ cup sugar
- ¼ cup unsalted butter, softened
- 1 egg yolk
- ½ tsp vanilla extract
- ½ cup dark chocolate chips

Directions:
1. Preheat the Air fryer to 360 F. Line the air fryer basket with parchment paper.
2. In a bowl, sift flour with baking powder and salt. In another bowl, combine sugar, butter, and honey; stir in egg yolk and vanilla until everything is well incorporated. Add in the dry ingredients until mixed. Fold in chocolate chips.
3. Spread the batter on the bottom of the air fryer basket and cook for 8 minutes until just set. Allow to cool on a wire rack and serve.

532.Simple Donuts

Servings:12
Cooking Time:25 Minutes
Ingredients:
- 2 cups all-purpose flour
- 2 teaspoons baking powder
- 1 egg
- 1 tablespoon butter, softened
- ½ cup milk
- Salt, to taste
- ¾ cup sugar
- 2 teaspoons vanilla extract
- 2 tablespoons icing sugar

Directions:
1. Preheat the Air fryer to 390 °F and grease an Air fryer basket lightly.
2. Sift together flour, baking powder and salt in a large bowl.
3. Add sugar and egg and mix well.
4. Stir in the butter, milk and vanilla extract and mix until a dough is formed.
5. Refrigerate the dough for at least 1 hour and roll the dough into ½ inch thickness onto a floured surface.

6. Cut into donuts with a donut cutter and arrange the donuts in the Air fryer basket in 3 batches.
7. Cook for about 8 minutes until golden and serve.

533.Double Chocolate Whiskey Brownies

Servings: 10
Cooking Time: 55 Minutes
Ingredients:
- 3 tablespoons whiskey
- 8 ounces white chocolate
- 3/4 cup almond flour
- 1/4 cup coconut flakes
- 1/2 cup coconut oil
- 2 eggs plus an egg yolk, whisked
- 3/4 cup monk fruit
- 2 tablespoons cocoa powder, unsweetened
- 1/4 teaspoon ground cardamom
- 1 teaspoon pure rum extract

Directions:
1. Microwave white chocolate and coconut oil until everything's melted; allow the mixture to cool at room temperature.
2. After that, thoroughly whisk the eggs, monk fruit, rum extract, cocoa powder and cardamom.
3. Next step, add the rum/egg mixture to the chocolate mixture. Stir in the flour and coconut flakes; mix to combine.
4. Mix cranberries with whiskey and let them soak for 15 minutes. Fold them into the batter. Press the batter into a lightly buttered cake pan.
5. Air-fry for 35 minutes at 340 degrees F. Allow them to cool slightly on a wire rack before slicing and serving.

534.Apple And Cinnamon Sauce

Servings: 6
Cooking Time: 30 Minutes
Ingredients:
- 6 apples, peeled, cored and cut into wedges
- 1 tablespoon cinnamon powder
- 1 cup sugar
- 1 cup red wine

Directions:
1. In a pan that fits your air fryer, place all of the ingredients and toss.
2. Place the pan in the fryer and cook at 320 degrees F for 30 minutes.
3. Divide into cups and serve right away.

535.Coconut Cake

Servings: 8
Cooking Time: 20 Minutes
Ingredients:
- 2 egg
- 3 tablespoons swerve
- 3 tablespoons coconut oil, melted
- ¼ cup coconut milk
- 4 tablespoons almond flour
- 1 tablespoon cocoa powder
- ½ teaspoon baking powder

Directions:
1. In a bowl, mix all the ingredients and stir well. Pour this into a cake pan that fits the air fryer, put the pan in the machine and cook at 340 degrees F for 20 minutes. Slice and serve.

536.Banana Chips With Chocolate Glaze

Servings: 2
Cooking Time: 20 Minutes
Ingredients:
- 2 banana, cut into slices
- 1/4 teaspoon lemon zest
- 1 tablespoon agave syrup
- 1 tablespoon cocoa powder
- 1 tablespoon coconut oil, melted

Directions:
1. Toss the bananas with the lemon zest and agave syrup. Transfer your bananas to the parchment-lined cooking basket.
2. Bake in the preheated Air Fryer at 370 degrees F for 12 minutes, turning them over halfway through the cooking time.
3. In the meantime, melt the coconut oil in your microwave; add the cocoa powder and whisk to combine well.
4. Serve the baked banana chips with a few drizzles of the chocolate glaze. Enjoy!

537.Plum Almond Cake

Servings: 8
Cooking Time: 30 Minutes
Ingredients:
- ½ cup butter, soft
- 3 eggs
- ½ cup swerve
- ¼ teaspoon almond extract
- 1 tablespoon vanilla extract
- 1 and ½ cups almond flour
- ½ cup coconut flour
- 2 teaspoons baking powder
- ¾ cup almond milk
- 4 plums, pitted and chopped

Directions:
1. In a bowl, mix all the ingredients and whisk well. Pour this into a cake pan that fits the air fryer after you've lined it with parchment paper, put the pan in the machine and cook at 370 degrees F for 30 minutes. Cool the cake down, slice and serve.

538.Coconut Almond Pies

Servings: 6
Cooking Time: 26 Minutes
Ingredients:
- 8 oz almond flour

- 1 teaspoon vanilla extract
- ¼ teaspoon salt
- 2 tablespoons Erythritol
- 2 eggs, beaten
- 1 tablespoon coconut butter, melted
- 1 tablespoon xanthan gum
- 1 teaspoon flax meal
- 2 oz blueberries
- Cooking spray

Directions:
1. In the mixing bowl mix up vanilla extract, eggs, and coconut butter. Then add almond flour, salt, xanthan gum, and flax meal. Knead the non-sticky dough and roll it up. Then cut the dough on 6 pieces. Put the blueberries on every dough piece. Sprinkle the berries with Erythritol. Fold the dough pieces to make the pockets and secure the edges of them with the help of the fork. Preheat the air fryer to 350F. Place the hand pies in the air fryer in one layer (4 pies) and cook them for 13 minutes. Then remove the cooked pies from the air fryer and cool them to the room temperature. Repeat the same steps with remaining uncooked pies.

539.Crispy Banana Split

Servings:8
Cooking Time: 14 Minutes
Ingredients:
- 3 tablespoons coconut oil
- 1 cup panko breadcrumbs
- ½ cup corn flour
- 2 eggs
- 4 bananas, peeled and halved lengthwise
- 3 tablespoons sugar
- ¼ teaspoon ground cinnamon
- 2 tablespoons walnuts, chopped

Directions:
1. In a medium skillet, heat the oil over medium heat and cook breadcrumbs for about 3-4 minutes or until golden browned and crumbled, stirring continuously.
2. Transfer the breadcrumbs into a shallow bowl and set aside to cool.
3. In a second bowl, place the corn flour.
4. In a third bowl, whisk the eggs.
5. Coat the banana slices with flour and then, dip into eggs and finally, coat evenly with the breadcrumbs.
6. In a small bowl, mix together the sugar and cinnamon
7. Set the temperature of air fryer to 280 degrees F. Grease an air fryer basket.
8. Arrange banana slices into the prepared air fryer basket in a single layer and sprinkle with cinnamon sugar
9. Air fry for about 10 minutes.
10. Remove from air fryer and transfer the banana slices onto plates to cool slightly
11. Sprinkle with chopped walnuts and serve.

540.Tangerine Cake Recipe

Servings: 8
Cooking Time:30 Minutes
Ingredients:
- 3/4 cup sugar
- 2 cups flour
- 1/2 tsp. vanilla extract
- 1/4 cup olive oil
- 1/2 cup milk
- 1 tsp. cider vinegar
- Juice and zest from 2 lemons
- Juice and zest from 1 tangerine
- Tangerine segments; for serving

Directions:
1. In a bowl; mix flour with sugar and stir
2. In another bowl, mix oil with milk, vinegar, vanilla extract, lemon juice and zest and tangerine zest and whisk very well
3. Add flour; stir well, pour this into a cake pan that fits your air fryer, introduce in the fryer and cook at 360 °F, for 20 minutes. Serve right away with tangerine segments on top.

541.Vanilla Mozzarella Balls

Servings: 8
Cooking Time: 4 Minutes
Ingredients:
- 2 eggs, beaten
- 1 teaspoon almond butter, melted
- 7 oz coconut flour
- 2 oz almond flour
- 5 oz Mozzarella, shredded
- 1 tablespoon butter
- 2 tablespoons swerve
- 1 teaspoon baking powder
- ½ teaspoon vanilla extract
- Cooking spray

Directions:
1. In the mixing bowl mix up butter and Mozzarella. Microwave the mixture for 10-15 minutes or until it is melted. Then add almond flour and coconut flour. Add swerve and baking powder. After this, add vanilla extract and stir the mixture. Knead the soft dough. Microwave the mixture for 2-5 seconds more if it is not melted enough. In the bowl mix up almond butter and eggs. Make 8 balls from the almond flour mixture and coat them in the egg mixture. Preheat the air fryer to 400F. Spray the air fryer basket with cooking spray from inside and place the bread rolls in one layer. Cook the dessert for 4 minutes or until the bread roll is golden brown. Cool the cooked dessert completely and sprinkle with Splenda if desired.

542.Soft Buttermilk Biscuits

Servings:4
Cooking Time: 25 Minutes

Ingredients:
- ½ tsp baking soda
- ½ cup cake flour
- ¾ tsp salt
- ½ tsp baking powder
- 4 tbsp butter, chopped
- 1 tsp sugar
- ¾ cup buttermilk

Directions:
1. Preheat the air fryer to 400 F and combine all dry ingredients, in a bowl. Place the chopped butter in the bowl, and rub it into the flour mixture, until crumbed. Stir in the buttermilk.
2. Flour a flat and dry surface and roll out until half-inch thick. Cut out 10 rounds with a small cookie cutter. Arrange the biscuits on a lined baking sheet. Cook for 8 minutes.

543. Dunky Dough Dippers & Chocolate Sauce

Servings: 5
Cooking Time: 45 Minutes
Ingredients:
- ¾ cup sugar
- 1 lb. friendly bread dough
- 1 cup heavy cream
- 12 oz. high quality semi-sweet chocolate chips
- ½ cup butter, melted
- 2 tbsp. extract

Directions:
1. Pre-heat the Air Fryer to 350°F.
2. Coat the inside of the basket with a little melted butter.
3. Halve and roll up the dough to create two 15-inch logs. Slice each log into 20 disks.
4. Halve each disk and twist it 3 or 4 times.
5. Lay out a cookie sheet and lay the twisted dough pieces on top. Brush the pieces with some more melted butter and sprinkle on the sugar.
6. Place the sheet in the fryer and air fry for 5 minutes. Flip the dough twists over, and brush the other side with more butter. Cook for an additional 3 minutes. It may be necessary to complete this step in batches.
7. In the meantime, make the chocolate sauce. Firstly, put the heavy cream into a saucepan over the medium heat and allow it to simmer.
8. Put the chocolate chips into a large bowl and add the simmering cream on top. Whisk the chocolate chips everything together until a smooth consistency is achieved. Stir in 2 tablespoons of extract.
9. Transfer the baked cookies in a shallow dish, pour over the rest of the melted butter and sprinkle on the sugar.
10. Drizzle on the chocolate sauce before serving.

544. Lemon Butter Pound Cake

Servings: 8
Cooking Time: 2 Hours 20 Minutes
Ingredients:
- 1 stick softened butter
- 1 cup sugar
- 1 medium egg
- 1 ¼ cups flour
- 1 tsp. butter flavoring
- 1 tsp. vanilla essence
- Pinch of salt
- ¾ cup milk
- Grated zest of 1 medium-sized lemon
- For the Glaze:
- 2 tbsp. freshly squeezed lemon juice

Directions:
1. In a large bowl, use a creamer to mix together the butter and sugar. Fold in the egg and continue to stir.
2. Add in the flour, butter flavoring, vanilla essence, and salt, combining everything well.
3. Pour in the milk, followed by the lemon zest, and continue to mix.
4. Lightly brush the inside of a cake pan with the melted butter.
5. Pour the cake batter into the cake pan.
6. Place the pan in the Air Fryer and bake at 350°F for 15 minutes.
7. After removing it from the fryer, run a knife around the edges of the cake to loosen it from the pan and transfer it to a serving plate.
8. Leave it to cool completely.
9. In the meantime, make the glaze by combining with the lemon juice.
10. Pour the glaze over the cake and let it sit for a further 2 hours before serving.

545. Red Velvet Pancakes

Servings: 3
Cooking Time: 35 Minutes
Ingredients:
- 1/2 cup flour
- 1 teaspoon baking powder
- 1/4 teaspoon salt
- 2 tablespoons white sugar
- 1/2 teaspoon cinnamon
- 1 teaspoon red paste food color
- 1 egg
- 1/2 cup milk
- 1 teaspoon vanilla
- Topping:
- 2 ounces cream cheese, softened
- 2 tablespoons butter, softened
- 3/4 cup powdered sugar

Directions:
1. Mix the flour, baking powder, salt, sugar, cinnamon, red paste food color in a large bowl.

2. Gradually add the egg and milk, whisking continuously, until well combined. Let it stand for 20 minutes.
3. Spritz the Air Fryer baking pan with cooking spray. Pour the batter into the pan using a measuring cup.
4. Cook at 230 degrees F for 4 to 5 minutes or until golden brown. Repeat with the remaining batter.
5. Meanwhile, make your topping by mixing the ingredients until creamy and fluffy. Decorate your pancakes with topping. Bon appétit!

546.Chocolate Soufflé

Servings:2
Cooking Time: 25 Minutes
Ingredients:
- ¼ cup butter, melted
- 2 tbsp flour
- 3 tbsp sugar
- 3 oz chocolate, melted
- ½ tsp vanilla extract

Directions:
1. Preheat the air fryer to 330 F.
2. Beat the yolks along with the sugar and vanilla extract; stir in butter, chocolate, and flour. and whisk the whites until a stiff peak forms.
3. Working in batches, gently combine the egg whites with the chocolate mixture. Divide the batter between two greased ramekins. Cook for 14 minutes.

547.Cashew Bars Recipe

Servings: 6
Cooking Time:25 Minutes
Ingredients:
- 1/4 cup almond meal
- 1 tbsp. almond butter
- 1 ½ cups cashews; chopped
- 4 dates; chopped
- 3/4 cup coconut; shredded
- 1/3 cup honey
- 1 tbsp. chia seeds

Directions:
1. In a bowl; mix honey with almond meal and almond butter and stir well.
2. Add cashews, coconut, dates and chia seeds and stir well again.
3. Spread this on a lined baking sheet that fits your air fryer and press well.
4. Introduce in the fryer and cook at 300 °F, for 15 minutes. Leave mix to cool down, cut into medium bars and serve

548.Fruity Crumble

Servings:4
Cooking Time:20 Minutes
Ingredients:
- ½ pound fresh apricots, pitted and cubed
- 1 cup fresh blackberries
- 7/8 cup flour
- 1 tablespoon cold water
- ¼ cup chilled butter, cubed
- 1/3 cup sugar, divided
- 1 tablespoon fresh lemon juice
- Pinch of salt

Directions:
1. Preheat the Air fryer to 390 °F and grease a baking pan lightly.
2. Mix apricots, blackberries, 2 tablespoons of sugar and lemon juice in a bowl.
3. Combine the remaining ingredients in a bowl and mix until a crumbly mixture is formed.
4. Pour the apricot mixture in the baking pan and top with the crumbly mixture.
5. Transfer the baking pan in the Air fryer basket and cook for about 20 minutes.
6. Dish out in a bowl and serve warm.

549.Avocado Chocolate Brownies

Servings: 12
Cooking Time: 30 Minutes
Ingredients:
- 1 cup avocado, peeled and mashed
- ½ teaspoon vanilla extract
- 4 tablespoons cocoa powder
- 3 tablespoons coconut oil, melted
- 2 eggs, whisked
- ½ cup dark chocolate, unsweetened and melted
- ¾ cup almond flour
- 1 teaspoon baking powder
- ¼ teaspoon baking soda
- 1 teaspoon stevia

Directions:
1. In a bowl, mix the flour with stevia, baking powder and soda and stir. Add the rest of the ingredients gradually, whisk and pour into a cake pan that fits the air fryer after you lined it with parchment paper. Put the pan in your air fryer and cook at 350 degrees F for 30 minutes. Cut into squares and serve cold.

OTHER AIR FRYER RECIPES

550. Easy Roasted Hot Dogs

Servings: 6
Cooking Time: 25 Minutes
Ingredients:
- 6 hot dogs
- 6 hot dog buns
- 1 tablespoon mustard
- 6 tablespoons ketchup
- 6 lettuce leaves

Directions:
1. Place the hot dogs in the lightly greased Air Fryer basket.
2. Bake at 380 degrees F for 15 minutes, turning them over halfway through the cooking time to promote even cooking.
3. Place on the bun and add the mustard, ketchup, and lettuce leaves. Enjoy!

551. Onion Rings Wrapped In Bacon

Servings: 4
Cooking Time: 25 Minutes
Ingredients:
- 12 rashers back bacon
- 1/2 teaspoon ground black pepper
- Chopped fresh parsley, to taste
- 1/2 teaspoon paprika
- 1/2 teaspoon chili powder
- 1/2 tablespoon soy sauce
- ½ teaspoon salt

Directions:
1. Start by preheating your air fryer to 355 degrees F.
2. Season the onion rings with paprika, salt, black pepper, and chili powder. Simply wrap the bacon around the onion rings; drizzle with soy sauce.
3. Bake for 17 minutes, garnish with fresh parsley and serve. Bon appétit!

552. Western Eggs With Ham And Cheese

Servings: 4
Cooking Time: 20 Minutes
Ingredients:
- 6 eggs
- 1/2 cup milk
- 2 ounces cream cheese, softened
- Sea salt, to your liking
- 1/4 teaspoon ground black pepper
- 1/4 teaspoon paprika
- 6 ounces cooked ham, diced
- 1 onion, chopped
- 1/2 cup cheddar cheese, shredded

Directions:
1. Begin by preheating the Air Fryer to 360 degrees F. Spritz the sides and bottom of a baking pan with cooking oil.
2. In a mixing dish, whisk the eggs, milk, and cream cheese until pale. Add the spices, ham, and onion; stir until everything is well incorporated.
3. Pour the mixture into the baking pan; top with the cheddar cheese.
4. Bake in the preheated Air Fryer for 12 minutes. Serve warm and enjoy!

553. The Best Sweet Potato Fries Ever

Servings: 4
Cooking Time: 20 Minutes
Ingredients:
- 1 1/2 tablespoons olive oil
- 1/2 teaspoon smoked cayenne pepper
- 3 sweet potatoes, peeled and cut into 1/4-inch long slices
- 1/2 teaspoon shallot powder
- 1/3 teaspoon freshly ground black pepper, or more to taste
- 3/4 teaspoon garlic salt

Directions:
1. Firstly, preheat your air fryer to 360 degrees F.
2. Then, add the sweet potatoes to a mixing dish; toss them with the other ingredients.
3. Cook the sweet potatoes approximately 14 minutes. Serve with a dipping sauce of choice.

554. Baked Eggs With Kale And Ham

Servings: 2
Cooking Time: 15 Minutes
Ingredients:
- 2 eggs
- 1/4 teaspoon dried or fresh marjoram
- 2 teaspoons chili powder
- 1/3 teaspoon kosher salt
- ½ cup steamed kale
- 1/4 teaspoon dried or fresh rosemary
- 4 pork ham slices
- 1/3 teaspoon ground black pepper, or more to taste

Directions:
1. Divide the kale and ham among 2 ramekins; crack an egg into each ramekin. Sprinkle with seasonings.
2. Cook for 15 minutes at 335 degrees F or until your eggs reach desired texture.
3. Serve warm with spicy tomato ketchup and pickles. Bon appétit!

555. Creamy Lemon Turkey

Servings: 4
Cooking Time: 2 Hours 25 Minutes
Ingredients:
- 1/3 cup sour cream

- 2 cloves garlic, finely minced
- 1/3 teaspoon lemon zest
- 2 small-sized turkey breasts, skinless and cubed
- 1/3 cup thickened cream
- 2 tablespoons lemon juice
- 1 teaspoon fresh marjoram, chopped
- Salt and freshly cracked mixed peppercorns, to taste
- 1/2 cup scallion, chopped
- 1/2 can tomatoes, diced
- 1 ½ tablespoons canola oil

Directions:
1. Firstly, pat dry the turkey breast. Mix the remaining items; marinate the turkey for 2 hours.
2. Set the air fryer to cook at 355 degrees F. Brush the turkey with a nonstick spray; cook for 23 minutes, turning once. Serve with naan and enjoy!

556.Creamed Cajun Chicken

Servings: 6
Cooking Time: 10 Minutes
Ingredients:
- 3 green onions, thinly sliced
- ½ tablespoon Cajun seasoning
- 1 ½ cup buttermilk
- 2 large-sized chicken breasts, cut into strips
- 1/2 teaspoon garlic powder
- 1 teaspoon salt
- 1 cup cornmeal mix
- 1 teaspoon shallot powder
- 1 ½ cup flour
- 1 teaspoon ground black pepper, or to taste

Directions:
1. Prepare three mixing bowls. Combine 1/2 cup of the plain flour together with the cornmeal and Cajun seasoning in your bowl. In another bowl, place the buttermilk.
2. Pour the remaining 1 cup of flour into the third bowl.
3. Sprinkle the chicken strips with all the seasonings. Then, dip each chicken strip in the 1 cup of flour, then in the buttermilk; finally, dredge them in the cornmeal mixture.
4. Cook the chicken strips in the air fryer baking pan for 16 minutes at 365 degrees F. Serve garnished with green onions. Bon appétit!

557.Mediterranean Roasted Vegetable And Bean Salad

Servings: 4
Cooking Time: 20 Minutes
Ingredients:
- 1 red onion, sliced
- 1 pound cherry tomatoes

- 1/2 pound asparagus
- 1 cucumber, sliced
- 2 cups baby spinach
- 2 tablespoons white vinegar
- 1/4 cup extra-virgin olive oil
- 2 tablespoons fresh parsley
- Sea salt and pepper to taste
- 8 ounces canned red kidney beans, rinsed
- 1/2 cup Kalamata olives, pitted and sliced

Directions:
1. Begin by preheating your Air Fryer to 400 degrees F.
2. Place the onion, cherry tomatoes, and asparagus in the lightly greased Air Fryer basket. Bake for 5 to 6 minutes, tossing the basket occasionally.
3. Transfer to a salad bowl. Add the cucumber and baby spinach.
4. Then, whisk the vinegar, olive oil, parsley, salt, and black pepper in a small mixing bowl. Dress your salad; add the beans and olives.
5. Toss to combine well and serve.

558.Potato Appetizer With Garlic-mayo Sauce

Servings: 4
Cooking Time: 19 Minutes
Ingredients:
- 2 tablespoons vegetable oil of choice
- Kosher salt and freshly ground black pepper, to taste
- 3 Russet potatoes, cut into wedges
- For the Dipping Sauce:
- 2 teaspoons dried rosemary, crushed
- 3 garlic cloves, minced
- 1/3 teaspoon dried marjoram, crushed
- 1/4 cup sour cream
- 1/3 cup mayonnaise

Directions:
1. Lightly grease your potatoes with a thin layer of vegetable oil. Season with salt and ground black pepper.
2. Arrange the seasoned potato wedges in an air fryer cooking basket. Bake at 395 degrees F for 15 minutes, shaking once or twice.
3. In the meantime, prepare the dipping sauce by mixing all the sauce ingredients. Serve the potatoes with the dipping sauce and enjoy!

559.Award Winning Breaded Chicken

Servings: 4
Cooking Time: 10 Minutes + Marinating Time
Ingredients:
- For the Marinade:
- 1 1/2 teaspoons olive oil
- 1 teaspoon red pepper flakes, crushed

- 1/3 teaspoon chicken bouillon granules
- 1/3 teaspoon shallot powder
- 1 1/2 tablespoons tamari soy sauce
- 1/3 teaspoon cumin powder
- 1 ½ tablespoons mayo
- 1 teaspoon kosher salt
- For the chicken:
- 2 beaten eggs
- Breadcrumbs
- 1 ½ chicken breasts, boneless and skinless
- 1 ½ tablespoons plain flour

Directions:
1. Butterfly the chicken breasts, and then, marinate them for at least 55 minutes.
2. Coat the chicken with plain flour; then, coat with the beaten eggs; finally, roll them in the breadcrumbs.
3. Lightly grease the cooking basket. Air-fry the breaded chicken at 345 degrees F for 12 minutes, flipping them halfway.

560.Spicy Omelet With Ground Chicken

Servings: 2
Cooking Time: 15 Minutes
Ingredients:
- 4 eggs, whisked
- 4 ounces ground chicken
- 1/2 cup scallions, finely chopped
- 2 cloves garlic, finely minced
- 1/2 teaspoon salt
- 1/2 teaspoon ground black pepper
- 1/2 teaspoon paprika
- 1 teaspoon dried thyme
- A dash of hot sauce

Directions:
1. Thoroughly combine all the ingredients in a mixing dish. Now, scrape the egg mixture into two oven safe ramekins that are previously greased with a thin layer of the vegetable oil.
2. Set your machine to cook at 350 degrees F; air-fry for 13 minutes or until thoroughly cooked. Serve immediately.

561.Dinner Turkey Sandwiches

Servings: 4
Cooking Time: 4 Hours 30 Minutes
Ingredients:
- 1/2 pound turkey breast
- 1 teaspoon garlic powder
- 7 ounces condensed cream of onion soup
- 1/3 teaspoon ground allspice
- BBQ sauce, to savor

Directions:
1. Simply dump the cream of onion soup and turkey breast into your crock-pot. Cook on HIGH heat setting for 3 hours.
2. Then, shred the meat and transfer to a lightly greased baking dish.

3. Pour in your favorite BBQ sauce. Sprinkle with ground allspice and garlic powder. Air-fry an additional 28 minutes.
4. To finish, assemble the sandwiches; add toppings such as pickled or fresh salad, mustard, etc.

562.Baked Eggs Florentine

Servings: 2
Cooking Time: 20 Minutes
Ingredients:
- 1 tablespoon ghee, melted
- 2 cups baby spinach, torn into small pieces
- 2 tablespoons shallots, chopped
- 1/4 teaspoon red pepper flakes
- Salt, to taste
- 1 tablespoon fresh thyme leaves, roughly chopped
- 4 eggs

Directions:
1. Start by preheating your Air Fryer to 350 degrees F. Brush the sides and bottom of a gratin dish with the melted ghee.
2. Put the spinach and shallots into the bottom of the gratin dish. Season with red pepper, salt, and fresh thyme.
3. Make four indents for the eggs; crack one egg into each indent. Bake for 12 minutes, rotating the pan once or twice to ensure even cooking. Enjoy!

563.Delicious Hot Fruit Bake

Servings: 4
Cooking Time: 40 Minutes
Ingredients:
- 2 cups blueberries
- 2 cups raspberries
- 1 tablespoon cornstarch
- 3 tablespoons maple syrup
- 2 tablespoons coconut oil, melted
- A pinch of freshly grated nutmeg
- A pinch of salt
- 1 cinnamon stick
- 1 vanilla bean

Directions:
1. Place your berries in a lightly greased baking dish. Sprinkle the cornstarch onto the fruit.
2. Whisk the maple syrup, coconut oil, nutmeg, and salt in a mixing dish; add this mixture to the berries and gently stir to combine.
3. Add the cinnamon and vanilla. Bake in the preheated Air Fryer at 370 degrees F for 35 minutes. Serve warm or at room temperature. Enjoy!

564.Rosemary Roasted Mixed Nuts

Servings: 6
Cooking Time: 20 Minutes

Ingredients:
- 2 tablespoons butter, at room temperature
- 1 tablespoon dried rosemary
- 1 teaspoon coarse sea salt
- 1/2 teaspoon paprika
- 1/2 cup pine nuts
- 1 cup pecans
- 1/2 cup hazelnuts

Directions:
1. Toss all the ingredients in the mixing bowl.
2. Line the Air Fryer basket with baking parchment. Spread out the coated nuts in a single layer in the basket.
3. Roast at 350 degrees F for 6 to 8 minutes, shaking the basket once or twice. Work in batches. Enjoy!

565.Family Favorite Stuffed Mushrooms

Servings: 2
Cooking Time: 16 Minutes
Ingredients:
- 2 teaspoons cumin powder
- 4 garlic cloves, peeled and minced
- 1 small onion, peeled and chopped
- 2 tablespoons bran cereal, crushed
- 18 medium-sized white mushrooms
- Fine sea salt and freshly ground black pepper, to your liking
- A pinch ground allspice
- 2 tablespoons olive oil

Directions:
1. First, clean the mushrooms; remove the middle stalks from the mushrooms to prepare the "shells".
2. Grab a mixing dish and thoroughly combine the remaining items. Fill the mushrooms with the prepared mixture.
3. Cook the mushrooms at 345 degrees F heat for 12 minutes. Enjoy!

566.Spicy Eggs With Sausage And Swiss Cheese

Servings: 6
Cooking Time: 25 Minutes
Ingredients:
- 1 teaspoon lard
- 1/2 pound turkey sausage
- 6 eggs
- 1 scallion, chopped
- 1 garlic clove, minced
- 1 bell pepper, seeded and chopped
- 1 chili pepper, seeded and chopped
- Sea salt and ground black pepper, to taste
- 1/2 cup Swiss cheese, shredded

Directions:
1. Start by preheating your Air Fryer to 330 degrees F. Now, spritz 4 silicone molds with cooking spray.
2. Melt the lard in a saucepan over medium-high heat. Now, cook the sausage for 5 minutes or until no longer pink.
3. Coarsely chop the sausage; add the eggs, scallions, garlic, peppers, salt, and black pepper. Divide the egg mixture between the silicone molds. Top with the shredded cheese.
4. Bake in the preheated Air Fryer at 340 degrees F for 15 minutes, checking halfway through the cooking time to ensure even cooking. Enjoy!

567.Parmesan-crusted Fish Fingers

Servings: 4
Cooking Time: 20 Minutes
Ingredients:
- 1 ½ pounds tilapia pieces (fingers)
- 1/2 cup coconut flour
- 2 eggs
- 1 tablespoon yellow mustard
- 1 cup parmesan cheese, grated
- 1 teaspoon garlic powder
- 1 teaspoon onion powder
- Sea salt and ground black pepper, to taste
- 1/2 teaspoon celery powder
- 2 tablespoons peanut oil

Directions:
1. Pat dry the fish fingers with a kitchen towel.
2. To make a breading station, place the coconut flour in a shallow dish. In a separate dish, whisk the eggs with mustard.
3. In a third bowl, mix parmesan cheese with the remaining ingredients.
4. Dredge the fish fingers in the flour, shaking the excess into the bowl; dip in the egg mixture and turn to coat evenly; then, dredge in the parmesan mixture, turning a couple of times to coat evenly.
5. Cook in the preheated Air Fryer at 390 degrees F for 5 minutes; turn them over and cook another 5 minutes. Enjoy!

568.Bagel 'n' Egg Melts

Servings: 3
Cooking Time: 25 Minutes
Ingredients:
- 3 eggs
- 3 slices smoked ham, chopped
- 1 teaspoon Dijon mustard
- 1/4 cup mayonnaise
- Salt and white pepper, to taste
- 3 bagels
- 3 ounces Colby cheese, shredded

Directions:
1. Place the wire rack in the Air Fryer basket; lower the eggs onto the wire rack.
2. Cook at 270 degrees F for 15 minutes.

3. Transfer them to an ice-cold water bath to stop the cooking. Peel the eggs under cold running water; coarsely chop them and set aside.
4. Combine the chopped eggs, ham, mustard, mayonnaise, salt, and pepper in a mixing bowl.
5. Slice the bagels in half. Spread the egg mixture on top and sprinkle with the shredded cheese.
6. Grill in the preheated Air Fryer at 360 degrees F for 7 minutes or until cheese is melted. Bon appétit!

569.Country-style Apple Fries

Servings: 4
Cooking Time: 20 Minutes
Ingredients:
- 1/2 cup milk
- 1 egg
- 1/2 all-purpose flour
- 1 teaspoon baking powder
- 4 tablespoons brown sugar
- 1 teaspoon vanilla extract
- 1/2 teaspoon ground cloves
- A pinch of kosher salt
- A pinch of grated nutmeg
- 1 tablespoon coconut oil, melted
- 2 Pink Lady apples, cored, peeled, slice into pieces (shape and size of French fries
- 1/3 cup granulated sugar
- 1 teaspoon ground cinnamon

Directions:
1. In a mixing bowl, whisk the milk and eggs; gradually stir in the flour; add the baking powder, brown sugar, vanilla, cloves, salt, nutmeg, and melted coconut oil. Mix to combine well.
2. Dip each apple slice into the batter, coating on all sides. Spritz the bottom of the cooking basket with cooking oil.
3. Cook the apple fries in the preheated Air Fryer at 395 degrees F approximately 8 minutes, turning them over halfway through the cooking time.
4. Cook in small batches to ensure even cooking.
5. In the meantime, mix the granulated sugar with the ground cinnamon; sprinkle the cinnamon sugar over the apple fries. Serve warm.

570.Cheese And Chive Stuffed Chicken Rolls

Servings: 6
Cooking Time: 20 Minutes
Ingredients:
- 2 eggs, well-whisked
- Tortilla chips, crushed

- 1 1/2 tablespoons extra-virgin olive oil
- 1 ½ tablespoons fresh chives, chopped
- 3 chicken breasts, halved lengthwise
- 1 ½ cup soft cheese
- 2 teaspoons sweet paprika
- 1/2 teaspoon whole grain mustard
- 1/2 teaspoon cumin powder
- 1/3 teaspoon fine sea salt
- 1/3 cup fresh cilantro, chopped
- 1/3 teaspoon freshly ground black pepper, or more to taste

Directions:
1. Flatten out each piece of the chicken breast using a rolling pin. Then, grab three mixing dishes.
2. In the first one, combine the soft cheese with the cilantro, fresh chives, cumin, and mustard.
3. In another mixing dish, whisk the eggs together with the sweet paprika. In the third dish, combine the salt, black pepper, and crushed tortilla chips.
4. Spread the cheese mixture over each piece of chicken. Repeat with the remaining pieces of the chicken breasts; now, roll them up.
5. Coat each chicken roll with the whisked egg; dredge each chicken roll into the tortilla chips mixture. Lower the rolls onto the air fryer cooking basket. Drizzle extra-virgin olive oil over all rolls.
6. Air fry at 345 degrees F for 28 minutes, working in batches. Serve warm, garnished with sour cream if desired.

571.Spicy Peppery Egg Salad

Servings: 3
Cooking Time: 20 Minutes + Chilling Time
Ingredients:
- 6 eggs
- 1 teaspoon mustard
- 1/2 cup mayonnaise
- 1 tablespoon white vinegar
- 1 habanero pepper, minced
- 1 red bell pepper, seeded and sliced
- 1 green bell pepper, seeded and sliced
- 1 shallot, sliced
- Sea salt and ground black pepper, to taste

Directions:
1. Place the wire rack in the Air Fryer basket; lower the eggs onto the wire rack.
2. Cook at 270 degrees F for 15 minutes.
3. Transfer them to an ice-cold water bath to stop the cooking. Peel the eggs under cold running water; coarsely chop the hard-boiled eggs and set aside.
4. Toss with the remaining ingredients and serve well chilled. Bon appétit!

572.Beef And Kale Omelet

Servings: 4
Cooking Time: 20 Minutes
Ingredients:
- Non-stick cooking spray
- 1/2 pound leftover beef, coarsely chopped
- 2 garlic cloves, pressed
- 1 cup kale, torn into pieces and wilted
- 1 tomato, chopped
- 1/4 teaspoon brown sugar
- 4 eggs, beaten
- 4 tablespoons heavy cream
- 1/2 teaspoon turmeric powder
- Salt and ground black pepper, to your liking
- 1/8 teaspoon ground allspice

Directions:
1. Spritz the inside of four ramekins with a cooking spray.
2. Divide all of the above ingredients among the prepared ramekins. Stir until everything is well combined.
3. Air-fry at 360 degrees F for 16 minutes; check with a wooden stick and return the eggs to the Air Fryer for a few more minutes as needed. Serve immediately.

573.Parmesan Broccoli Fritters

Servings: 6
Cooking Time: 30 Minutes
Ingredients:
- 1 1/2 cups Monterey Jack cheese
- 1 teaspoon dried dill weed
- 1/3 teaspoon ground black pepper
- 3 eggs, whisked
- 1 teaspoon cayenne pepper
- 1/2 teaspoon kosher salt
- 2 ½ cups broccoli florets
- 1/2 cup Parmesan cheese

Directions:
1. Blitz the broccoli florets in a food processor until finely crumbed. Then, combine the broccoli with the rest of the above ingredients.
2. Roll the mixture into small balls; place the balls in the fridge for approximately half an hour.
3. Preheat your Air Fryer to 335 degrees F and set the timer to 14 minutes; cook until broccoli croquettes are browned and serve warm.

574.The Best London Broil Ever

Servings: 8
Cooking Time: 30 Minutes + Marinating Time
Ingredients:
- 2 pounds London broil
- 3 large garlic cloves, minced
- 3 tablespoons balsamic vinegar
- 3 tablespoons whole-grain mustard
- 2 tablespoons olive oil
- Sea salt and ground black pepper, to taste
- 1/2 teaspoon dried hot red pepper flakes

Directions:
1. Score both sides of the cleaned London broil.
2. Thoroughly combine the remaining ingredients; massage this mixture into the meat to coat it on all sides. Let it marinate for at least 3 hours.
3. Set the Air Fryer to cook at 400 degrees F; Then cook the London broil for 15 minutes. Flip it over and cook another 10 to 12 minutes. Bon appétit!

575.Cottage Cheese Stuffed Chicken Rolls

Servings: 2
Cooking Time: 20 Minutes
Ingredients:
- 1/2 cup Cottage cheese
- 2 eggs, beaten
- 2 medium-sized chicken breasts, halved
- 2 tablespoons fresh coriander, chopped
- 1 teaspoon fine sea salt
- 1/2 cup parmesan cheese, grated
- 1/3 teaspoon freshly ground black pepper, to savor
- 3 cloves garlic, finely minced

Directions:
1. Firstly, flatten out the chicken breast using a meat tenderizer.
2. In a medium-sized mixing dish, combine the Cottage cheese with the garlic, coriander, salt, and black pepper.
3. Spread 1/3 of the mixture over the first chicken breast. Repeat with the remaining ingredients. Roll the chicken around the filling; make sure to secure with toothpicks.
4. Now, whisk the egg in a shallow bowl. In another shallow bowl, combine the salt, ground black pepper, and parmesan cheese.
5. Coat the chicken breasts with the whisked egg; now, roll them in the parmesan cheese.
6. Cook in the air fryer cooking basket at 365 degrees F for 22 minutes. Serve immediately.

576.Masala-style Baked Eggs

Servings: 6
Cooking Time: 25 Minutes
Ingredients:
- 6 medium-sized eggs, beaten
- 1 teaspoon garam masala
- 1 cup scallions, finely chopped
- 3 cloves garlic, finely minced
- 2 cups leftover chicken, shredded
- 2 tablespoons sesame oil
- Hot sauce, for drizzling
- 1 teaspoon turmeric

- 1 teaspoon mixed peppercorns, freshly cracked
- 1 teaspoon kosher salt
- 1/3 teaspoon smoked paprika

Directions:
1. Warm sesame oil in a sauté pan over a moderate flame; then, sauté the scallions together with garlic until just fragrant; it takes about 5 minutes. Now, throw in leftover chicken and stir until thoroughly warmed.
2. In a medium-sized bowl or a measuring cup, thoroughly combine the eggs with all seasonings.
3. Then, coat the inside of six oven safe ramekins with a nonstick cooking spray. Divide the egg/chicken mixture among your ramekins.
4. Air-fry approximately 18 minutes at 355 degrees F. Drizzle with hot sauce and eat warm.

577. Keto Rolls With Halibut And Eggs

Servings: 4
Cooking Time: 25 Minutes
Ingredients:
- 4 keto rolls
- 1 pound smoked halibut, chopped
- 4 eggs
- 1 teaspoon dried thyme
- 1 teaspoon dried basil
- Salt and black pepper, to taste

Directions:
1. Cut off the top of each keto roll; then, scoop out the insides to make the shells.
2. Lay the prepared keto roll shells in the lightly greased cooking basket.
3. Spritz with cooking oil; add the halibut. Crack an egg into each keto roll shell; sprinkle with thyme, basil, salt, and black pepper.
4. Bake in the preheated Air Fryer at 325 degrees F for 20 minutes. Bon appétit!

578. All-in-one Spicy Spaghetti With Beef

Servings: 4
Cooking Time: 30 Minutes
Ingredients:
- 3/4 pound ground chuck
- 1 onion, peeled and finely chopped
- 1 teaspoon garlic paste
- 1 bell pepper, chopped
- 1 small-sized habanero pepper, deveined and finely minced
- 1/2 teaspoon dried rosemary
- 1/2 teaspoon dried marjoram
- 1 ¼ cups crushed tomatoes, fresh or canned
- 1/2 teaspoon sea salt flakes

- 1/4 teaspoon ground black pepper, or more to taste
- 1 package cooked spaghetti, to serve

Directions:
1. In the Air Fryer baking dish, place the ground meat, onion, garlic paste, bell pepper, habanero pepper, rosemary, and the marjoram.
2. Air-fry, uncovered, for 10 to 11 minutes. Next step, stir in the tomatoes along with salt and pepper; cook 17 to 20 minutes. Serve over cooked spaghetti. Bon appétit!

579. Famous Cheese And Bacon Rolls

Servings: 6
Cooking Time: 10 Minutes
Ingredients:
- 1/3 cup Swiss cheese, shredded
- 10 slices of bacon
- 10 ounces canned crescent rolls
- 2 tablespoons yellow mustard 6

Directions:
1. Start by preheating your air fryer to 325 degrees F.
2. Then, form the crescent rolls into "sheets". Spread mustard over the sheets. Place the chopped Swiss cheese and bacon in the middle of each dough sheet.
3. Create the rolls and bake them for about 9 minutes.
4. Then, set the machine to 385 degrees F; bake for an additional 4 minutes in the preheated air fryer. Eat warm with some extra yellow mustard.

580. Cornbread With Pulled Pork

Servings: 2
Cooking Time: 24 Minutes
Ingredients:
- 2 ½ cups pulled pork, leftover works well too
- 1 teaspoon dried rosemary
- 1/2 teaspoon chili powder
- 3 cloves garlic, peeled and pressed
- 1/2 recipe cornbread
- 1/2 tablespoon brown sugar
- 1/3 cup scallions, thinly sliced
- 1 teaspoon sea salt

Directions:
1. Preheat a large-sized nonstick skillet over medium heat; now, cook the scallions together with the garlic and pulled pork.
2. Next, add the sugar, chili powder, rosemary, and salt. Cook, stirring occasionally, until the mixture is thickened.
3. Preheat your air fryer to 335 degrees F. Now, coat two mini loaf pans with a cooking spray. Add the pulled pork mixture and spread over the bottom using a spatula.

4. Spread the previously prepared cornbread batter over top of the spiced pulled pork mixture.
5. Bake this cornbread in the preheated air fryer until a tester inserted into the center of it comes out clean, or for 18 minutes. Bon appétit!

581.Zesty Broccoli Bites With Hot Sauce

Servings: 6
Cooking Time: 20 Minutes
Ingredients:
- For the Broccoli Bites:
- 1 medium-sized head broccoli, broken into florets
- 1/2 teaspoon lemon zest, freshly grated
- 1/3 teaspoon fine sea salt
- 1/2 teaspoon hot paprika
- 1 teaspoon shallot powder
- 1 teaspoon porcini powder
- 1/2 teaspoon granulated garlic
- 1/3 teaspoon celery seeds
- 1 ½ tablespoons olive oil
- For the Hot Sauce:
- 1/2 cup tomato sauce
- 3 tablespoons brown sugar
- 1 tablespoon balsamic vinegar
- 1/2 teaspoon ground allspice

Directions:
1. Toss all the ingredients for the broccoli bites in a mixing bowl, covering the broccoli florets on all sides.
2. Cook them in the preheated Air Fryer at 360 degrees for 13 to 15 minutes. In the meantime, mix all ingredients for the hot sauce.
3. Pause your Air Fryer, mix the broccoli with the prepared sauce and cook for further 3 minutes. Bon appétit!

582.Spring Chocolate Doughnuts

Servings: 6
Cooking Time: 20 Minutes
Ingredients:
- 1 can (16-ounce can buttermilk biscuits
- Chocolate Glaze:
- 1 cup powdered sugar
- 4 tablespoons unsweetened baking cocoa
- 2 tablespoon butter, melted
- 2 tablespoons milk

Directions:
1. Bake your biscuits in the preheated Air Fryer at 350 degrees F for 8 minutes, flipping them halfway through the cooking time.
2. While the biscuits are baking, make the glaze.

3. Beat the ingredients with whisk until smooth, adding enough milk for the desired consistency; set aside.
4. Dip your doughnuts into the chocolate glaze and transfer to a cooling rack to set. Bon appétit!

583.Onion Rings With Mayo Dip

Servings: 3
Cooking Time: 25 Minutes
Ingredients:
- 1 large onion
- 1/2 cup almond flour
- 1 teaspoon salt
- 1/2 teaspoon ground black pepper
- 1 teaspoon cayenne pepper
- 1/2 teaspoon dried thyme
- 1/2 teaspoon dried oregano
- 1/2 teaspoon ground cumin
- 2 eggs
- 4 tablespoons milk
- Mayo Dip:
- 3 tablespoons mayonnaise
- 3 tablespoons sour cream
- 1 tablespoon horseradish, drained
- Kosher salt and freshly ground black pepper, to taste

Directions:
1. Cut off the top 1/2 inch of the Vidalia onion; peel your onion and place it cut-side down. Starting 1/2 inch from the root, cut the onion in half. Make a second cut that splits each half in two. You will have 4 quarters held together by the root.
2. Repeat these cuts, splitting the 4 quarters to yield eighths; then, you should split them again until you have 16 evenly spaced cuts. Turn the onion over and gently separate the outer pieces using your fingers.
3. In a mixing bowl, thoroughly combine the almond flour and spices. In a separate bowl, whisk the eggs and milk. Dip the onion into the egg mixture, followed by the almond flour mixture.
4. Spritz the onion with cooking spray and transfer to the lightly greased cooking basket. Cook for 370 degrees F for 12 to 15 minutes.
5. Meanwhile, make the mayo dip by whisking the remaining ingredients. Serve and enjoy!

584.Spicy Potato Wedges

Servings: 4
Cooking Time: 23 Minutes
Ingredients:
- 1 ½ tablespoons melted butter
- 1 teaspoon dried parsley flakes
- 1 teaspoon ground coriander
- 1 teaspoon seasoned salt

- 3 large-sized red potatoes, cut into wedges
- 1/2 teaspoon chili powder
- 1/3 teaspoon garlic pepper

Directions:
1. Dump the potato wedges into the air fryer cooking basket. Drizzle with melted butter and cook for 20 minutes at 380 degrees F. Make sure to shake them a couple of times during the cooking process.
2. Add the remaining ingredients; toss to coat potato wedges on all sides. Bon appétit!

585.Italian Cheese Chips

Servings: 4
Cooking Time: 15 Minutes
Ingredients:
- 1 cup Parmesan cheese, shredded
- 1 cup Cheddar cheese, shredded
- 1 teaspoon Italian seasoning
- 1/2 cup marinara sauce

Directions:
1. Start by preheating your Air Fryer to 350 degrees F. Place a piece of parchment paper in the cooking basket.
2. Mix the cheese with the Italian seasoning.
3. Add about 1 tablespoon of the cheese mixture (per crisp) to the basket, making sure they are not touching. Bake for 6 minutes or until browned to your liking.
4. Work in batches and place them on a large tray to cool slightly. Serve with the marinara sauce. Bon appétit!

586.Greek Omelet With Halloumi Cheese

Servings: 2
Cooking Time: 17 Minutes
Ingredients:
- 1/2 cup Halloumi cheese, sliced
- 2 teaspoons garlic paste
- 2 teaspoons fresh chopped rosemary
- 4 well-whisked eggs
- 2 bell peppers, seeded and chopped
- 1 ½ tablespoons fresh basil, chopped
- 3 tablespoons onions, chopped
- Fine sea salt and ground black pepper, to taste

Directions:
1. Spritz your baking dish with a canola cooking spray.
2. Throw in all ingredients and stir until everything is well incorporated.
3. Bake for about 15 minutes at 325 degrees F. Eat warm.

587.Chicken Drumsticks With Ketchup-lemon Sauce

Servings: 6
Cooking Time: 20 Minutes + Marinating Time
Ingredients:

- 3 tablespoons lemon juice
- 1 cup tomato ketchup
- 1 ½ tablespoons fresh rosemary, chopped
- 6 skin-on chicken drumsticks, boneless
- 1/2 teaspoon ground black pepper
- 2 teaspoons lemon zest, grated
- 1/3 cup honey
- 3 cloves garlic, minced

Directions:
1. Dump the chicken drumsticks into a mixing dish. Now, add the other items and give it a good stir; let it marinate overnight in your refrigerator.
2. Discard the marinade; roast the chicken legs in your air fryer at 375 degrees F for 22 minutes, turning once.
3. Now, add the marinade and cook an additional 6 minutes or until everything is warmed through.

588.Peppery Roasted Potatoes With Smoked Bacon

Servings: 2
Cooking Time: 15 Minutes
Ingredients:
- 5 small rashers smoked bacon
- 1/3 teaspoon garlic powder
- 1 teaspoon sea salt
- 2 teaspoons paprika
- 1/3 teaspoon ground black pepper
- 1 bell pepper, seeded and sliced
- 1 teaspoon mustard
- 2 habanero peppers, halved

Directions:
1. Simply toss all the ingredients in a mixing dish; then, transfer them to your air fryer's basket.
2. Air-fry at 375 degrees F for 10 minutes. Serve warm.

589.Steak Fingers With Mushrooms And Swiss Cheese

Servings: 4
Cooking Time: 25 Minutes
Ingredients:
- 2 eggs, beaten
- 4 tablespoons yogurt
- 1 cup parmesan cheese, grated
- 1 teaspoon dry mesquite flavored seasoning mix
- Coarse salt and ground black pepper, to taste
- 1/2 teaspoon onion powder
- 1 pound cube steak, cut into 3 inch long strips
- 1 pound button mushrooms
- 1 cup Swiss cheese, shredded

Directions:

1. In a shallow bowl, beat the eggs and yogurt. In a resealable bag, mix the parmesan cheese, mesquite seasoning, salt, pepper, and onion powder.
2. Dip the steak pieces in the egg mixture; then, place in the bag, and shake to coat on all sides.
3. Cook at 400 degrees F for 14 minutes, flipping halfway through the cooking time.
4. Add the mushrooms to the lightly greased cooking basket. Top with shredded Swiss cheese.
5. Bake in the preheated Air Fryer at 400 degrees F for 5 minutes. Serve with the beef nuggets. Bon appétit!

590.Cheddar Cheese And Pastrami Casserole

Servings: 2
Cooking Time: 20 Minutes
Ingredients:
- 4 eggs
- 1 bell pepper, chopped
- 2 spring onions, chopped
- 1 cup pastrami, sliced
- 1/4 cup Greek-style yogurt
- 1/2 cup Cheddar cheese, grated
- Sea salt, to taste
- 1/4 teaspoon ground black pepper

Directions:
1. Start by preheating your Air Fryer to 330 degrees F. Spritz the baking pan with cooking oil.
2. Then, thoroughly combine all ingredients and pour the mixture into the prepared baking pan.
3. Cook for 7 to 9 minutes or until the eggs have set. Place on a cooling rack and let it sit for 10 minutes before slicing and serving.

591.Easy Fried Button Mushrooms

Servings: 4
Cooking Time: 15 Minutes
Ingredients:
- 1 pound button mushrooms
- 1 cup cornstarch
- 1 cup all-purpose flour
- 1/2 teaspoon baking powder
- 2 eggs, whisked
- 2 cups seasoned breadcrumbs
- 1/2 teaspoon salt
- 2 tablespoons fresh parsley leaves, roughly chopped

Directions:
1. Pat the mushrooms dry with a paper towel.
2. To begin, set up your breading station. Mix the cornstarch, flour, and baking powder in a shallow dish. In a separate dish, whisk the eggs.
3. Finally, place your breadcrumbs and salt in a third dish.
4. Start by dredging the mushrooms in the flour mixture; then, dip them into the eggs. Press your mushrooms into the breadcrumbs, coating evenly.
5. Spritz the Air Fryer basket with cooking oil. Add the mushrooms and cook at 400 degrees F for 6 minutes, flipping them halfway through the cooking time.
6. Serve garnished with fresh parsley leaves. Bon appétit!

592.Italian Creamy Frittata With Kale

Servings: 3
Cooking Time: 20 Minutes
Ingredients:
- 1 yellow onion, finely chopped
- 6 ounces wild mushrooms, sliced
- 6 eggs
- 1/4 cup double cream
- 1/2 teaspoon cayenne pepper
- Sea salt and ground black pepper, to taste
- 1 tablespoon butter, melted
- 2 tablespoons fresh Italian parsley, chopped
- 2 cups kale, chopped
- 1/2 cup mozzarella, shredded

Directions:
1. Begin by preheating the Air Fryer to 360 degrees F. Spritz the sides and bottom of a baking pan with cooking oil.
2. Add the onions and wild mushrooms, and cook in the preheated Air Fryer at 360 degrees F for 4 to 5 minutes.
3. In a mixing dish, whisk the eggs and double cream until pale. Add the spices, butter, parsley, and kale; stir until everything is well incorporated.
4. Pour the mixture into the baking pan with the mushrooms.
5. Top with the cheese. Cook in the preheated Air Fryer for 10 minutes. Serve immediately and enjoy!

593.Snapper With Gruyere Cheese

Servings: 4
Cooking Time: 25 Minutes
Ingredients:
- 2 tablespoons olive oil
- 1 shallot, thinly sliced
- 2 garlic cloves, minced
- 1 ½ pounds snapper fillets
- Sea salt and ground black pepper, to taste
- 1 teaspoon cayenne pepper
- 1/2 teaspoon dried basil
- 1/2 cup tomato puree
- 1/2 cup white wine
- 1 cup Gruyere cheese, shredded

Directions:

1. Heat 1 tablespoon of olive oil in a saucepan over medium-high heat. Now, cook the shallot and garlic until tender and aromatic.
2. Preheat your Air Fryer to 370 degrees F.
3. Grease a casserole dish with 1 tablespoon of olive oil. Place the snapper fillet in the casserole dish. Season with salt, black pepper, and cayenne pepper. Add the sautéed shallot mixture.
4. Add the basil, tomato puree and wine to the casserole dish. Cook for 10 minutes in the preheated Air Fryer.
5. Top with the shredded cheese and cook an additional 7 minutes. Serve immediately.

594. Winter Baked Eggs With Italian Sausage

Servings: 4
Cooking Time: 30 Minutes
Ingredients:
- 1 pound Italian sausage
- 2 sprigs rosemary
- 1 celery, sliced
- 1/2 pound broccoli, cut into small florets
- 2 sprigs thyme
- 1 bell pepper, trimmed and cut into matchsticks
- 2 garlic cloves, smashed
- 2 tablespoons extra-virgin olive oil
- 1 leek, cut into halves lengthwise
- A pinch of grated nutmeg
- Salt and black pepper, to taste
- 4 whole eggs

Directions:
1. Arrange vegetables on the bottom of the Air Fryer baking dish.
2. Sprinkle with the seasonings and top with the sausage.
3. Roast approximately 20 minutes at 375 degrees F, stirring occasionally. Top with eggs and reduce the temperature to 330 degrees F.
4. Bake an additional 5 to 6 minutes. Bon appétit!

595. Country-style Pork Meatloaf

Servings: 4
Cooking Time: 25 Minutes
Ingredients:
- 1/2 pound lean minced pork
- 1/3 cup breadcrumbs
- 1/2 tablespoons minced green garlic
- 1½ tablespoon fresh cilantro, minced
- 1/2 tablespoon fish sauce
- 1/3 teaspoon dried basil
- 2 leeks, chopped
- 2 tablespoons tomato puree
- 1/2 teaspoons dried thyme
- Salt and ground black pepper, to taste

Directions:
1. Add all ingredients, except for breadcrumbs, to a large-sized mixing dish and combine everything using your hands.
2. Lastly, add the breadcrumbs to form a meatloaf.
3. Bake for 23 minutes at 365 degrees F. Afterward, allow your meatloaf to rest for 10 minutes before slicing and serving. Bon appétit!

596. Traditional Onion Bhaji

Servings: 3
Cooking Time: 40 Minutes
Ingredients:
- 1 egg, beaten
- 2 tablespoons olive oil
- 2 onions, sliced
- 1 green chili, deseeded and finely chopped
- 2 ounces chickpea flour
- 1 ounce all-purpose flour
- Salt and black pepper, to taste
- 1 teaspoon cumin seeds
- 1/2 teaspoon ground turmeric

Directions:
1. Place all ingredients, except for the onions, in a mixing dish; mix to combine well, adding a little water to the mixture.
2. Once you've got a thick batter, add the onions; stir to coat well.
3. Cook in the preheated Air Fryer at 370 degrees F for 20 minutes flipping them halfway through the cooking time.
4. Work in batches and transfer to a serving platter. Enjoy!

597. Grilled Cheese Sandwich

Servings: 1
Cooking Time: 15 Minutes
Ingredients:
- 2 slices artisan bread
- 1 tablespoon butter, softened
- 1 tablespoon tomato ketchup
- 1/2 teaspoon dried oregano
- 2 slices Cheddar cheese

Directions:
1. Brush one side of each slice of the bread with melted butter.
2. Add the tomato ketchup, oregano, and cheese. Make the sandwich and grill at 360 degrees F for 9 minutes or until cheese is melted. Bon appétit!

598. Hearty Southwestern Cheeseburger Frittata

Servings: 2
Cooking Time: 30 Minutes
Ingredients:
- 3 tablespoons goat cheese, crumbled

- 2 cups lean ground beef
- 1 ½ tablespoons olive oil
- ½ teaspoon dried marjoram
- 2 eggs
- ½ onion, peeled and chopped
- ½ teaspoon paprika
- ½ teaspoon kosher salt
- 1 teaspoon ground black pepper

Directions:
1. Set your air fryer to cook at 345 degrees F.
2. Melt the oil in a skillet over a moderate flame; then, sweat the onion until it has softened. Add ground beef and cook until browned; crumble with a fork and set aside, keeping it warm.
3. Whisk the eggs with all the seasonings.
4. Spritz the inside of a baking dish with a pan spray. Pour the beaten egg mixture into the baking dish, followed by the reserved beef/onion mixture. Top with the crumbled goat cheese.
5. Bake for about 27 minutes or until a tester comes out clean and dry when stuck in the center of the frittata. Bon appétit!

599.Celery Fries With Harissa Mayo

Servings: 3
Cooking Time: 30 Minutes
Ingredients:
- 1/2 pound celery root
- 2 tablespoons olive oil
- Sea salt and ground black pepper, to taste
- Harissa Mayo
- 1/4 cup mayonnaise
- 2 tablespoons sour cream
- 1/2 tablespoon harissa paste
- 1/4 teaspoon ground cumin
- Salt, to taste

Directions:
1. Cut the celery root into desired size and shape.
2. Then, preheat your Air Fryer to 400 degrees F. Now, spritz the Air Fryer basket with cooking spray.
3. Toss the celery fries with the olive oil, salt, and black pepper. Bake in the preheated Air Fryer for 25 to 30 minutes, turning them over every 10 minutes to promote even cooking.
4. Meanwhile, mix all ingredients for the harissa mayo. Place in your refrigerator until ready to serve. Bon appétit!

600.Classic Egg Salad

Servings: 3
Cooking Time: 20 Minutes + Chilling Time
Ingredients:
- 6 eggs
- 1 teaspoon mustard
- 1/2 cup mayonnaise
- 1 tablespoons white vinegar
- 2 carrots, trimmed and sliced
- 1 red bell pepper, seeded and sliced
- 1 green bell pepper, seeded and sliced
- 1 shallot, sliced
- Sea salt and ground black pepper, to taste

Directions:
1. Place the wire rack in the Air Fryer basket; lower the eggs onto the wire rack.
2. Cook at 270 degrees F for 15 minutes.
3. Transfer them to an ice-cold water bath to stop the cooking. Peel the eggs under cold running water; coarsely chop the hard-boiled eggs and set aside.
4. Toss with the remaining ingredients and serve well chilled. Bon appétit!

CPSIA information can be obtained
at www.ICGtesting.com
Printed in the USA
BVHW051936220221
600779BV00002B/91